HOLY WAR

HOLY WAR

*The Rise of Militant
Christian, Jewish and
Islamic Fundamentalism*

DAVID S. NEW

McFarland & Company, Inc., Publishers
Jefferson, North Carolina, and London

ISBN 0-7864-1336-0 (softcover : 50# alkaline paper) ∞

Library of Congress cataloguing data are available

British Library cataloguing data are available

Cover photograph © 2001 Photodisc

Manufactured in the United States of America

*McFarland & Company, Inc., Publishers
Box 611, Jefferson, North Carolina 28640
www.mcfarlandpub.com*

Contents

Preface

On September 11, 2001, the twin towers of New York City's World Trade Center succumbed to a terrorist attack, presumably by Muslim fundamentalists. Thousands of people, most of whom likely knew virtually nothing about Islam and harbored no dislike for Muslims, died. American president George W. Bush asked, Why did this happen? Why do these people hate Americans? We are good people.

To Muslim fundamentalists, however, the United States is the leader of a Western culture that is the very embodiment of evil. As a prominent symbol of this culture, the World Trade Center became a logical target.

To understand this madness we need to understand religious fundamentalism. Just as there are Muslim fundamentalists, there are Christian and Jewish fundamentalists, some with terrorist plans of their own. The acts of September 11 were a response to, among other things, such plans.

This book is an account of Christian and Jewish terrorist plans, of the recent rise of Christian, Jewish, and Muslim fundamentalisms and how they are interacting to endanger peace in the Middle East and the world.

For some time apocalypticist fundamentalists—Christians in America, Jews in Israel and America—have been working together, in the hope of hastening the coming of the Messiah, to bring about a Holy War to end all Holy Wars—nuclear Armageddon in the Middle East. They have been attempting to provoke and draw out a violent Muslim fundamentalist response. As September 11 witnessed, their endeavors have clearly begun to bring forth fruit.

The Middle East is a powder keg awaiting a lighted match. Religious fundamentalism is that lighted match. Religious extremism and polarization are on the increase both in the United States and in the Middle East, and some political scientists think we truly are headed for a nuclear Armageddon. The flash point is Temple Mount, the site of Islam's third most holy shrine, believed by Jews to be the locus of their ancient Temple. Jewish fundamentalists want to destroy the mosques on Temple Mount and rebuild the Temple. Christian apocalypticists are financing and supporting their efforts.

The mosques on Temple Mount are the very soul of Islam, the symbolic equivalent of the World Trade Center. Destruction of the mosques would rally Muslims the world over behind the extremists who vow to annihilate Israel. But Israel is not going to disappear — memories of the Holocaust are too fresh. Israel would use its nuclear weapons if necessary.

Russian intelligence confirms that Osama Bin Laden, head of the terrorist Muslim network al-Qaida, has nuclear weapons, obtained in a trade for heroin with the Chechnyan mafia. The Harvard Center for International Affairs ran a simulation game regarding Temple Mount and concluded that if the mosques are destroyed World War III will follow. Experts believe that the possibility of nuclear weapons being used is the greatest since the Cuban Missile Crisis of 1962.

A professor of political science at the Hebrew University of Jerusalem and fellow at the Center for International Development and Conflict Management says that Temple Mount is the most volatile spot in the Middle East, perhaps in the whole world. A former deputy mayor of Jerusalem fears the apocalyptic dimensions of Temple Mount.

All of this sounds unbelievable, mad — for religious fundamentalism *is* madness to those on the outside. So in this book we go inside, to understand the fundamentalist mind, what fundamentalists want to do and why.

We begin with the story of one group of Christian apocalypticists and the religious excitement surrounding the new millennium, and then go back in time to trace the recent history of Christian apocalypticism, noting how the dawning of the nuclear age in 1945 and the 1967 Six Day War in the Middle East gave impetus to this contemporary religious phenomenon. For the first time in almost two thousand years the Jews were in possession of the holy Mount. Surely Christ's return was imminent.

The burgeoning, yet hidden, culture of Christian fundamentalism has entered American politics, exerting a potent influence on the foreign policy of the United States with respect to the Middle East. In considering this influence this book focuses on three figures: Jerry Falwell, Ronald Reagan, and Pat Robertson — all ardent apocalypticists.

The astounding political success of these three demonstrates the powerful influence of Christian fundamentalism in America. Forty-four percent of Americans now believe in a biblical Armageddon, and one American in three believes the Second Coming will occur within a few decades. American fundamentalists believe it is God's will and command that we fight a nuclear Armageddon. Few people knew that Ronald Reagan, as his biographer notes, was "hooked on Armageddon." As president he made secret plans for a nuclear war. Fundamentalists believed Reagan's presidency would hasten Jesus' return. Pat Robertson says God speaks to him: "I have chosen you to usher in the coming of my Son." Robertson is a political genius. Political scientists say he has the most powerful political organization in America and that he is on the verge of seizing control of the Republican Party.

Falwell, Reagan, and Robertson are only the tip of the iceberg. This book traces the support and financial assistance rendered by other American Christian apocalypticists — individuals and organizations — in the promotion and subsidizing of terrorist acts by Israeli Jewish fundamentalists who wish to promote Holy War and the coming of their Messiah. The groundwork has already begun for the rebuilding of the Temple that will stand on the ground now occupied by the two mosques. Several minor failed attempts to destroy the mosques have already taken place.

Muslim fundamentalists are more aware of these facts than secular Americans. Osama Bin Laden and others like him are responding with a new type of warfare. That warfare gives small groups leverage against military giants like the United States. It is terrorism, the terrorism of Holy War — war to the bitter end, a war where suicide has its religious reward.

The recent surge in the three religious fundamentalisms occurs within an increasingly nervous political environment in the Middle East. Separate chapters in this book are devoted to Israel's nuclear program and political psychology, and to the fact that nuclear weapons are leaving the new nation-states resulting from the breakup of the former Soviet Union and finding their way to Islamic nations and Islamic terrorists. Nuclear terrorism is thought to be the wave of the future. These ingredients present a dangerous mix even *without* the addition of apocalypticist efforts. The book concludes with a possible future — a nightmare scenario, the self-fulfillment of apocalypticist dreams.

Since the events of September 11 and the resulting actions by the United States, Muslim fundamentalists have been mobilizing and gathering support. We can expect Christian and Jewish apocalypticists to step up their own terrorist timetables, confident that all the pieces are in place for the coming of the End Time.

The Middle East is always close to exploding. Even should today's political leaders manage to engineer a peace accord, it would be no guarantee for the future. Indeed, this would only drive religious fundamentalists on both sides to extreme acts—for peace runs counter to their agenda.

1

Time Bomb

In the evening hours of January 3, 1999, Israeli police and members of Shin Bet (General Security Service) raided two houses just outside Jerusalem. Three men were taken in for interrogation concerning conspiracy to bomb holy places. Official police statements accused them of intending "to carry out violent and extreme acts ... to bring about the Second Coming" of Jesus Christ.[1] Spokesman for the Israeli police Brigadier General Elihu Ben-Onn was certain they "planned to carry out violent and extreme acts in the streets of Jerusalem at the end of 1999 to start the process of bringing Jesus back to life."[2] The men were soon released when it was agreed that all fourteen of the occupants of the two homes would leave Israel immediately.

The fourteen Americans, including six children, were members of Concerned Christians, a Denver-based "Doomsday cult." Of all such groups under surveillance, Concerned Christians was considered the "most dangerous" by Israeli security.[3] Seventy-eight Concerned Christians had disappeared from Denver in September 1998. Where the other sixty-four were no one seemed to know for sure. "Prepare to follow me and die," leader Monte Kim Miller had said to the seventy-eight.[4] But where was Miller now? Guesses ranged from Libya to Mexico's Yucatan Peninsula to Toronto. However, the most likely place seemed to be London, from where, some said, he was running the organization by phone.

A former husband of a Concerned Christian called Miller "a scam

1

artist." "Real prophets don't get involved in shootouts. Jesus didn't come with a machine gun."[5] If Miller is a violent man his physical appearance betrays nothing out of the ordinary. One would pass him by on any city street without a second glance. Clean-shaven, neatly groomed, glasses, forty-four years of age, otherwise nondescript — the very picture of the marketing executive he had formerly been for Procter & Gamble. Nor would Miller's followers stand out in a crowd. A neighbor in the hilltop village of Mevasseret Zion noted only that they appeared not to have jobs: "You could see them here sitting around all day. You could call it idleness. The children, of course, were not registered at any school around here."[6]

In 1996, according to a Denver police officer, Miller pretended to go into a trance. The veins of his neck protruded; his mouth contorted: "I am the Lord your God ... you need to bow down to me, and if you don't, you will die."[7] Miller sees himself as the complete godhead, the Trinity. Because one doesn't question the whims of the Lord, members of Concerned Christians follow their leader slavishly. The sixteen-year-old daughter of a Concerned Christian said, "My mother told me that if Kim Miller told her to kill me, she would."[8]

Miller has a particular thing about black helicopters. His paranoia is shared by groups known as militia. These militia are not the government-financed military reserves that meet on weekends. They are independent vigilante groups — Robert Boston calls them "band[s] of heavily armed Rambo-wannabees"[9] — scattered throughout the United States. These militia believe black helicopters are operated by the federal government of the United States and by the United Nations. They believe the United States government and the United Nations are virtually identical and that they intend to institute a one-world government that would strip freedom-loving Americans of their rights. This one-world will be ruled over by the Antichrist and Satan. As the Lord God, Miller wages a continual and cosmic battle against Satan. Hence, his paranoia regarding black helicopters.

Miller has told Concerned Christians that the United States will soon be destroyed. On the night of the raid on the Concerned Christians' home an audiotape — dated June 25, 1997, titled "Time of the End," number 30, series 18 — was found at the doorstep.[10] In the tape the United States is called the "dragon kingdom." America will get "double the judgment" Japan got at Hiroshima and Nagasaki. American President Bill Clinton is called the "counterfeit son of man" for his involvement in the 1993 Israeli-Palestinian peace treaty and the subsequent Israel-Jordan peace accords. The tape talks about biblical prophecy, the Second Coming, and God's final judgment of the earth to show that the time of such false messengers and counterfeit religious figures is about to end.

The tape continues: "This is looking to be like the final message of our time together, at least as it concerns the Manson murders."[11] Charles Manson? The phrase "I am the Lawmaker"—the subtitle of the tape—had been used in a Manson interview in 1988. Manson saw himself as divine lawmaker and Son of man (Manson → Man Son → Son of man—one of Christ's titles in the New Testament).

Miller and Manson were both fascinated with the biblical book of Revelation and its End Time scenario. Both saw themselves as playing a significant role in End Time events. Miller claimed to be one of the prophets mentioned in the eleventh chapter of Revelation who "shall prophesy a thousand two hundred and threescore days"—about 40 months. In August 1996 a Concerned Christian said, "We have only forty months left on earth."[12] Forty months after August 1996 is late 1999. At this time, Revelation says, the prophets will be killed. Three and a half days later they will be resurrected. Miller expected to be killed in Jerusalem late in 1999 and to rise from the dead three days later.

Concerned Christians are one variety of apocalypticists—those who hold a religious belief in, and eagerly anticipate, the imminent end of the world. Like Concerned Christians, other Christian apocalypticists find their End Time scenario in the biblical book of Revelation: the Second Coming of Christ and other events, including the war to end it all—Armageddon. Miller and most other apocalypticists are not the cartoon figures of years gone by—the bearded doomsday sayers who walked the downtown streets of major cities with placards warning that the End was near. They are far more sophisticated. Groups like Concerned Christians are likely to be found on the internet. One quick survey found 239 web-sites on the topic.[13]

Southern Baptist minister Tim LaHaye is a typical apocalypticist. He believes that we are irrevocably headed for a nuclear Armageddon. He and evangelical writer Jerry B. Jenkins have coauthored six "Left Behind" novels, all using plots based on the apocalyptic notion of the Rapture—where Christ rescues his people from the horrors of the End Time. With an initial printing of one million,[14] the latest installment placed second on the *New York Times* best-seller list only three weeks after publication. By 1998 the series had already sold over two and a half million copies and garnered five million dollars for its creators.[15] As 1999 was coming to a close sales had jumped to nine million, with two books of the series published that year.[16] A movie based on the first book of the series, *Left Behind*, was scheduled for release in October 2000.

Some readers seem hardly to realize that these books are fiction. One reader remarked, "I think the books are so real that *Left Behind* could happen today, this minute, to all of us."[17] Author Jenkins notes, "We've had many unsaved people say they have accepted Christ because of reading

Left Behind or one of the other books."[18] But LaHaye and Jenkins have their critics. Randall Balmer, a professor of religion at Barnard College, is appalled at the faulty theology underpinning the novels: "They don't see this [biblical book of Revelation] as allegory but as literal truth."[19] University of Wisconsin professor of religious history Paul Boyer says, "It feeds the most paranoid strands in American life today."[20]

Most Christian apocalypticists live in the United States. As Peter L. Berger, University Professor at Boston University, writes, "By any measure, the United States is the most religious country among the Western democracies."[21] And apocalypticism is a significant thread in American Protestantism. Daniel Wojcik writes, "Beliefs about worldly destruction and transformation have been an ongoing and significant part of the cultural and religious heritage of the United States."[22] Two out of three Americans believe in the Second Coming of Christ (part of the End Time scenario), including one third of those who never attend church. A 1994 survey found that one in three Americans expected the Second Coming to occur within a few years, or at least within a few decades.[23] Thirty-six million Americans—almost one in eight — expect the world to end (which follows some time after the Second Coming) within their lifetime, according to a *Newsweek* poll.[24]

As the year 2000 approached the number believing in the Second Coming grew rapidly — by eight percent in only three years.[25] Up to one half of all Americans believed that Christ might "possibly" return around the year 2000.[26] The Christian Research Institute reports that there are thousands of "millennial madness cults." Some 350 organizations predicted the world would end in the year 2000.[27] A *Time*/CNN poll found that almost one in ten Americans thought the world would come to an end in the year 2000.[28] Many Americans were so sure The End was imminent they hoarded food and other goods. A photograph in *Time* magazine posed one family in front of their stockpile. The caption read, "God's going to protect us. But...."[29]

The religious significance apocalypticists gave to anno Domini 2000 — as the two-thousandth "year of the Lord"—was misguided. The anno Domini system of counting years was initiated in the sixth century by the monk Dionysius Exiguus (Denis the Short). Denis miscalculated Christ's birth as 753 years—rather than 750 years, as we now know—after the founding of Rome. Unless the Bible is wrong, Jesus was born while Herod was still alive, which would put the date of his birth at least three years earlier than Denis had figured — historians place it between 7 B.C.and 3 B.C., 4 B.C. being most likely. So the real year 2000 — 2000 years after the birth of Christ — would be the year we designate 1997.[30] Notwithstanding this logic, round numbers like 2000 continue to possess a certain magic.

Most apocalypticists are content to wait patiently for the End Time events to transpire. Some are not. Some seek to hasten the End by their own actions. People fixated on the Second Coming might be "predisposed to act in abnormal and foolish ways,"[31] warned dispensationalist (a type of apocalypticist) professor C. Marvin Pate of Moody Bible Institute in Chicago, along with Calvin Haines, in their book *Doomsday Delusions*.

The Christian Reconstructionist movement is one apocalypticist group which seeks to hasten the End. Reconstructionists believe that before Christ returns society must be reconstructed along godly lines. Gary North is the son-in-law of Reconstructionist founder Rousas John Rushdoony. "Scary Gary" believes it is his duty to destroy present society and replace it with a Bible-based state that will impose the death penalty on blasphemers, heretics, adulterers, gay men, and women who have abortions or partake of sex before marriage.[32] The death penalty would be executed by stoning, for Reconstructionists believe in Old Testament law. Reconstructionists, along with televangelist Pat Robertson, praise Zambia — an African dictatorship rife with intolerance and censorship — as a "Christian nation" and an experiment in theocracy.[33]

As the year 2000 and a new millennium drew near, the predisposition to hasten the End increased. Because Christian apocalypticists expect the Second Coming to occur in Jerusalem, security regarding foreign religious groups and individuals in Israel was stepped up. Israeli security became increasingly watchful for Doomsday cults and individuals. Israeli officials kept in touch with American authorities: Were any religious groups about to fly to Israel? The FBI set up a system so that Israel could track American millennialist cultists and other religious extremists. After Concerned Christians were deported the FBI stepped up its surveillance. As part of Project Megiddo — named after the region in Israel that gives us the word "Armageddon"— the order went out to all field offices to investigate organizations and individuals who might take violent action related to the millennium.

Beginning in 1998 Israeli Tourism Ministry official in charge of planning millennial events Shabtai Shay alerted tour guides and hotel managers concerning signs of suspicious behavior. They knew their task would not be easy. The ministry had been expecting an influx of up to three million people of various religions, especially Christians, to mark the year 2000.[34] Minister of Tourism Moshe Katsav says the Israeli government earmarked $500 million to be used in preparation for that special year.[35] In Nazareth alone two thousand new hotel rooms were built in anticipation of the incoming crowds.[36] When the pope proclaimed 2000 a "holy year" and "world pilgrimage to the Holy Land year" the Vatican told Israel to anticipate six million Roman Catholic visitors. To that number could be added Protestant Christians: Rick Ricart of TTI Travel in Wheeling, Illinois, noted that his mainly Protestant clientele had increased its booking to the Holy Land by 35 percent.[37] Even given a head start it was clear that the ministry would be pressed to keep up.

Most of those coming to Israel would be innocent tourists coming to see the places where Jesus had walked. But not all, it was feared. The Interreligious Coordinating Council in Israel issued a press release: "Apocalypse? Armageddon? Religious cults and Mass Suicides? What can we expect as millions of Christian pilgrims from around the globe flock to Jerusalem to mark the year 2000?"[38] Tel-Aviv University's Inter-University Center for Terrorism Studies announced a conference titled "Millennial Terrorism: Religious, Political, Security and Legal Perspectives."

In a climate of millennialist tensions Shin Bet and Mossad (Israel's external spy agency) closely monitored any organization or individual they felt might threaten the peace. One such individual was an American who called himself Elijah after the biblical prophet. He had been living in Jerusalem for most of the 1990s and was considered crazy, but harmless. For several years he had been proclaiming the year 2000 as the End. Nobody listened. Until 1999. That year he began to attract a following. Israeli security became nervous, and he was asked to leave the country. As a result, one apocalypticist website blasted Israel for its harsh treatment of Christians.

Another individual who had come from the States in 1980 called himself Brother David. He discarded his surname and passport and was jailed as an illegal alien. The police could not deport him because they could not find proof of his country of origin. After his release from prison Brother David moved to al-Azariya just below the Mount of Olives to await Christ's Second Coming. He began to attract followers. Their numbers increased, particularly in 1999. One follower expected the Rapture (a divine act eagerly anticipated by apocalypticist Christians) in the year 2000, with World War III in November of that year.

Concerned Christians represented only a fraction of the people who took up residence in Jerusalem in the months preceding the turn of the millennium. Estimates placed the total at around one hundred and fifty — all born-again Christians, mostly from the United States. Shin Bet and Mossad watched an American group which was scattered among a number of residences around Jerusalem. Every member was designated "the chosen man for the mission" and had an assigned portfolio — Justice, and so on[39] — which he would assume in the End Time, expected shortly. But try as they might, Israeli security forces couldn't watch everybody. In the words of former chief of Shabak (the Israeli general security service) Carmi Gillon, "This is going to be a mission impossible. There are too many crazies in Jerusalem."[40]

Nevertheless, Israeli security did what it could. There was every reason to err on the side of caution, for Israeli-Arab relations have been sensitive since large numbers of Jews began to settle in the Middle East after the First World War. In Jerusalem fanatical apocalypticists could cause trouble on an international scale. As Richard Landes, head of Boston University's Center for Millennial Studies notes, "Israel can't afford a Waco."[41] Jewish and Muslim holy sites have became focal points for religious dissension and Arab-Israeli relations. Chief among these is Temple Mount in Jerusalem.

Temple Mount is the Western name for a raised terrace known to Muslims as Haram al-Sharif, the Noble Sanctuary. It is called Temple Mount because Jews believe that Haram al-Sharif is directly above the site of their two ancient temples — the first destroyed by the Babylonians, and the second by the Romans. Archaeologists have been unable to locate any artifacts which would indicate that this is the exact location of either of these ancient temples. Nevertheless, a portion of the wall surrounding the terrace of Temple Mount — known as the Western Wall or the Wailing Wall — has become a holy shrine for Jews who believe it is the last remaining part of their ancient temple.

Perched upon Temple Mount/Haram al-Sharif are two mosques. These resplendent examples of Muslim architecture are significant for more than their aesthetic appeal. The Mosque of Omar is the third most holy shrine in all of Islam. Thirteen hundred years old, it is built over what is alleged to be the site of the peak of Mount Moriah — the first place God created, where Adam drew his first breath, and where Abraham brought Isaac to be sacrificed. This mosque is also known as the Dome of the Rock — for Muslims believe that it is from this site that Muhammad, the prophet of Islam, ascended to heaven. Inside the Dome is preserved a large rock, upon which Muhammad's holy feet last made earthly contact. The second mosque on Temple Mount is al-Aqsa, dating from the eighth century.

Today devout Jews pray at the Wailing Wall, kissing the worn stones only shouting distance from crowds of Muslims worshiping at the two mosques. Former security boss Gillon laments, "Every day in Jerusalem that ends peacefully is a miracle. I am afraid of what could happen on the Temple Mount."[42]

The propinquity of the two holy sites has long been a source of conflict. In 1930, years before the creation of the modern nation of Israel, the British convened a commission to determine the causes of intercommunal rioting sparked by conflict over the Western Wall a year earlier. The leading Islamic religious leader, in a memorandum to the commission, cited "widespread propaganda undertaken by the Jews with a view to influencing the London Government and other powers … in order to take possession of the Western Wall." He went on: "Having realized by bitter experience the unlimited greedy aspirations of the Jews in this respect, Moslems believe that the Jews' aim is to take possession of the Mosque of al-Aqsa gradually on the pretense that it is the temple, by starting with the Western Wall of this place, which is an inseparable part of the Mosque of al-Aqsa."[43] To give the Palestinians a nationalist cause, the writer of these words mounted a campaign to protect the sanctity of Haram al-Sharif. Ever since, Temple Mount has been the locus of the conjunction of religious and political motifs. There is an interesting footnote: Yasser Arafat belongs to this man's extended family and received his initial political education at the man's home.

Today the Western Wall is both a holy site for Jewish worshipers and, according to Charles S. Liebman and Eliezer Don-Yehiya, "the central shrine in the Israeli civil religion."[44] Israel's elite military units undergo ritualistic initiations at the wall. Here, too, memorial festivals are celebrated: Holocaust Memorial Day, Jerusalem Day, Independence Day, and the memorial day for fallen soldiers. Hence, the Western Wall has become as much a religiopolitical symbol for Jews as has Haram al-Sharif for Muslims. And there they stand, side by side.

In the mid–1970s the potential of Temple Mount for dangerous confrontation drew the attention of the United Nations Security Council. It held a debate on what should be done concerning the inflammatory situation there. After extensive research and discussion it was concluded that holy places like Temple Mount, "constitute a dangerous flash point which can quickly inflame religious-cum-political fanaticism into violence and indeed another major war."[45]

It is little wonder the former deputy mayor of Jerusalem summed up the situation: "A time bomb with a destructive force of apocalyptic dimensions is ticking in the form of the Temple Mount."[46] Ehud Sprinzak has taught political science at the Hebrew University of Jerusalem and has been a fellow at the Center for International Development and Conflict Management, among other honors. A Ph.D. from Yale, he is a noted authority on extremism, violence, and terrorism both in Israel and abroad. In his opinion Temple Mount "is today the most volatile spot in the Middle East, perhaps on Earth."[47] Using almost identical words journalist Jeffrey Goldberg says Temple Mount is "the single-most-explosive piece of real estate on the planet."[48]

As the year 2000 approached, time and place coincided. On the cusp of the year 2000 journalist Susan Sappir called Temple Mount "such a volatile place at such a volatile time."[49] Israeli officials became doubly nervous. December 31, 1999, was the last Friday of Ramadan — Islam's holy fast month. Three hundred thousand Muslim worshipers were expected to crowd Temple Mount for this busiest religious service of the year. Security worried about confrontation between them and the thousands of apocalypticist Christians who might gather close by. Provocative acts by religiously motivated Westerners was a major concern.

Temple Mount remains the focal point for apocalyptic anticipation, but was especially so as the year 2000 approached. Israeli security feared that Monte Kim Miller and Concerned Christians or other similar groups might be planning to destroy the mosques on Temple Mount in the hope of instigating war between Jews and Muslims which would lead to Armageddon and hasten the return of Christ.[50] In just a few months of 1999 Israeli police arrested five "mentally ill" people — three Christians and two Jews — each of whom independently planned to enact their own suicide on Temple Mount or planned to attack it. Two of these were regarded as "provocation" intended to bring on the End Time war of wars, Armageddon. Two European tourists were not even allowed to set foot in Israel. Suspected of plotting "anti–Muslim provocation" at al-Aqsa, they were denied entry at Ben Gurion Airport.[51]

The Israeli government earmarked $11 million to upgrade security around Temple Mount[52] and was careful to keep the details of its security planning for the approach of the millennium under wraps. Israeli authorities are fully aware of the significance of Temple Mount for the survival of their nation and for any hope of peace in the Middle East. As one security official bluntly states: "The next war can come not from our borders but from here in Jerusalem, from the Temple Mount."[53]

Miller and his followers are only the thin edge of the wedge. There are those who so seriously want the world to come to an end that they are dedicating their time and their money and their lives in this direction. Gerard Straub writes, "The threat of a nuclear holocaust looms large on humanity's horizon because of the swelling number of people who believe that God wants it to happen, and they are, quietly and almost unnoticed, taking steps to hurry that happy day along."[54]

Those who are seriously dedicated to bringing the world to an end are not cultists, and do not belong to a sect. Unlike Concerned Christians, they are respectable Christians and Jews. They have considerable influence, financial backing, and political clout. These religious hardliners are vigorously promoting politically explosive activities in the Middle East. They hope their actions will lead to Armageddon, to a nuclear war to end all wars. As Arthur P. Mendel writes in *Vision and Violence*, "Until now, the world could afford the fantasy of Apocalypse…. No longer is that so. Tens of thousands of nuclear warheads … make that prophecy disturbingly realistic, especially given the current worldwide revival of fundamentalism."[55]

Walter Laqueur, chairman of the International Research Council at the Center for Strategic and International Studies, writes in the prestigious journal *Foreign Affairs*, "Extremist millenarians would like to give history a push, helping create world-ending havoc replete with universal war.... It is possible that members of certain Christian and Jewish sects that believe in Armageddon ... or the Muslims ... who harbor related extreme beliefs could attempt to play out a doomsday scenario. A small group of Israeli extremists, for instance, firmly believes that blowing up Temple Mount in Jerusalem would bring about a final (religious) war and the beginning of redemption with the coming of the Kingdom of God."[56]

A former FBI agent who used to track terrorists warned that Israel and Temple Mount would not be out of danger after New Year's Day, 2000: "It might take a year or two because it depends on whose calendar they're using and how they interpret it."[57] One group in Texas had been keying on the date May 5, 2000, even back in the 1970s. Some look to the year 2033 — the beginning of the third millennium after the Crucifixion and the Resurrection.

With the passing of the year 2000 — or 2001, or 2002, or 2010, or ... — fanatical apocalypticists will not cease their activities. As Daniel Wojcik says, apocalypticism is "an enduring way of interpreting the world" because it "fulfill[s] important religious and psychological needs." Hence, he goes on to say, "Despite predictions to the contrary, apocalyptic belief systems will not become outdated or 'collapse from exhaustion' in the near future.... endtimes enthusiasts have consistently updated eschatological beliefs and made them relevant and will continue to transform such ideas creatively in the years ahead."[58] The date for the End has constantly been moved forward in the past, and it will continue to be moved forward in the future. The specific date changes; apocalypticism remains.

Journalist Gershom Gorenberg has studied End Time movements. Here is what he has to say in this regard: "The fact that millions of people regard Israel as the stage for the End, and the Jews as leading actors, does present some problems. But they won't go away after January 1, 2000, or even after the whole year passes.... 2000 is just the start."[59]

Countdown

July 16, 1945. 5:29:45 A.M.

Countdown: zero.

Searing brilliance rends the darkness. A seething fireball bright as several noonday suns makes the hills of the New Mexico desert glare ghastly white. A roiling conflagration surges forth, hungrily consuming the ground at its rapidly expanding circumference. Agitated dust swirls desperately as it feeds the fiery vortex, igniting a second explosion. Billowing into a fullblown sphere, the ponderous mass of unrestrained fury and unfettered power slowly ascends, casting against the clouds above an ever-changing palette of colors: from garish yellow to orange to blood red to unearthly green. Finally, a mushroom-shaped tumescence that glows spectral violet.

Official observers of the detonation of the first atomic bomb are located six to twenty-seven miles from ground zero. It seems forever before the shock-wave of sound and wind relieves the spell of silent tension. The time lapse between the initial flash and the thunderous bang echoing back and forth among the hills gives measure. It seems impossible that anything so bright could be so far away. Might the fireball take on a life of its own, out of control?

One observer momentarily loses his sight, having disregarded the warning to use tinted eye protection.[1] So bright is the blast it is observed 120 miles away.[2] A blind woman sees its light.[3] It is calculated that the flash could be seen from the moon. Ten miles away an observer likens the heat from the explosion to the rush of hot air from an opened oven.[4]

The test proved successful beyond the most optimistic expectations. Thirteen and a half pounds of material at the core of the bomb had released a force equivalent to 18,600 tons of TNT.[5]

Meanwhile, another atomic bomb was being loaded onto the U.S.S. *Indianapolis* in San Francisco Bay. This bomb was of a different design and used different materials. No one could be certain of its success. It, too, would have to be tested.

The test took place twenty-one days later, on August 6. Once again, success. It exploded with a force comparable to that of the first bomb — more than 2,000 times that of any bomb previously used in warfare.[6] But this time its explosive might was not expended over the empty spaces of a remote desert. Instead, three fifths of a large Japanese city was obliterated, the major portion of her population killed or injured — 140,000 dead up to the end of 1945,[7] 200,000 bomb-related deaths by 1950.[8] The *Times* remarked that where the bomb "landed had been the city of Hiroshima; what is there now has not been learned."[9]

Three days later another atomic bomb, this one similar in design to that tested in New Mexico, wreaked similar destruction on Nagasaki.

The destruction was unprecedented; the graphic imprint nightmarish. The image of a spiral ladder was traced in unscorched paint on an adjacent steel tank.[10] A vine's leaf shielded what lay in its shadow from burning radiation.[11] Miles from the blast unprotected human skin was instantly sunburned, often displaying the pattern of an intervening object. The searing heat produced startling etchings: flower patterns were burned from a blouse[12]; letters had been punched out from their white background as by an invisible press.[13] The closer to ground zero, the more hellish the artwork. In undisturbed asphalt the image of a man and his handcart.[14] Hellish heat boiled the surrounding asphalt and instantly transformed man and cart into small clumps of carbon. Any closer to ground zero and the clumps would have been vaporized.

On November 1, 1952, a hydrogen bomb was detonated. Its fireball measured three miles in diameter.[15] Where once was an island, now a crater over a mile wide and more than a hundred feet deep.[16] Moreover, this was only the beginning. The explosive force of individual bombs increased as the years passed — to more than a thousand times that of the bombs dropped on Hiroshima and Nagasaki.[17] One such bomb had the force of all of the explosives used in all of the wars in all of history,[18] ten times the force delivered by all the Allied air forces in the Second World War[19] — an immensity of destructive force equivalent to a freight train of TNT stretching across North America.[20] At one time the United States had a sufficient stockpile to drop the equivalent of one Hiroshima bomb for every day since the time of Jesus Christ.[21] Likewise for the Russians. The superpowers armed themselves with a collective capacity of more than one million Hiroshimas.[22] This is 1,000 times all the explosive power expended in all the wars in history,[23] the equivalent of more than three tons of TNT for every man, woman, and child on this planet.[24] More than 50,000 nuclear warheads[25] come in all shapes and sizes and methods of delivery — a veritable catalogue of death. Some can be fired from artillery: an eight-inch shell can deliver a punch of one half Hiroshima.[26] One submarine can deliver a thousand Hiroshimas[27] and destroy every large and medium-sized city in all the territory that once comprised the Soviet Union.[28] The collective arsenal is enough to kill, eight times over, all of the citizens of every city in the world with a population of more than 100,000.[29] One thirtieth of this stockpile would effectively annihilate modern civilization.

Human history had passed a point of no return. What had been done could not be undone. A new era had dawned. There now existed a gargantuan threat to the future of humankind. In the days following the bombing of Hiroshima and Nagasaki a feeling of finality oppressed public consciousness. The *New York Herald Tribune* noted that Americans were consumed with fear that "the foundations" of the universe were "trembling." The *Washington Post* speculated that the life expectancy of the human species had decreased immeasurably in only two weeks. The *Chicago Tribune* envisioned the whole Earth a "barren waste" following nuclear war, people crouched in caves. The *New Republic* looked ahead to nuclear war and the end of civilization. Thinking was global, universal: the Earth, the universe, the human species, the future. Was there a future?

Had scientists tampered with forces best left unknown? Had we tasted the forbidden fruit of the tree of the knowledge of good and evil? In Genesis, God had promised death for this, but mercifully temporized. Would God now make good on this promise? Of that fateful morning in the New Mexico desert, physicist I. I. Rabi mused, "Suddenly the Day of Judgment was the next day and has been ever since."

From the beginning of the atomic age religious imagery gave dimension to nuclear thought, and religious language furnished categories for nuclear speculation. The site of the detonation of the first atomic bomb was designated Trinity. A later nuclear test was named Mighty Oak. Surely it was mere coincidence that both the military and scientific leaders of the project to develop the first atomic bomb were sons of Protestant ministers. The Vatican spoke of "apocalyptic surprises"[30] and "catastrophic conclusion." To many there seemed some elemental, rudimentary, and rock-bottom connection between things atomic and religious. The awesomeness, the power, the finality.

The advent of the atomic bomb fostered visions of religious finality. The words "apocalyptic" and "Armageddon" were tossed about recklessly. The *Philadelphia Inquirer* trumpeted the atomic bomb as "the new beast of the apocalypse."[31] "Armageddon" was the title for the last section of William L. Laurence's history of the bomb project. Apocalypticism became an increasingly prevalent feature of the nuclear age.

The bomb gave new life to outdated theologies. Preachers of doom zealously searched Scripture for the slightest hint of anything that might be interpreted with nuclear flavor. With perverted genius they spotted here a word, there a phrase. Again and again into words wrenched totally out of context they read an allusion to atomic destruction. In their minds Zechariah's "small things" (4:10) was clear reference to the atom. Religious scenarios of the End Time were dusted off. Second Peter 3:10 was quoted over and over, lending scriptural significance to prevalent concerns: "The heavens shall pass away with a great noise, and the elements shall melt with fervent heat, the earth also and the works that are therein shall be burned up." Heretofore this passage was assumed to be a description of natural events. The atomic bomb had provided new ears for ancient words.

Religious hawkers and hucksters found ample audience. "Catastrophe," "cataclysm," "devastation," "annihilation," "obliteration," "desolation"—any designation for the ultimate and final—became instant catchwords. The public ate up this new apocalyptic sensationalism and seemed to relish pessimistic predictions of gloom and doom. Accept Christ today and escape the imminent holocaust!

The atomic bomb has now nourished two generations of doomsday prophecies. Many Americans have come to believe that the end of the world will be nuclear. In a 1984 poll 39 percent agreed with the statement "When the Bible predicts that the earth will be destroyed by fire, it's telling us that a nuclear war is inevitable."[32]

Careful and elaborate collations of biblical evidence for the precise date of the final demise have become instant bestsellers, making their authors wealthy. Carefully calculated dates have come and gone, only to be replaced by newly calculated dates. In 1990 Bantam Books reported that *Armageddon—Appointment with Destiny* was its "hottest single religious title."[33] Since its publication in 1970 Hal Lindsey's *The Late Great Planet Earth* has been a bestseller. This account of the Last Days has been *the* all-time nonfiction bestseller (excluding the Bible) with over thirty-one million copies sold.[34]

Apocalypticism is ready to burst into the forefront at any hint of international crisis. When the Persian Gulf War was making headlines, I answered the telephone to a bizarre question: Was Saddam Hussein the Antichrist (a figure prominent in the apocalyptic scenario)? The answer was available by dialing 900-4-MESSIAH[35]; the Jews for Jesus organization would be happy to assist. The same topic was subject for a sermon at First Baptist Church in Dallas.[36] The Gulf War proved a bonanza for End Time hucksters. Faculty member Charles Dyer of fundamentalist stronghold Dallas Theological Seminary rushed to press with *The Rise of Babylon: Sign of the End Times*. Evangelical publishing houses were suddenly drunk with glorious profit.

For evangelical publishers the coming of the year 2000 had money written all over it. Clergymen who tried to stem the tide failed. The Evangelical Lutheran Church in America circulated a pastoral letter in the autumn of 1998 stating that "there is no biblical basis for equating a year with Jesus' return, the coming of the kingdom of God, or the end of the world."[37] Did those using Scripture to calculate the date of the End Time not notice that Scripture itself made a lie of the process?: "But of that day and that hour knoweth no man" (Mark 13:32).

Apocalypticist books predicting the date of The End continue to roll off the press. Always there is some new twist, some connection with contemporary culture and events. Michael Drosnin's *The Bible Code* asserts that World War III will begin in the year 2000, or the year 2006. He cites the Old Testament like many others, but uses the latest in technology — a computer analysis of the text to find his evidence.

3

Religious Hardliners

In the state of Montana several thousand people paid up to $12,000 each for a place in a concrete bomb shelter topped by a watchtower armed with gun turrets.[1] Americans separated from America; they set up their own church, their own subdivisions, their own private school, their own university, their own publishing house, their own stockpile of guns and gold for what they believed to be the cataclysm of the soon-to-be End Time. They owed their allegiance to the "Mother of the Universe," "The Mother of the Flame," Guru Ma, a woman who claimed to be the only person who speaks to Jesus.[2] She had several times earlier predicted the date of Armageddon — the war to end all wars, to end everything — and the date when the world would end.[3] Those dates had come and gone, but her flock remained faithful. It never occurred to them that she might be one of the false prophets against which the Bible so loudly and vigorously proclaims, so they continued to wait for the End.

American culture has been speckled with such groups for the past century and a half. Most are religious apocalypticists. They make the news usually only if they commit mass suicide or if one of their members commits publicly violent acts: David Koresh and the Branch Davidians; Monte Kim Miller and his Concerned Christians. At a certain place and time such groups could pose a serious threat to the public peace. But, in general, members of these cults and sects are not the real danger.

The real danger lies with apocalypticists within the major world

16

religions. They have the power, the money, the influence, the numbers. Forty percent of American adults believe the world will end in the battle of Armageddon as depicted in the biblical book of Revelation.[4] In the United States such apocalyptic beliefs are predominantly held by evangelical and fundamentalist Christians.

The term "fundamentalist" has come to be applied to the hardliners of any major religion.[5] Hence, there are Christian fundamentalists, Jewish fundamentalists, and Muslim fundamentalists. Fundamentalists insist that it is necessary to take a hard line on the "fundamentals"—specific statements of belief which the fundamentalists assert to be the essential propositions of their respective religion. Fundamentalists gratuitously and presumptuously arbitrate the definition of what it is to be a Christian ... or a Jew, or a Muslim. It should come as no surprise, then, that what a fundamentalist calls a "Christian" turns out to be no more, and no less, than a *fundamentalist* Christian. In recent times "fundamentalist" has come to be a scare word, associated with violent behavior, although it need not be.

Christian fundamentalism, and hence Christian apocalypticism, is known formally as dispensationalist premillennialism. As William Martin remarked in his monumental study *With God on Our Side*, dispensationalist premillennialism is "a relatively new scheme of biblical interpretation that would have an incalculable impact on evangelical theology."[6] That dispensationalist premillennialism is virtually a theological creation of the nineteenth century is something many apocalypticists would rather gloss over, or simply deny. They prefer to think that their beliefs are identical with original Christian doctrine, the true Christian doctrine. But some dispensationalists admit the truth. Two professors at Dallas Theological Seminary, Craig A. Blaising and Darrell L. Bock, in their recent book *Progressive Dispensationalism* "concede that dispensationalism is both recent and different from most of what went before it."[7]

Evangelical Christians had traditionally held the optimistic view that humankind was so rapidly improving that God would soon inaugurate a millennium of peace and prosperity, after which Christ would return. But then, somewhat more than a century ago, along came the new theology of premillennialism. Americans had always looked with hope to the future, but now premillennialist apocalypticists viewed the future with a pessimistic fatalism.[8] Premillennialists hold a pessimistic view of their fellow humans and their future. People are bad, not good; immoral or amoral, not moral. They think things are getting worse, not better. Hence, Christ will return to destroy this sinful world, and *then* inaugurate the millennium. Dispensationalist premillennialists—apocalypticists—maintain that certain biblical prophecies, particularly those in Revelation, tell us when

Christ will come back to inaugurate the millennium. As it turns out, the worse things get, the more enthusiastic these apocalypticists become — it means that Christ's return is just around the corner.

So much for the premillennial part. Dispensationalism is the belief that time — from the beginning of creation, to the End Time — is divided by God into dispensations. The Jews had their dispensation, their time in the sun, if you will, before the appearance of Jesus Christ. Their time has now past; they are has-beens in the eyes of Christian fundamentalists, although they still have an important role in Last Days events.

The basic institutions of apocalypticism were developed in the United States, and today the bedrock, the homebase of Christian apocalypticism is still found in the United States. When Peter Gardella speaks of "the American drive toward apocalypse"[9] and writes, "Apocalyptic is the characteristic literature of the United States,"[10] he goes perhaps too far. Nevertheless, it is here that apocalypticists have the numbers and the political power to influence national and international affairs. Charles B. Strozier puts their number at up to one third of the American population.[11]

Dispensationalism had been nourished at the bosom of conferences on prophecy and the Bible held in the latter decades of the nineteenth century. The "fundamentals" — the propositional beliefs to which one must adhere to be considered a "Christian" — were ironed out and then chiseled in stone in the early years of the twentieth century. Those open to dialogue were replaced by rigid, unbending, militant hardliners — the fundamentalists.

Organization and institutionalization were crucial if the movement was to survive. First-century Christians had recognized the necessity of two institutions — the biblical canon and the church. Dispensationalist fundamentalists believed the traditional church was in the hands of Satan. Hence, they devised parallel institutions to function in the same way as the traditional Bible and church.

The first of these institutions was the *Scofield Reference Bible*, the brainchild of Cyrus I. Scofield. Scofield had no formal biblical education. He learned from his pastor, who took the younger man under his wing. Scofield's pastor was the individual who had led the Bible conferences in their dispensationalist direction. Scofield was not shy about giving credit: "During the last twenty years of his life Dr. Brookes was perhaps my most intimate friend, and to him I am indebted more than to all other men in the world for the establishment of my faith."[12]

Scofield found the Bible far from the perfect word of God. He prefaced his Bible by speaking of "a perfected text,"[13] noting that up until this point "the many excellent and useful editions of the Word of God left much to be desired."[14] The *Scofield Reference Bible* has been called "the most effective tool for the dissemination of dispensationalism in America,"[15] and acclaimed by one historian to be "perhaps the most influential single publication in millenarian and Fundamentalist historiography."[16] Certainly the *Scofield Reference Bible* has been "the Bible" for fundamentalists for several generations. It has sold over ten million copies[17] and continues to be updated and revised for today's readers. Scofield added copious editorial notes to the text which functioned as dispensationalist eyeglasses, focusing the biblical text into neat dispensational divisions for the reader. But because the notes are on the same page as the biblical text, they have come to acquire some of the latter's authority. Readers often find it difficult to differentiate between dispensationalist doctrine and the words of Scripture. Scofield's project had the backing of a large group of influential men and was financed for the purpose of spreading the dispensationalist message. Clearly, financial backers got full value for their money.

Because fundamentalists chafed at the restrictions imposed by the traditional church, the second type of institutionalization devised by dispensationalists took the form of parachurch organizations. One of these was the Bible institute. Bible institutes had been started by Dwight L. Moody, "Mr. Evangelical." Moody's fame is carried forward today in the institutions which bear his name. At the World's Christian Fundamentals Association conference an attempt was made to standardize Bible institutes.

The Bible institute has become the vanguard in the propagation of dispensationalist fundamentalism. Here ministers, evangelists, and missionaries get the "proper" slant on biblical understanding, which they then promote around the world. Instead of "wasting time" on the niceties of Hebrew and Greek like traditional church seminaries, Bible institutes focus on Armageddon, Last Days, and the End Time — apocalypticism through and through. Roughly 200 Bible institutes graduate approximately 100,000 students.[18] Without these institutes fundamentalism might not have survived such crises as the Scopes fiasco of the 1920s or the stresses and strains of the ensuing decades.

If Bible institutes are the mission centers for dispensationalism, Dallas Theological Seminary is its Vatican. Those who staff the Bible institutes are often Dallas men. This seminary has counted, and continues to count, many of the leading dispensationalist luminaries among its faculty. It is the largest nondenominational seminary in the world. With its extension schools in Philadelphia and San Antonio it boasts 2000 students.[19]

Dallas Theological Seminary was the realized dream of Lewis Sperry Chafer. It had been his dream for more than a decade before the first sod was turned. He was the driving force behind its establishment; he was a principal in the phrasing of its doctrinal statement; he chose its location.

In 1924 Chafer's vision was realized. The seminary was molded to Chafer's liking and in every way it bore his image. Originally known as the Evangelical Theological College, the seminary assumed its present name twelve years later. Chafer served as theology professor and the seminary's first president until his death in 1952.

Chafer wanted his seminary to be nondenominational. Students would come from various denominations to study, and then return to their denominations to spread the dispensationalist message. All of the faculty were devoted dispensationalists. Chafer had no formal theological education, yet he wrote the definitive systematic theology of dispensationalism — an eight-volume work (2,700 pages) titled *Systematic Theology*, structured after the curriculum of the school. In the first volume Chafer negated almost two thousand years of Christian exegesis when he bluntly asserted, "Apart from a sane recognition of the great purposes and time-periods of God, no true understanding of the Bible has ever been received."[20]

Chafer had pedigree. He had learned his lessons at the feet of C. I. Scofield. Scofield had spent most of his pastoring years in Dallas and Chafer would later minister in the same church. Scofield became the father Chafer had lost as a child, and no one had greater influence on his life. Scofield was Chafer's mentor in the fullest sense of the word, and Chafer was Scofield's associate for several years at various Bible institutes and schools and on his travels. Some historians trace the roots of Dallas Theological Seminary back to educational endeavors started by Scofield in Dallas. When Scofield died, Chafer was his logical heir apparent as the leading luminary among dispensationalists.

In such a unique position, Chafer could tinker with the dispensationalist doctrine he had received and over which he was curator. It was his belief that Armageddon would involve Iran, Iraq, and Israel, and this belief was passed along to future generations.

To this day Dallas remains the hotbed of dispensationalism, and not only because it is the site of Dallas Theological Seminary. Scofield had twice pastored a church in Dallas, and had headed the Southwestern School of the Bible in that city. Today Scofield's old church has been renamed Scofield Memorial Church.

Dispensationalist minister W. A. Criswell continued to preach the party line at First Baptist Church of Dallas at an age in life when most men would be content to reminisce. So celebrated a figure was this millionaire minister — his luxurious home had iron grates over the windows to protect his antiques and art collection — in the huge metropolis of Dallas that he was known simply as "the pastor." When he surrendered the helm to a younger man in 1990 after almost half a century, the membership of his church stood at 28,000, surpassing the population of many good-sized towns and the total membership of many religious denominations.[21] It was the largest congregation in the largest Protestant denomination in the United States. Billy Graham himself was counted among its membership.

Criswell was described as "the definitive picture of Texas-sized confidence and Scotch-Irish resolve,"[22] and when he spoke people listened. When he made a request people responded — one Sunday $1.85 million came in on the collection plates.[23] Criswell pounded home apocalyptic rhetoric. Armageddon must be fought, and so should be welcomed. He was a staunch supporter of Israel. Such interests merited him the title "the Protestant pope of this generation" from public apocalypticist figure Jerry Falwell. Criswell delivered a commencement address at Falwell's Liberty University (then Liberty Baptist College) and spoke on his "Old Time Gospel Hour," and Falwell was invited to speak from Criswell's home pulpit.

Criswell carried the flag for apocalypticism. He preached for three straight years from Revelation. People didn't get tired of the same old thing; his church grew. In time it became almost an independent city in itself — a Christian day school for grades one through twelve, two gymnasiums, a roller-skating rink, bowling alleys, a sauna, fitness machines, racquetball courts, and a restaurant. A member could virtually live life there. Multilevel garages provide ample parking, and during weekdays bring in supplementary income by serving Dallas businesses.

Criswell pounded apocalypticism from the pulpit. His Sunday morning sermons went out over radio and television. (The church owns its own radio station.) Armageddon is close at hand. Armageddon is close at hand. Armageddon is close at hand. In the forty years before retiring he published a book a year promulgating the dispensationalist message. Criswell used his influence to get dispensationalists into office in the Southern Baptist Convention, the nation's largest and most evangelical denomination, and to get dispensationalism taught at Convention seminaries. So that certain things would be taught exactly according to the party line, he founded the Criswell Center for Biblical Studies which included Criswell Bible College and the Graduate School of the Bible, for preparing ministers.

In his younger years Criswell had led a coalition of Protestant clergy who fought John Kennedy's nomination and election to the presidency. Why? Because Kennedy was Roman Catholic. Yet from Criswell's viewpoint there may have been stronger motivation. Kennedy stood for many of the things fundamentalists are against; he was against many of the things fundamentalists hold dear. Fundamentalists have traditionally espoused racism, ranted against Roman Catholicism, denigrated social welfare, thwarted efforts at world peace, and frustrated attempts to bring humanity

into closer community. The antihumanist sentiment of Christian fundamentalists does much to kill the legacy of Kennedy's spirit in American
life today.

Christians have a reputation for doing good works and getting
involved in various charities. They are thought of as peacemakers. But
these are the mainline Christians, those who worship at the traditional
churches which fundamentalists term "Satanic." Fundamentalists are not
big on peacemakers, for, as Grace Halsell notes, "Far from working to make
peace, all dispensationalists believe that it is God's will, indeed, His command, that we fight a nuclear Armageddon."[24]

4

End Time Scenario

In 1970 a manuscript was submitted to the Zondervan Publishing House in Grand Rapids, Michigan. The editor was a former classmate, but he felt obligated to warn the author not to get his hopes up too high. "Hal, I'd like to tell you right now that we'll publish your work. But the publishing business is extremely competitive and the editorial staff must be sure the book will sell. And you are, after all, a neophyte writer. This is your first manuscript. You're unpublished. No track record. We'll have to see. It'll depend on editorial opinion. We'd be taking a chance ... you understand."

Well, they took a chance. The manuscript did get published, and the book was a publisher's dream. The presses churned, the money flowed in. Printrun followed printrun. Orders kept coming. Total sales climbed and climbed. Bestseller. Blockbuster. Major publishing milestones were exceeded, and still the orders came in. One million. Two million. Three million.... It was nothing short of a publishing phenomenon. By the end of the decade the book had become the best-selling nonfiction book of the 1970s. In just ten years the book had been translated into thirty-one languages and circulated in over fifty countries.[1] Total sales continue to increase to this day. Estimates put sales for the 1970s at fifteen million, with the total to date more than double that number.[2] Assessments are replete with superlatives, sometimes bordering on the exaggerated and unverifiable: "the most widely read writer on prophetic themes in history"[3]; "the bestselling Christian book in history"[4] (other than the Bible).

The author of the book is Hal Lindsey; the book is *The Late Great Planet Earth*. *The Late Great Planet Earth* is *the* book when it comes to outlining the apocalyptic scenario. When a book makes a big splash, more and more people want to read it. Curiosity, if nothing else. There is really nothing new in the book; it is basically a rehash of the End Time scenario Lindsey heard in lectures as a student at Dallas Theological Seminary.[5] He refined his material as well as he could and then had an experienced and professional columnist and free-lance journalist polish it into the fast-paced, hard-hitting prose of newspapers and magazines. The title was copped from a potboiler on earthquakes, *The Late Great State of California*. If it works don't change it.

Lindsey demonstrates a sophisticated knowledge of the market. Businesslike, pragmatic, purposeful, realistic, a former riverboat captain among other things, Lindsey is wise to the ways of the world. Baptized three times before demonstrating any serious piety, he came late to his faith. He likes to recount that before discovering the Bible he experienced a "taste for wine, women, and song." In seven years of preaching with the evangelistic Campus Crusade for Christ, Lindsey learned the psychology of salesmanship and persuasion. He learned how to stimulate interest in jaded youths and hold the attention of the capricious. He learned how to debate with agile young minds. He learned what would, and what would not, succeed. After years of carefully listening to the heartbeat of the American soul Lindsey knew people, how they felt. He knew that most people lived on emotion, not intellect. He would address the soul, the emotions. So he honed his rhetorical skills and added a bold and sassy southern–California style.

The Late Great Planet Earth deals with biblical prophecy, but its author couldn't be more different from the typical caricature of the prophets of old. No bearded eccentric here. Instead, a suave, meticulously coiffed and attired, Madison Avenue type of figure. Where the biblical prophets were otherworldly, Lindsey is this-worldly and has the material accouterments to prove it: a Mercedes 450 SL, a sumptuous home in one of the West Coast's choice neighborhoods, a lavish motorhome in which to conduct transcontinental junkets.[6]

Anyone this obviously successful is going to arouse both curiosity and envy. Journalists have been quick to characterize Lindsey as "shameless," "confident," "undaunted," with an "instinct for the topical and marketable." Lindsey owns a management firm, the Generation Company, which invests his book royalties and administers Hal Lindsey Ministries. Is this an overweening focus on the bottom line, or just good personal stewardship? Journalists prod Lindsey concerning his royalties, insinuating a tendency toward moneygrubbing, that he writes for profit and not for prophecy. But Lindsey refuses to divulge his income and insists that he has every right to whatever profits his writing brings. On occasion he has threatened to take a swipe at journalists who pry too closely into personal matters.

Lindsey might not approve, but *The Late Great Planet Earth* is usually found shelved among books on UFOs and science fiction. The cover shows an incandescent earth against a red-orange background, and promotes the fact that the book is a #1 bestseller, giving the number sold. The book isn't long — starts on page 11, ends on 188. Not much print per page. Most paragraphs are three to five lines in length. The content is broken into bite-sized sections, some only three lines long. Puns and twists abound; titles are snappy, hip, and to the point: "Tell It Like It Will Be"; "C'est la Vie"; "God's Woodshed"; "Russia Is a Gog"; "Sheik to Sheik"; "How to Make Enemies and Influence People"; "Scarlet O'Harlot."

The Late Great Planet Earth is peppered with biblical quotes. Anyone trying to follow Lindsey in either of the two standard Bibles of the English-speaking church — the centuries-old and highly revered King James Version, or the contemporary Revised Standard Version — would have trouble. That's because dispensationalists have their own versions of the Bible, not those used in the pews of mainline churches on Sunday mornings. Lindsey is a true dispensationalist here; the church is of the devil: "Satan ... invades certain churches on Sunday."[7] Dispensationalists have proclaimed the Revised Standard Version of the Bible the work of the devil, so Lindsey uses the Amplified Bible. "To amplify," says the dictionary, is "to expand in order to clarify one's ideas."

Lindsey begins by challenging his reader with all the art of a carnival pitchman: "This [*The Late Great Planet Earth*] is a book about prophecy.... If you have no interest in the future, this isn't for you."[8] Who, after all, is *not* interested in the future? Just inside the cover is a long quote from one of his documentary films: "You know, I used to come to the beach to get away from things.... But now even the ocean is a reminder that man may be running out of time." Lindsey says the Secretary General of the United Nations gives us ten years to solve the problem of survival. His tone suggests we won't solve it. The End is nigh.

Computers, witchcraft, astrology. The solution isn't here, warns Lindsey. We need to heed the words of the biblical prophets. These men of ancient times predicted certain patterns would emerge just before the End. Pieces of that pattern are already forming.

In Lindsey's scenario for the End Time, a ten-nation European Common Market guarantees Israel peace and security by treaty sometime before 1988, the fortieth anniversary of the founding of Israel. During this period Israel rebuilds its Temple, but to do so it must first clear the site by destroying Islam's holy shrine, the Dome of the Rock. The destruction of the Dome of the Rock precipitates an Arab-African attack. Russia and its allies become involved and gain control of the Middle East. Realizing that the Common Market forces will soon come to Israel's aid, the Russians begin a genocide of the Jews. Because the Jews have been God's special people since early biblical times, this provokes God's wrath. Russia and its allies are destroyed. China uses the opportunity offered by the ensuing chaos to challenge the Common Market for world supremacy. The opposing forces meet at Armageddon for the final battle. Great destruction results. Major cities are annihilated, possibly by nuclear weapons. Just before "it appears that all life will be destroyed on earth"[9] Jesus Christ returns to save humankind from self-extinction and establish his millennial kingdom.

Christians (read dispensationalist fundamentalists) need not fear all the chaos and violence of the Last Days, Lindsey says, because Jesus will come and remove them beforehand in an act called the Rapture. Lindsey is forced to concede that the word "Rapture" cannot be found anywhere in the Bible.[10] Nonetheless, that has never stopped other dispensationalists, and it doesn't stop Lindsey.

Charles B. Strozier says the Rapture "is probably the single most significant theological innovation in contemporary fundamentalism."[11] He credits this idea as giving new meaning to, and reshaping fundamentalism. It is "a crucial part" of the End Time scenario. The Rapture allows fundamentalist Christians to view the End Time with anticipation. They actually look forward to the end of the world, and would gladly hasten the day. All because of the Rapture. Take the Rapture away, and the whole End Time scenario becomes a nightmare rather than a shining dream.

Not all dispensationalists agree with Lindsey's approach. C. Marvin Pate, a dispensationalist and a professor at the Moody Bible Institute in Chicago warns: "Anachronistically correlating current events" with Bible prophecies is "an obsession" that has "undoubtedly caused more harm than good."[12] At the time of the Gulf War, a University of Minnesota graduate student said, The End "is definitely coming. It's freaky but it doesn't scare me, because I'm a Christian. It'll be other people who will suffer."[13] Thanks to books like Lindsey's *The Late Great Planet Earth* an astounding 44 percent of Americans believe in the Rapture — the same percent as believe in Armageddon.[14] Clearly, there is a connection. It is ironical that Lindsey himself writes, "Satan loves religion.... Religion is a great blinder of the minds of men."[15]

5

The Dawning of
the Last Days

Since the creation of the state of Israel Jerusalem had been divided in two—the western half under Israel's jurisdiction and the eastern half, containing the Old City, in Jordanian hands. On June 7, 1967, Israeli paratroopers of the 55th Parachute Brigade changed that. They captured the Old City of Jerusalem.

Standing by the Western (Wailing) Wall—reputed to be the last remnant of Judaism's ancient Temple—in the Old City of Jerusalem, victorious General Moshe Dayan declared: "We have returned to our holiest of holy places, never to leave her again."[1] Israeli soldiers kissed the worn stones of this most holy shrine of Judaism; they wept with joy and prayed with a new religious fervor. A rabbi in soldier's uniform blew the symbolic ram's horn at the Wailing Wall. Proclaimed one rabbi, a military chaplain, "We are entering the messianic era."[2]

This was the final and most triumphant scene in what history would call the Six Day War. It had started in the spring of 1967 with the buildup of Egyptian and Arab military forces close to Israel's borders. Since the founding of Israel on May 14, 1948, Palestinians had continually tried to upset the newly declared state. At times they were assisted by local Arab states, and the greatest Arab alliance occurred preceding the Six Day War.

The Egyptian head of state vowed to annihilate the young nation, and it seemed that his words might prove true. Israel decided not to await its fate and struck first — with lightning speed. After only a single day 400 warplanes of five Arab nations — Egypt, Syria, Iraq, Lebanon, and Jordan — lay shattered and burned; they had not had time to become airborne. Israel had lost only nineteen aircraft. Deprived of air support, the Arab tank forces proved ineffective against the better-trained and more highly coordinated Israeli armor; in many cases they turned and ran, abandoning expensive military materiel which the Israelis were quick to confiscate. Seven hundred of Egypt's 900 tanks were lost in the sands of the Sinai Peninsula, and within only sixty hours the Israeli army was in sight of the Suez Canal.

When the Six Day War was over, Arab casualties outnumbered those of Israel twenty to one. A nation of less than three million had defeated an alliance with a population of over 110 million. Religious Jews saw the hand of God in this twentieth-century struggle of David against Goliath. Philosopher Martin Buber made a comparison with the biblical story of the salvation of the ancient Israelites at the Red Sea. For many, the sudden turn of events and the dramatic reversal of fortune demanded more than a mundane explanation. One Israeli scholar perhaps best summed up the mood of his fellow citizens: "It was a truly religious movement, the experience of a miracle. It had a special metaphysical character."[3]

The success of Hal Lindsey's *The Late Great Planet Earth* was founded on the Israeli victory of 1967 and on its conquest of Jerusalem. The miraculous pace of the victory, and the fact that the Jews were at long last in possession of the ancient city of Jerusalem, was what gave Hal Lindsey's End Time scenario credibility. Without these events of 1967 his description of the Last Days would have been nothing more than a cleverly packaged rehash of century-old dogma. Instead, his book excited millions of readers and won many new converts to apocalypticism.

Lindsey candidly admits that he would have had no audience had he been writing fifteen years earlier. But this was not mere coincidence or lucky timing. It took Lindsey to spot the potential gold mine that the situation of 1967 presented. Here was an unprecedented opportunity to give credence to the dispensationalist apocalyptic scenario he had been taught at Dallas Theological Seminary. It was his task to neatly weave words of Scripture with current events.

In *The Late Great Planet Earth* Lindsey makes Israel's possession of Jerusalem the primary event in the dawning of the Last Days. For thousands of years the Jews were without a homeland. When this homeland was finally created in 1948, the new state of Israel did not include the city of Jerusalem. The Six Day War of 1967 changed that. Lindsey predicted that soon the Israelis would rebuild the Temple and offer blood sacrifices.

But what about Islam's Dome of the Rock, which stood on the site where the Temple would be built? No problem. "Obstacle or no obstacle, it is certain that the Temple will be rebuilt. Prophecy demands it,"[4] wrote Lindsey confidently. Three decades later Lindsey has come to avoid specific dates regarding the End Time, but as he lectures a group of sixty born-again American tourists on Temple Mount, he still insists that the Temple will be rebuilt during the generation that was alive in 1967.

Opponents of the state of Israel in the Middle East were unlikely to take the results of the Six Day War sitting down. There would be a reprisal. This seemed as likely a time as any for the battle of Armageddon, which was prophesied to occur in the Middle East. Such a dramatic possibility was not lost on Lindsey. He published quickly and his book rode the crest of Middle East tensions.

Hal Lindsey was not the only dispensationalist to focus on the events of the Middle East. The significance of the Six Day War was not lost on American dispensationalists in general. The events of those few days in the sunny Middle East breathed new life into a tired dispensationalist theology. "Armageddon," "apocalypse," and "the Rapture" soon became the common vocabulary of a wider public. Christian fundamentalism's sleeping giant — dispensationalist premillennialism — had been awakened. Its fondest dreams were coming true.

The quick and decisive victory of the Israelis in this war was final proof to dispensationalists that Jewish restoration to the Holy Land was legitimate. No more confirmation was needed to demonstrate that the Lord had given Palestine to the Jews. The hand of the Lord was clearly visible. As one editorial said, "Christians and Jews both recognize a supernatural dimension to this struggle."[5] The author of one article saw God's plan, as prophesied, coming to fruition: "One cannot help thinking that in all of this God was working out his own purposes, far above and beyond the capabilities of men or nations!... It is a thrilling thing to see a segment of prophecy being fulfilled!"[6]

Christian evangelicals and fundamentalists exulted in the Jewish conquest, not for the Jews' sake, but for the vindication of dispensationalist theology. L. Nelson Bell, Billy Graham's father-in-law and an editor of the evangelical periodical *Christianity Today* gloated: "That for the first time in more than 2,000 years Jerusalem is now completely in the hands of the Jews gives the student of the Bible a thrill and a renewed faith in the accuracy and validity of the Bible."[7] Surely the events of June 1967 were a clear fulfillment of Luke 21:24: "And Jerusalem shall be trodden down of the Gentiles, until the times of the Gentiles be fulfilled." The apocalypticist Christian awaited his imminent reward with breathless eagerness. The long-awaited time was just around the corner: "The prophetic clock of

God is ticking while history moves inexorably toward the final climax. And as that clock ticks, the Christian believer lifts his head high, for he knows that a glorious redemption draws near."[8] American televangelist Pat Robertson treated the news as "a direct sign from God"[9] that his destiny as an apocalypticist, and Israel's, were one and the same.

Organized by the editor of the prominent evangelical periodical *Christianity Today*, a prophecy conference reminiscent of those which gave birth to American Christian fundamentalism was struck to celebrate the victory of 1967. Israel's first prime minister and 1,500 delegates from thirty-two nations were invited. Among those individuals and organizations in attendance were the Reverend W. A. Criswell of First Baptist Church of Dallas, faculty members from Dallas Theological Seminary, officials from the National Association of Evangelicals, Youth for Christ, and Inter-Varsity Christian Fellowship, singer Anita Bryant, and the Jerusalem Symphony.

Since June 1967 headlines from the Middle East have riveted the attention of dispensationalists. The year 1967 brought the apocalyptic scenario alive, and it has experienced a vibrant existence ever since.

The rapid victory of Israel's forces against seemingly invincible odds assured the Israelis that God was on their side. Nothing could stop them now. In those first few days speculation about the immediate future ran rampant. The *Jerusalem Post* said that some believed the Messiah was already present among God's chosen people. The individual believed to be the Messiah was named, his ancestry provided. Many people believed that the Messiah would appear exactly one week after the conquest of Jerusalem — on June 14 — at the Feast of Weeks (Shavuot). In preparation for the expected crowd authorities went into action just hours before a pilgrimage through Jerusalem ending at the Wailing Wall was to take place. Bulldozers "swept out slum dwellings that reached to within feet of the Wall, opening up a huge square to accommodate the pilgrims."[10] Starting at 4 A.M. some 200,000 marched under the Israeli flag to their destination at the base of the wall.

"Military takeover of the 'old' city from Jordan raised immediate hope that the Jews ... could rebuild the Temple on its original site."[11] Such was the expectation expressed in one Christian editorial. Many Jews were just as hopeful. If the Messiah was not already among them, he would come at the Feast of Weeks exactly seven years hence, at which time he would rebuild the Temple.

The Israeli conquest of Jerusalem in 1967 gave extremist religious Zionists, both Christian and Jewish, a sense of power and overwhelming confidence that they had not before experienced. Despite glaring traditional differences in belief, Christian and Jewish fundamentalists would henceforth see their cause as one.

Christian Zionists

Apocalypticist fundamentalists cited the events of 1967 as conclusive evidence that their End Time scenario was correct. The possibility that the whole matter was little more than self-fulfilling prophecy seems not to have occurred to these true believers. For Christian Zionist fundamentalists had initiated the process of Jewish restoration and fostered its every step. Israel did not exist, as one evangelical claimed, "plainly and simply ... because God decreed she should,"[1] but because Christian apocalypticists had unceasingly advocated and promoted her existence.

It started back in the early nineteenth century when one Lewis Way found himself the recipient of a generous and surprise bequest. Freed from the bondage of having to spend his days making a living, he set out to play the role of philanthropic Christian gentleman. In his travels Way came to hear of a special grove of trees mentioned in a landowner's will: "These oaks shall remain standing, and the hand of man shall not be raised against them till Israel returns and is restored to the Land of Promise."[2] What did this mean? Way set out to learn whatever he could concerning the notion of the restoration of the Jews to Palestine.

He soon discovered the London Society for Promoting Christianity among the Jews. This organization was in dire financial straits, but Way resolved these difficulties and infused new energy into the group's activities. The Society began to publish a monthly journal, the *Jewish Expositor*, in which the issue of the restoration of the Jews to the Holy Land was discussed and promoted.

Through his association with the society, his contacts with several European rabbis, and intense personal study of biblical prophecies Way was responsible for associating two ideas: the restoration of the Jews, and the Second Coming of Christ. He wove these concepts into the fabric of an End Time scenario and his thoughts on these matters were propagated in the pages of the fledgling *Jewish Expositor*. In Lewis Way, Christian and Jewish perspectives on the issue of Jewish restoration in the Holy Land met for the first significant time.

The next step was to translate abstruse religious doctrine into political action. Convinced that the return of the Jews to Palestine must precede the Second Coming of Christ, the Earl of Shaftesbury set Great Britain on a path that would eventually result in the modern state of Israel: In 1839 a British consulate was established in Jerusalem. The first consul was a staunch evangelical. From the beginning of modern Western meddling in the Middle East the notion that those who protect the Jews will be blessed with worldly success made it remarkably easy to confuse selfish national ambitions with apparent religious magnanimity.

Without the Jews there would be no dispensations; they were at the heart of dispensationalism right from the beginning.[3] Dispensationalists on both sides of the Atlantic laid the groundwork for the Zionist movement. In the United States major dispensationalist figures advocated the Jews' restoration to Palestine. James Brookes and Arno Gaebelein were particularly influential in this regard.

In Israel there is a grove of trees dedicated by citizens of that nation to the man who had been recognized a generation earlier at a Zionist conference as a "father of Zionism." William E. Blackstone was just that. A disciple of Britain's John Nelson Darby, he spread the message to millions of Americans with his best-selling book *Jesus Is Coming* (1878 — the first of three editions). He brought Jews and Christians together on the subject of Zionism. In 1891 he organized the first Zionist lobbying effort in the United States. He gathered the signatures of 413 leading Americans, including the chief justice of the Supreme Court, the speaker of the House, and the mayors of Chicago, New York, and Boston. He enlisted J. P. Morgan, John D. Rockefeller, Charles B. Scribner, and other financiers to underwrite a massive newspaper campaign requesting President Benjamin Harrison to support the establishment of a Jewish state in Palestine. Harrison was petitioned "to further the purposes of God concerning His ancient people."[4]

Friends of Blackstone, Horatio and Anna Spafford, along with sixteen other Americans had gone to the Holy Land in 1881 to establish a Christian presence there in the Muslim quarter of the Old City of Jerusalem and to witness the Second Coming. Every day they journeyed to the Mount of Olives with tea and cakes, hoping to be the first to welcome their Messiah and to offer him refreshment.

In Britain the preacher John Cumming's books "outsold those of any other writer of his day,"[5] according to a contemporary biographer. Titles like *The End* grabbed the public's attention. Pointing out that only in the last thirty years had the Jews been allowed to live in Jerusalem, Cumming proclaimed this as a sign that the Last Days were fast approaching. He observed that Jews in London were collecting money to purchase Palestine and that American Jews had accumulated "enormous sums" to rebuild the Temple in Jerusalem. This was exciting news for apocalypticists, for they believed that without a Jewish presence in the Holy Land God's plan for the End Time could not proceed. Jesus could not return to an Israel which did not exist.

On the Jewish side much of the credit for the founding of a Jewish state in Palestine goes to Theodor Herzl. Herzl did not care where the Jewish state was to be located, as long as the Jews had some safe haven from their persecutors. He took as his motto the words coined by the same Lord Shaftesbury who had earlier established the British consulate in Jerusalem — "A land of no people for a people with no land."[6] He published the influential *Der Judenstaat* (*The Jewish State*), convened the First Zionist Congress in 1897, and tried to get various heads of state interested in the concept of a Jewish homeland. He was willing to try any angle. He approached the Russian Minister of the Interior — a renowned anti–Semite responsible for that nation's dreaded pogroms— on the pretext that a Jewish state would get the Jews out of Russia. He was unsuccessful.

Then he turned to Britain, where apocalypticist Christians had over many decades carefully prepared the way. Herzl's unstinting efforts finally paid off years after his death when his cause was championed by Christian Zionists. On November 2, 1917, the Foreign Office issued the famous Balfour Declaration: "His Majesty's Government views with favour the establishment in Palestine of a national home for the Jewish people, and will use their best endeavours to facilitate the achievement of this object, it being clearly understood that nothing shall be done which may prejudice the civil and religious rights of existing non–Jewish communities in Palestine, or the rights and political status enjoyed by Jews in any other country."[7] With the collapse of the Ottoman empire after World War I, Britain established a Mandate over Palestine, pledging to implement the Balfour Declaration. Both British Prime Minister David Lloyd George and Lord Arthur Balfour (author of the Balfour Declaration)— the two most powerful figures in British foreign policy at the end of the war — were raised in dispensationalist churches and were publicly committed to Zionist agenda for "biblical" reasons. Decades later when the British put down an Arab uprising which backed Palestinian complaints, the British evangelical Christian Colonel Orde Wingate was training a generation of Israeli military officials including Moshe Dayan who would later be Defense Minister.

Early Jewish Zionists were not religiously motivated. This was somewhat disappointing for their Christian supporters. Herzl, for example, was an atheist. When a Christian apocalypticist sent him an Old Testament with the key prophecies marked he was no doubt amused. The reason the first large wave of Jewish immigrants came to Palestine, in 1882, was to escape Russian persecution. Twenty years later a second wave of Jews emigrated from Russia. These people were imbued with a strictly secular idealism. They wanted to create a socialist society which would serve as a model for the revolutionary struggle of other peoples.

On May 14, 1948, the state of Israel came into being, and with it the renewal of Christian apocalypticism. As one faculty member of the Bible Institute of Los Angeles asserted in a radio address, the proclamation of the state of Israel was "the greatest piece of prophetic news that we have had in the twentieth century."[8] It was heralded as "the most significant event since Jesus Christ was born."[9] Israel and the Jews had become a focal point for apocalyticists: "All prophetic truth revolves around the Jews."[10] Israel was "the only nation on earth to have its history written in advance."[11] "The Jew is God's timeclock."[12] One recent survey found that forty-six percent of all Americans, not just fundamentalists, believe the establishment of Israel to be the fulfillment of prophecy.[13]

Looking back in time apocalypticists saw the hand of the Lord behind every phase of the reconstitution of the Jewish people in the Holy Land. After General Allenby had freed the land from the grip of the Ottoman Turks in the final days of the First World War, making it available for the Jews, one evangelical wrote concerning "the real purpose that God had in permitting the war to take place. It was not until the peoples of the world had done something for Israel that God permitted the war to stop."[14] The taking of Jerusalem had been an elaborate military procedure, but the myths that grew up around Allenby's victory credited everything to the Lord: Allenby prayed, and "the fiendish Turk"[15] withdrew without a shot being fired.

Christian apocalypticists sided with the Jews in their conflict with the Palestinians. All that really mattered was the fulfillment of biblical prophecy. The Christian's argument went this way. The land had rightfully belonged to the Jews since the beginning of biblical history: "In the same day the Lord made a covenant with Abram, saying, Unto thy seed have I given this land, from the river of Egypt unto the great river, the river Euphrates" (Genesis 15:18). There was no excuse for Arab intransigence and hostility. They had usurped what wasn't theirs. The Jew-Arab squabble was a modern continuation of the biblical feud between Isaac and Ishmael, Jacob and Esau. The Arabs had descended from Ishmael, the illegitimate offspring of Abraham, who had been cast out from the land. Had not the Lord said, "I hated Esau" (Malachi 1:3)? Arab resistance was seen as Satanic. In the minds of Christian apocalypticists the case against Palestinian Arabs was closed.

However, that does not mean that Christian apocalypticists have warm personal feelings toward the Jews. On the contrary, American professor and long time student of Christian fundamentalism Charles B. Strozier observes, "Fundamentalism is theologically pro–Jewish and at the same time anti–Semitic."[16] It's the old saw that Jews are Christ-killers. Back in 1870 one of dispensationalism's founders, James Brookes, stated that in the Last Days "an unequalled visitation of wrath"[17] would fall on the Jews, "a people still so inveterate in their prejudices, and so obstinate in their rejecting the Messiah."[18] An Episcopal bishop at one of the early prophecy conferences noted, concerning the restoration of the Jews to Palestine, "The object of their gathering is ... primarily their chastisement and suffering."[19]

During the early years, especially the 1920s, dispensationalists were virulently anti–Semitic. Many leading Christian fundamentalists championed the notoriously scurrilous *The Protocols of the Elders of Zion*. The *Protocols* was alleged to have been written by a Jewish conspiracy which was plotting to destroy Christian civilization and take over the world. It is considered the epitome of anti–Semitic literature. Arno Gaebelein, one of dispensationalism's most prominent figures, found *The Protocols* consistent with biblical prophecy. James M. Gray, the president of Moody Bible Institute, proclaimed *The Protocols* "a clinching argument for premillennialism."[20] As one shocked pastor protested, "*The Protocols* are being used ... by some fundamentalist Christians to stir up suspicion and hatred against the Jewish people as a whole."[21]

In the 1930s dispensationalists found reason to feel optimistic about Nazi persecution of the Jews. According to the 1937 editor of the dispensationalist *Sunday School Times* the Jews were being punished by God, just as the Bible prophesied. The Nazi persecution was their payment for "deliberate, persistent, and continued apostasy."[22] Seeming finally to feel some human compassion, in 1939 dispensationalist leaders called for an international day of prayer on behalf of the Jews. But, as professor of church history and dean at Northern Theological Seminary in Lombard, Illinois, Timothy P. Weber writes, these dispensationalists prayed "not that the persecutions stop, but that in their despair they [the Jews] turn to Christ."[23]

Weber notes that "dispensationalists received news of the Holocaust with a combination of horror, resignation, and hope."[24] Hope? They believed that God was using the Holocaust to increase the Jews' desire for a homeland in Palestine. The logic was simple. The Jews had as yet shown too little interest in Christian Zionist efforts to implement God's plan for the reestablishment of a Jewish nation in the Holy Land. God was, therefore, giving them a nudge in the appropriate direction. As Weber put it, "Prophetically speaking, the most crucial point was not that millions were dying, but that some would survive."[25] It was hoped that those who survived would enthusiastically do whatever was needed to move God's plan forward, so that the Christian End Time and the Rapture could take place in the near future.

Dispensationalists seemed to enjoy pointing out that what the Jews suffered in Germany would pale in comparison to what awaited them in the Last Days. Hal Lindsey said that the horrors the Jews would experience in the End Time would make Hitler and his cohorts "look like Girl Scouts weaving a daisy chain."[26]

Jews are not unaware of Christian fundamentalist anti–Semitism or of the real direction of their theology. Rabbi Chaim Richman remarks, "The whole rapture thing ... which calls for a fulfillment of hard times for Jacob, is essentially an invitation to genocide."[27] The Jews will die while the true Christians are spared in the Rapture. Christian apocalypticists will allow Jews a way out, however. But not as Jews. They must be converted to Christians. Tim LaHaye and Jerry Jenkins sprinkle their *Left Behind* novels with Jewish characters, but these are nearly always converts to Christianity. Nonetheless, apocalypticists expect only a small number of Jews to convert before the End Time. Jews are aware of this proselytizing aspect of Christian apocalypticism and do not appreciate it.

In the early 1980s the president of the Union of American Hebrew Congregations, Rabbi Alexander Schindler, criticized Jewish collaboration with Christian fundamentalism: "We cannot be blind to the fact that the deepest reasons for the backing given to Israel by evangelical fundamentalists are theologically self-serving. They believe Jesus cannot return for the Second Coming until the Jews are regrouped in their biblical homeland to Christianity."[28]

Schindler is right. Dispensationalist Christians believe that the Jews have only been allowed to exist during the intervening centuries since Christ's crucifixion for this very reason: "The New Testament teaches that he [God] is keeping the Jews in the world so that they may participate as a nation in the events connected with Jesus Christ's return."[29] Schindler also notes that Christian fundamentalists "believe further that even devout Jews are not welcome in heaven."[30] But there's more. Schindler did not mention that some Christian apocalypticists believe that the Messiah whom Jews await in Israel with the rebuilding of the Temple is the false Messiah, the Antichrist — a figure prominent in the Christian apocalyptic scenario.[31]

Mark Bruzonsky is an American Jew who worked for Zionist organizations because he saw Israel as "the Jewish version of self-determination."[32] Eventually disillusioned by Zionism's dangerous tendencies toward extremism, he quit the movement. His diagnosis of Christian Zionists is crystal clear: "Zionism would never have been started without Christians wanting to put Jews in a ghetto—called a Jewish state, exclusively for Jews. The tragedy is that after resisting the idea for about 200 years the Jews went along with it."[33] A Palestinian Christian thinks Christian Zionists are rabidly anti–Semitic. These "Christians are saying, quietly, to each other, 'And the Jews can go to Israel and stay *there*.' They believe that God is going to gather all the Jews in Palestine and then the unspoken end of the sentence is 'So they can all be killed in Armageddon....' That is the part of the sentence that is not always emphasized."[34]

The same Balfour responsible for the Balfour Declaration had a few years earlier introduced the Aliens Bill in Parliament which aimed to limit Jewish immigration into Britain. It seems that one reason he wanted the Jews in Palestine was that he did not want them living down the street. A religious Zionist, Balfour tried to compensate for the discomfort his own anti–Semitic tendencies caused his conscience with his famous declaration. Its strongest opponents were Jews. One, Lord Montagu, accused Balfour of promoting Zionism in order to get the Jews out of Britain.

It did not bother Balfour that Jews settling in Palestine would be in conflict with Arabs living there. Unlike many of his contemporaries, Balfour was fully aware that there were Arab inhabitants in the land (he even knew how many), but "in Palestine we do not propose even to go through the form of consulting the wishes of the present inhabitants of the country.... Zionism, be it right or wrong, good or bad, is rooted in age-long traditions, in present needs, in future hopes, of far profounder import than the desires and prejudices of the 700,000 Arabs who now inhabit that ancient land."[35] Like today's dispensationalist Zionists, Balfour was going to settle the Jews in Palestine for strictly selfish reasons. The "age-long traditions" and "future hopes" were those of the Christian Zionists— that the Jews be in the Holy Land so that Christ could return. Included among the "present needs" was the desire of Christian Zionists and others that the Jews find any other place than *here* to take up their abode. Palestine offered a solution that would satisfy traditions and hopes and needs all at one time.

Jerry and the Jews

Not just anyone gets his picture on the cover of *Time* magazine. By September 2, 1985, the Reverend Jerry Falwell's name and face were well known to Americans. People either hated him or idolized him, but he got their attention.

Called the American "Ayatollah Khomeini," the "Robespierre" of the twentieth century, and "the potential dictator of the New Christian Nation," Jerry Falwell was synonymous with Moral Majority, and Moral Majority was synonymous with the New Christian Right, a movement which sought to amalgamate the forces of fundamentalist Christianity and political conservatism in order to promote their common interests.

By the mid 1980s Falwell was traveling 8,000 miles a week in a private jet owned by his ministry. *U.S. News & World Report* had named him one of the twenty most powerful figures in America. The readers of *Good Housekeeping* had voted him the most admired citizen, second only to Ronald Reagan. He had been featured, often more than once, by a wide gamut of periodicals: *Atlantic Monthly, Chic, Esquire, Harpers, Hustler, Life, Newsweek, Penthouse, Playboy, Screw, The New Yorker, Village Voice,* to name only a few. He had been constant news for the major papers. The talk shows could not get enough of him. The president heaped praise upon him.

Falwell loved the attention. He courted the eyes and ears of the media. He teased and tantalized the press. He toyed with journalists. He constantly went out of his way to be in the public spotlight, uttering challenging and scandalous remarks which often shocked and created controversy. Falwell seemed determined to draw headlines, to get into the news and stay there.

Jerry Falwell had come a long way from his local pastorate in Lynchburg, although it remained the center of his life. The vehicle for his larger fame was his television ministry. Although Falwell's audience was surpassed numerically by those of several other televangelists, his attempt to put Christian fundamentalism on the political map set him apart from his broadcasting colleagues in the late 1970s and early 1980s.

Falwell is well aware that Christian fundamentalists have long had a reputation for being anti–Semitic. President of the Southern Baptist Convention Bailey Smith baldly states, "God does not hear the prayers of the Jews."[1] Despite much contrary evidence, Falwell claims things are changing: "In the past twenty years, Fundamentalists and Evangelicals, at a very rapid pace, have been 'converting' to support for Israel. This has not been a traditional position.... Leading pastors and preachers across the nation have begun taking a very courageous stand on what they have always believed theologically but have never been willing to take a stand on practically."[2] The reason for this change in attitude can be found in Falwell's own words: The creation of the state of Israel is "the single greatest sign indicating the imminent return of Jesus Christ."[3]

Even though he insists the Antichrist will be a Jew, Falwell asserts, "I doubt the Jewish people and the state of Israel have a better friend outside their own community than Jerry Falwell."[4] In 1984 he testified before the United States House of Representatives' Foreign Affairs Committee on behalf of Israel and in cooperation with the America Israel Political Affairs Committee, the leading Israeli lobby organization, in support of an attempt to get the United States embassy moved from Tel Aviv to Jerusalem. Falwell claimed to be backed by 50 million American evangelical Christians in his statement that Jerusalem and the West Bank belonged to Israel and the Jewish people.

Jerry Falwell is big on Israel, and Israel is big on Jerry Falwell. Falwell travels in a private plane — a gift from Israel. Value? About four million dollars, when spare parts are included — a token of the value Israel places on Falwell's friendship. For Falwell constantly gained the ears of the media with his views on Israel and events in the Middle East. Falwell never failed to put in a good word for the Israelis, never missed an opportunity to cast them in shining light. All this good publicity was worth the price of an airplane.

Falwell's motives are held in common with other Christian dispensationalists. Israel must be kept strong, because if there is no Israel Christ will have no place to return to. Falwell is on record as favoring an Israel which would incorporate chunks of what now belongs to Iraq, Syria, Turkey, Saudi Arabia, Egypt, and Sudan, as well as all of Lebanon, Jordan, and Kuwait.

A strongly armed Israel, surrounded by unfriendly nations, offers the best opportunity for war in the Middle East — Armageddon. Falwell is sure that war is coming. He anticipates this eventuality, rather than fears it. Back in 1979 he said, with regard to President Jimmy Carter's attempts to promote peace in the region, "In spite of the rosy and utterly unrealistic expectations by our government, this treaty will not be a lasting treaty.... You and I know that there's not going to be any real peace in the Middle East until the Lord Jesus sits down upon the throne of David in Jerusalem."[5]

After bombing Iraq in 1981, Israel's Prime Minister Menachem Begin knew he would be the target of criticism in the West. He had an upcoming interview on American television and wanted help to quash the criticism he expected. He made an urgent telephone call to Jerry Falwell: "Get to work for me."[6] Falwell promised that he would. Only then did Begin phone President Reagan. Later the same year Begin visited Falwell.

A year earlier at a gala dinner in New York Begin had rewarded Falwell for all that he said and wrote, for the influence he had with American President Reagan, and for the positive picture of Israel he painted for American conservative Christians, by presenting him with the Jabotinsky Medal. Only a few had received this award previously, all Jews. When Begin was a young man Jabotinsky had been his mentor; his admiration for the man remained strong. Jabotinsky's legacy was the militarization of Zionism. He had envisioned an expanded Israel with land on both sides of the river Jordan. His nationalism was so strongly racist that even some Jewish Zionists likened him to the Nazis. Jabotinsky was renowned for saying that Israel would rise in blood and fire. Did Begin see Falwell — who was known to have said, "Peaceful intentions are acts of stupidity"[7] — as a Jabotinsky?

Falwell supported the right-wing Likud Party during the 1984 Israeli elections. He addressed Americans for a Safe Israel at its annual conference that year. Americans for a Safe Israel is known for its smear campaigns against liberal Jewish organizations. In March 1995 Falwell spoke before the conservative Rabbinical Assembly in Miami. Here he pledged to "mobilize seventy million conservative Christians for Israel."[8] Falwell was responsible for converting Republican Senator from North Carolina Jesse Helms into one of Israel's staunchest allies as chair of the Senate Foreign Relations Committee.

In January 1998 Israel's Prime Minister Benjamin Netanyahu paid a visit to Washington. To meet with President Clinton? No. Bill Clinton stood alone in his position on the Middle East, against a Republican Congress and the New Christian Right. He had little leverage with Netanyahu's

Likud government. No, Netanyahu had come to see someone who did have leverage — Jerry Falwell. He'd pay a dutiful visit to Clinton only after the important business.

Falwell had arranged a meeting between Netanyahu and over one thousand leading Christian fundamentalists. The enthusiastic crowd greeted Netanyahu as "the Ronald Reagan of Israel." This gathering was persuaded to pledge that they would mobilize the evangelical community against the Clinton administration's continual pressure on Israel to give land up to the Palestinians. These leaders would contact more than 200,000 evangelical pastors in the United States. The pastors would be asked to "tell President Clinton to refrain from putting pressure on Israel"[9] and to use their pulpits to get the message across that Israel must be supported.

A few months later, in April, Netanyahu was back in the United States again, this time to speak to several evangelical organizations. One of these was the National Unity Coalition for Israel. On this occasion Jerry Falwell also addressed those in attendance. He spoke against the internationalization of Jerusalem, something Christian apocalypticists were dead set against. Jerusalem belonged to the Jews, and only to the Jews. It was their holy city, the site of David's throne and the two Temples of antiquity.

Falwell's Christ is a militant Christ, so it is not surprising that Falwell takes vicarious pride in the strength and effectiveness of Israel's military machine. Falwell describes himself as "a Zionist" and "one who, in the Christian community, is probably the most outspoken supporter of Israel ... I would say that I have become a radical on this issue."[10] He likes to boast that "the Jewish people in America and Israel and all over the world have no dearer friend than Jerry Falwell."[11] Like Hal Lindsey he believes that America's fate is bound up with that of Israel. If America blesses Israel with a plentiful and constant supply of arms and dollars, America in turn will be blessed. Certainly God would not look kindly on an America which ignored his chosen people in their quest for a strong and expanded homeland. Hence, Falwell has never ceased beating the drum of American support for Israel.

To promote Christian support for a strong and expanding military Israel, Falwell runs tours to the Middle East. Tourism nets Israel about a billion U.S. dollars a year, mostly from evangelical groups like Falwell's.[12] A billion dollars can buy a lot of weapons, and a lot of influence in the United States. A billion dollars is equivalent to one fifth of the aid given to Israel annually by the United States government.[13]

A Christian tourist on a Christian tour might expect to walk in the footsteps of Jesus, to stop where he had stopped, and to hear Jesus' words in places familiar to him during his stay upon this earth. But Falwell's tours emphasize Israel's David-amidst-Goliaths image — despite the fact that Israel has the best fighting force in the Middle East and one of the best in the world. Falwell knows this; he has stated that Israel has "the third largest air force in the world."[14] Nevertheless, Israel is painted as a brave little country desperately trying to hold its own in a world full of evil terrorists and warmongers. One disappointed Christian tourist found that for every hour spent at Christian sites and hearing about Jesus, thirty were spent extolling the political and military achievements of Israel.[15]

Just how much the Jews appreciate Falwell's support can be seen between the covers of *Jerry Falwell and the Jews*. Begin had introduced Falwell to the book's Jewish author, Merrill Simon. Simon sets the tone of his book right at the beginning: "A double standard of judgment has effectively been established: one for Israel and a second for the rest of the nations of the world."[16] In "a climate increasingly hostile toward Israel" Israel is the "bad guy" and the Arabs are the "good guys."[17] Israel versus the world, but for one man. "During this period, however, there has emerged one man who has become an outspoken supporter of Israel's policies and political positions, a person whose public support of the State of Israel has been tendered consistently, without apology, and without Jewish solicitation, no matter how controversial the issue. This man is Jerry Falwell."[18]

Falwell clearly supports Israel's conflict with her Muslim neighbors. He describes the problem of Islamic fundamentalism as "one of the most dangerous movements on the face of the earth.... I feel that the spread of Fundamentalist Islamic religion must be looked on as a very dangerous phenomenon."[19] When Menachem Begin telephoned in 1981 to explain why he had bombed Iraq, Falwell replied, "Mr. Prime Minister, I want to congratulate you for a mission that made us very proud that we manufacture those F-16s. In my opinion, you must've put it right down the smokestack."[20]

So pro–Israel is Falwell he backed for office a liberal Democrat ... one who was in favor with the Israeli lobby. That a fundamentalist would support a liberal indicates how much dispensationalists are governed in everything by their apocalypticism.

8

Militant Apocalypticism

Almost sixteen million Southern Baptists[1] comprise the largest Protestant denomination in the United States, and they are expanding at a faster rate than the national population. One out of every four seminarians in the nation is enrolled at a Southern Baptist seminary. The denomination is conservative both theologically and politically. In every state in the Deep South the white Baptist swing to Ronald Reagan was the highest for any voting group. Southern Baptists have traditionally been evangelical, but the trend in recent times is more and more toward the fundamentalist right. The denomination has always had a strong leaning toward dispensationalism. Many now want to make this the exclusive viewpoint. W. A. Criswell of First Baptist Church in Dallas is one of the leaders of this movement.

While there is a movement to the fundamentalist right within the Southern Baptist Convention, this has never been fast enough or complete enough for many. The alternative to reformation is to opt out. Hence, there has been constant attrition as millions of dissatisfied archconservatives have left, and continue to leave, the denomination to form independent Baptist churches and associations of Baptist churches which make up the core of fundamentalism.

Jerry Falwell's roots are found among these independent fundamentalist Baptists. He received his theological education at Baptist Bible College, which was run on the pattern of the earlier fundamentalist Bible institutes. Springfield, Missouri, is home for both the college and the head-quarters of the affiliated Baptist Bible Fellowship. This is the largest fundamentalist group in the United States, and a legacy of none other than J. Frank Norris. In his monumental *A History of Fundamentalism in America*, George W. Dollar, himself a fundamentalist, names Norris as one of only four "prima donnas of fundamentalism."[2] Concerning these four he writes, "Most Fundamentalists on the scene today are directly or indirectly indebted to their loyal stand and their magnificent defense of the Faith."[3] Falwell's fundamentalist pedigree is clearly of good standing.

Falwell's boyhood gave no indication that he would someday become a religious leader. He played hooky from Sunday School — it was sissy stuff. Religion was "something women did."[4] Echoes remain in the man: "We have to show people that Christianity is not some sissy religion."[5] "Jesus was a he-man."[6] This macho rationale slid easily into martial imagery. Here is how Falwell describes his conversion experience: "It was all so new and exciting to me! Suddenly all of life became a kind of battlefield. God and Satan were waging war.... At my conversion I was changing sides.... My brothers and sisters at Park Avenue Baptist were my fellow Christian soldiers marching as to war. Christ was our Commander-in-Chief. The Bible was my guide, my strategy for warfare.... And those front porches on which we witnessed were scenes of battle."[7]

Like other dispensationalists Falwell sees the cosmos as divided into two forces—good and evil. There are no shades of gray for the fundamentalist. You are either on the side of good, or you are on the side of evil. Either you are a committed Christian, or you are not a Christian at all. The logic of apocalypticism forces polarization. It divides human beings into two camps: us and them.

A few years after his conversion Falwell was called upon to begin a new church. Here was an opportunity to follow his "Commander-in-Chief" into the cosmic war of good against evil. He could hardly suppress his excitement: "That morning I sat at my small wooden desk feeling exactly like Eisenhower as he plotted D-Day and the invasion of Europe."[8] An aggressive campaign utililizing the air waves, the public mail service, and the tried-and-true traditional door-to-door method of solicitation, proved Falwell an apt field general. Thomas Road Baptist Church grew from thirty-five people to become one of the nation's largest congregations at 22,000 members[9] (equal to one quarter of Lynchburg's population). On special occasions its Sunday School has drawn over 10,000 people and has been held in the local municipal stadium. More than one thousand people are employed by the church and there are seventy-five assistant ministers.[10]

Speaking to church workers, Falwell elaborates on the military imagery: "The local church is an organized army equipped for battle, ready to charge the enemy. The Sunday School is the attacking squad. The church should be a disciplined, charging army. Christians, like slaves and soldiers, ask no questions."[11] In 1974 Falwell launched a program called the Student Missionary Intern Training for Evangelism — SMITE.

Religious broadcasting would be part of the battle. Right from the beginning Falwell went on the air with his church service — "The Old Time Gospel Hour." He boasts that his nationwide ministry of evangelism comprises over five million families.[12] This dwarfs the membership of many major Protestant denominations. Direct mail campaigns would also be part of the battle: "It is important to bombard the territory, to move out near the coast and shell the enemy. It is important to send in the literature. It is important to send that radio broadcast and to use the dial-a-prayer telephone.... But, ultimately some Marines have to march in, encounter the enemy face-to-face, and put the flag up.... Marines who have been called to God to move in past the shelling, the bombing and the foxholes.... You and I are called to occupy until He comes."[13]

In Falwell's eyes the battle between good and evil demanded that God's troops be given stricter and more pertinent training. Falwell began to build an empire of ministry centered in Lynchburg, Virginia. Because the real strength and influence of any religious movement lies in the seeds which are planted in today's children, and because the greatest potential for growth resides in future generations, Falwell sought to provide "a total education for young people."[14] The first phase was Lynchburg Christian Academy. It would ensure that students from elementary school through high school graduation were imbued with "the vision for Christ."[15]

The second phase was and remains, next to Thomas Road Baptist Church itself, Falwell's pride and joy. Liberty University began as Lynchburg Baptist College in 1971. It rapidly acquired a reputation as a fundamentalist "boot camp." Chapel and church attendance is compulsory for everyone. Rules are strict, and there is a long, long list of these. There are curfews and restrictions on dating. There is a dress code. Drugs, drinking, dancing, and rock music are out. So are a great many other things. Students are encouraged to report the infractions of their fellows. Faculty must be born-again Christians. Knowledge comes in "Christian" packaging—courses on fundamentalism are mandatory, and books illustrating the spectrum of modern biblical scholarship are conspicuously absent from a library which boasts almost 300,000 volumes.[16]

Members of the university administration see no reason to be defensive about the strictures of life at Liberty U. Students know what they are getting into before they arrive in Lynchburg. Besides, those from fundamentalist homes are accustomed to life on the narrow pathway, and Liberty

University draws mainly from such homes. Ninety percent of applicants are granted admission.[17] Incoming students must profess to a belief in the "verbal inspiration, inerrancy, and authority" of Scripture, and to a belief in the imminent Second Coming of Christ. It is not enough to believe that Christ will come a second time; you must believe that he will be returning soon.

Falwell carries the war between good and evil to the podium of Liberty University. He enjoys a challenge, a fight. Wrestling with an opponent is the essence of life for Falwell. Combat is in his blood. He loves to win. He encourages this militant spirit in the students: "Winning is not a sometime thing; it's an all-the-time thing. You don't win once in a while. You don't do things right once in a while. You do them all of the time. Winning is a habit."[18] "I believe in God and I believe in human decency.... I firmly believe that any man's finest hour — his greatest fulfillment to all he holds dear — is that moment when he has worked his heart out in a good cause and lies victorious in the field of battle."[19] Falwell proudly holds up a recent newspaper to show his audience of students. The title reads, "Science Loses One to Creationism." "We are winning, we are winning, we are winning...."[20] Falwell gleefully shouts the same phrase over and over from the podium. The students have been taught when to applaud; the cheers are deafening.

Falwell hoped that the day would come when "the fundamentalist kid will look on Liberty Baptist [now Liberty University] the same way a Roman Catholic youngster looks on Notre Dame."[21] Although the 1992 enrollment had reached only 12,000, Falwell envisioned a student body numbering 50,000 by the year 2000. Still operated as one of the ministries of Thomas Road Baptist Church, Liberty University has failed to completely fulfill Falwell's cherished dreams. By 1996 enrollment had dropped to 10,550.[22] By 1999 it had dropped further to just over 7,000, including part-time students.[23]

Christian education in Lynchburg does not end with a degree from Liberty U. Falwell's Lynchburg Baptist Theological Seminary provides graduate training for fundamentalist preachers. Most of its students are Liberty University graduates. Even by 1980 Falwell's students had founded two hundred new churches. During the following year he organized the Liberty Baptist Fellowship for Church Planting. Its purpose was to provide financial support for pastors who started autonomous fundamentalist Baptist churches.

The battle, Falwell believes, will soon end in victory. He sees abundant signs that we are now "in the last of the last days"[24]: hedonism, divorce, drugs, pornography, abortion, homosexuality. In *Listen, America!* he notes that moral decay in the United States has increased to the point where "if God does not judge America soon, He will have to apologize to Sodom and Gomorrah."[25] A few words from chapter eleven of the biblical book of Revelation — "all the world" — Falwell believes refer to the instant worldwide communication made possible by Cable News Network.

Falwell emphasizes that the believing fundamentalist does not fear, but rather joyfully anticipates, the End Time. The key to this confidence is belief in the Rapture. Falwell's pamphlet, "Armageddon and the Coming War with Russia," features a nuclear mushroom cloud on its cover. Is Falwell afraid of nuclear war? "Heck no, I'm going to meet the Lord in the air."[26] "I ain't gonna be here."[27]

Falwell speaks of "the soft landing." "If you are saved, you will never go through one hour, not one moment of the Tribulation."[28] The End Time is a stock-in-trade topic for sermons at Thomas Road Baptist Church and on "The Old Time Gospel Hour." Falwell's titles demonstrate that he never grows tired of this subject: *Nuclear War and the Second Coming of Jesus Christ* (book and cassette tape), "The Twenty-First Century and the End of the World." Although he is aware of the pitfalls involved in predicting a precise date, he did say in 1981 that he believed there were less than fifty years remaining. In *The Future, the Bible and You* he predicts that the End will come about 2007. As the century was drawing to a close he announced that the Antichrist was "probably" already among us.[29] It seemed that in that final year before the turn of the millennium Falwell too succumbed to the common fever, if only temporarily. In a sermon posted on his website he cited two arguments for the world ending in the year 2000. First, the world will be 6,000 years old. Second, the "three-day theory" — because Jesus rose on the third day he will return at the beginning of the third millennium.

In *The Fundamentalist Phenomenon* Falwell states his stand on a "vital issue": "We believe that a strong national defense is the best deterrent to war.... Therefore we support Reagan administration efforts to regain our position of military preparedness."[30] In full-page ads in the major newspapers Falwell's people warned, "We cannot afford to be number two in defense! But, sadly enough, that's where we are today. Number two. And fading!" In point of fact, the United States was number one.[31]

The build-up of nuclear weapons is a favorite Falwell hobbyhorse. Falwell finds it a "sad fact" that in an all-out nuclear war the United States would kill several million fewer Soviets than they would kill Americans. Hence, he has been a vehement activist against any freeze on the escalation of nuclear weapons. Conveniently ignoring what the Bible has to say about making swords into ploughshares, and Jesus's warning that those who live by the sword will die by the sword, Falwell insists that "nowhere in the Bible is there a rebuke for the bearing of armaments."[32] "The Bible is absolutely infallible, without error in all matters pertaining to faith and practice, as well as in areas such as geography, science, history, etc.,"[33] and nowhere does the Bible say anything explicitly against nuclear weapons.

9

In from the Political Cold

For more than a century Christian fundamentalists were by nature separatists. Defining themselves as the true Christians, they lived apart from the wider culture, awaiting the day when Christ would return.

In recent years there has been a change in this pattern of behavior. A few prominent fundamentalists began to flood the airwaves with news of Christ's Second Coming and the proximity of the Last Days. They preached an era of chaos and confusion, of declining moral values, just before the final battle of Armageddon and Christ's return. On the evening news ... behold!: chaos, confusion, and declining moral values.

Soon fundamentalist televangelists were reaching one half of the nation's population every week — more than attended church. About one fifth of all Americans subscribed to one religious network alone. This same network brought in four million dollars a week, half of which was in gifts.

Fundamentalist efforts were not in vain. At the end of the 1980s Isabel Rogers, former moderator of the Presbyterian Church (USA), conceded that the mainline churches were "no longer the primary shapers of values in American society."[1] American Christians were becoming more conservative.

Evangelicals were an increasing sector of the American population. By 1987 professor of religion Ronald H. Nash cited "forty to fifty million evangelicals in the United States."[2] In *Under God: Religion and American Politics*, published in 1990, historian Garry Wills stated that "evangelicals make up the largest number of Christians in America."[3] Evangelicals are moderately conservative Christians with apocalyptic beliefs—93 percent "have no doubts" about the Second Coming of Christ.[4] Gallup surveys showed that in the eight years preceding 1984 evangelicals had increased by almost one quarter.[5]

These freshly minted evangelicals represented Christians searching for a new spiritual home. Jerry Falwell saw a vast reservoir waiting to be tapped. He would attempt to convert these evangelicals into fundamentalists. Many evangelicals had moved away from mainline religious liberalism: the trick was to keep them moving in the same direction until they were part of the fundamentalist camp.

"Fundamentalist" is often a term of opprobrium. Falwell set out to change that. He himself wears the designation proudly. "I have always made it clear that I am a Fundamentalist—big F!"[6] Stifling his obvious pride, he remarks on fundamentalists' irresponsibility "as Christian citizens": "For too many years now, we have been sitting back waiting for apostasy to take over."[7] It is time to change. "We Fundamentalists have much to offer our Evangelical brethren that they need. We preach the Bible with authority and conviction. Where they hesitate and equivocate, we loudly thunder, 'Thus saith the Lord!'"[8]

Falwell needed to convince evangelicals that they had much in common with fundamentalists: "In reality, there is little difference theologically between Fundamentalists and Evangelicals."[9] "We Fundamentalists appeal to you to reacknowledge your Fundamentalist roots.... Evangelicals need to reaffirm the foundation. Come back to the fundamentals of the Christian faith, and stand firm on that which is essential."[10]

Falwell's efforts and those of his fellow fundamentalists brought the previously hidden culture of conservative Christianity into the open. Hal Lindsey's *The Late Great Planet Earth* had sold over thirty-one million copies,[11] and had been made into a film featuring Orson Welles which played in commercial theaters throughout the United States. He had three books simultaneously on the *New York Times* bestseller list. His other half-dozen books totaled another seventeen million sales. He had a regular television program on prophecy and the news which was syndicated throughout the United States on several Christian networks. Yet the name "Hal Lindsey" meant nothing to a vast number of people. Even many professors of religious studies had never heard of him. Thanks to Jerry Falwell and others like him, that changed.

For too long the secular press virtually ignored the "Christian" print media. Only in the last few years, for example, has the *New York Times* consulted religious bookstores when it makes up its bestseller lists. Recently there has been a belated attempt to play catch-up. *Publishers*

Weekly now lists "Christian Bestsellers"— ten hardcovers and ten paperbacks.

The efforts of fundamentalists like Jerry Falwell were paying dividends. The Christian Booksellers Association was soon boasting over 3,500 members.[12] There were over seventy evangelical publishing houses.[13] With every passing year the number of evangelical periodicals increased by two dozen.[14] During the 1980s member stores affiliated with the Christian Booksellers Association doubled their sales, and doubled them again.[15] 50 million Americans were reading at least one Christian book other than the Bible every year.[16] Considering that the United States was an embarrassing twenty-fourth in per capita book sales compared to other nations,[17] and that nationally there were 72 million illiterates,[18] the evangelical book business was successfully penetrating the market.

More important to the long-term growth of conservative Christianity was its youth. The young are the future; their education the principal force in acculturation. Between 1971 and 1978 the number of "Christian" schools (defined as employing born-again teachers and using a "Christ-centered curriculum," among other things[19]) increased by 47 percent and the number of teachers and students approximately doubled.[20] By 1984 the number of students had doubled again, and there were at least 10,000 Christian private primary and secondary schools in the United States, a doubling in five years.[21] This represents expansion at the rate of three new schools a day.[22] Whereas at midcentury more than ninety percent of school-aged children attended public schools, now that fraction had dropped to less than three quarters.[23] Over one and a half million students were enrolled in "Christian" schools[24] and a further half million to one million were being educated at home.[25] The motivation for home education in almost all cases was religious.

Now that the hidden culture of conservative Christianity had begun to merge with the dominant culture, the next step was political empowerment. Televangelist Pat Robertson spoke to President-elect Jimmy Carter just after his election: "I suggested to Governor Carter that he, as a strong evangelical, might want to include some evangelical Christians among his appointments."[26] Robertson submitted a list of possible candidates but the new electee turned thumbs down.

Where Robertson failed, Jerry Falwell would succeed. Falwell began his foray into the wider public scene by capitalizing on the potential he saw in America's bicentennial celebrations. The United States had recently come through two traumas: Vietnam and Watergate. The previous few years had witnessed great social and economic upheaval. The national spirit badly needed a morale booster. The bicentennial could be just the ticket.

On July 4, 1976, Falwell rallied 25,000 people on Liberty Mountain near his college campus. It was a sight for sore patriotic eyes. Fifteen hundred clean-cut young men and women marched energetically forward with heads held high and eyes clearly raised to the future, fervently singing about their proud land and the God they loved. Local religious and political leaders offered prayers and proclaimed a new day for America. The United States would once again be God's country.

This was only the first of over one hundred "I love America" rallies that Falwell and his youthful troupe conducted throughout the nation. Everywhere they were received warmly and enthusiastically. Religious and patriotic emotions proved a potent mix. Falwell had struck a sensitive and responsive chord. As a biblical theme he had chosen 2 Chronicles 7:14, "If my people, which are called by my name, shall humble themselves, and pray, and seek my face, and turn from their wicked ways; then will I hear from heaven, and will forgive their sin, and will heal their land." "My people." God's people. The United States as God's chosen nation.

Jerry Falwell carried this theme into the political sphere. His Moral Majority was innovative in its attempt to build a political consensus upon the existing evangelical and fundamentalist network. Herein lay its strength — mobilization at the grass roots. Falwell avowed that "seventy-two thousand pastors, priests, rabbis, and Mormon elders are a direct part of the Moral Majority."[27] This may sound ecumenical, but for all that Falwell denied it, the real heart and soul of Moral Majority was its fundamentalist preachers. All but two of Moral Majority's state chairmen were conservative clergymen. Most of these were pastors of independent Baptist churches; more than half of the total were affiliated with Baptist Bible Fellowship. Not only was the fundamentalist clergy the backbone of Moral Majority's hierarchy, the ground troops came from the same bailiwick. Research on the Indiana chapter revealed that eighty percent of the membership was independent Baptist or from some fundamentalist denomination. There was not a single Jew, Roman Catholic, or Mormon in this group.[28]

In independent Baptist churches the pastor was indeed shepherd of his flock. His potential for political influence was overwhelming. Falwell himself devised a socially effective means of getting members of his congregation to register. He would ask everyone to stand, would tell those who had registered to be seated, and then would lecture those who remained standing on their political duties, warning them that the whole procedure would be repeated every Sunday until election day. His actions were copied at other fundamentalist churches. In some cases voter registration booths were set up immediately after the service.

So neatly did Falwell's church ministry dovetail with his political efforts that it became difficult to know where the one ended and the other began. For example, in the year in which Moral Majority began, his "The Old Time Gospel Hour," which was carried by 373 television stations, raised $35 million from its mailing lists of 2.5 million people.[29] Most of this was earmarked for nonpolitical funding, but the potential for harnessing this well-organized machine for political purposes was obvious. After only one month of fundraising Moral Majority took in over $1 million from a list of 250,000 prime donors selected from the larger lists of "The Old Time Gospel Hour."[30] *Moral Majority Report* began with a circulation that would have normally taken a lifetime to achieve. But it did not start from scratch. It simply incorporated *Journal Champion*, the publication hitherto distributed to contributors to "The Old Time Gospel Hour."

Falwell claimed, "We support principles, not people or parties."[31] Yet he always maintained that "Moral Majority is a political, not a religious, movement,"[32] despite the fact that Moral Majority state leaders were given bags of "Christians for Reagan" buttons, and "Christians for Reagan" bumper stickers were handed out at Moral Majority's Capitol Hill office.

In 1980 Falwell claimed that there were four million newly registered Christian voters and that Moral Majority had won the election for Reagan.[33] As well, polls showed that Reagan had 58 percent of the Protestant vote to Carter's 28 percent, despite the fact that Carter had drawn 46 percent of the Protestant vote in 1976. Estimates suggest that between five and eight million evangelicals switched their vote from the previous presidential election.[34] Carter did much better among Roman Catholic voters (43 percent, compared to Reagan's 48 percent).[35] Reagan won 51 percent of the popular vote, but 61 percent of the white born-again vote.[36] Moral Majority also took credit for defeating six senators and several congressmen.

Falwell and Moral Majority had an even greater impact in the 1984 election. Among born-agains, 69 percent voted for Reagan and only 30 percent for Mondale.[37] For congressional races these figures were 60 percent Republican and 34 percent Democrat respectively.[38] Compare this with the 58 percent of nonevangelicals who supported Reagan. A few numbers indicate affirmation of Falwell's entry into the political sphere: Falwell's church budget increased by more than half in the period between the two presidential elections. His own people seem to have approved. His television viewership increased by five million, and membership in Moral Majority more than trebled.

Without Falwell and his Moral Majority would Reagan have been elected? Pollster Lou Harris thinks not: Jimmy Carter would have been returned to office in 1980 by a margin of one percentage point.[39] Harris is certain that Falwell's efforts had put Reagan into the White House. Harry

Cook, religion editor for the *Detroit Free Press*, observed that never before
in the nation's history had a religious leader had such impact on a presidential race.[40] Apocalypticism had come in from the political cold.

In 1987 Jerry Falwell resigned as president of Moral Majority. Reagan
had just about completed his maximum two terms, and George Bush (or
anyone else, for that matter) was no Ronald Reagan. Bush needed to be
educated on why evangelicals think America should be strongly pro–Israel,
for example. He just didn't get it. In addition, the fallout from the religious Watergate of Jim and Tammy Faye Bakker had dimmed the lens for
all televangelists; Falwell was no exception. There were financial fences to
be mended in Falwell's home Lynchburg ministry: "The Old Time Gospel
Hour" revenues had dropped over $5 million. Besides, the percentages
were just not there for any continued political efforts in Washington. It
was time to enjoy once more the simple pleasures of pastoring at Thomas
Road — the fellowship, the weddings, the potluck suppers. His congregation of 17,000 were his kind of people. They needed him. Jerry Falwell had
been born in Lynchburg and had spent most of his life there. It was time
to go home again.

Two years after Falwell resigned, Moral Majority ceased to exist. Falwell wasn't disappointed. He felt satisfied. The fundamentalist venture
into politics had been entirely successful. It had aimed to get evangelicals
and fundamentalists involved politically and this had been accomplished.

It appears that he was right. Before Moral Majority only 55 percent
of Christian fundamentalists were registered to vote, compared with 72
percent of the general population.[41] Moral Majority claimed to have registered as many as eight million new voters.[42] Clearly, Moral Majority had
a significant effect on American political history.

In addition to the fact that large numbers of evangelicals and fundamentalists became politically mobilized for the first time, polls indicate that
between 1976 and 1984, 22 million evangelical and fundamentalist voters
shifted from Democrat to Republican.[43] The Republicans now had good
reason to give ear to evangelicals and fundamentalists. Here was the beginning of real political influence. In 1984 three hundred conservative ministers were invited to the White House to meet with the president and
vice-president and two cabinet members. At the Republican convention
in Dallas that year there was at least some surface wooing. Televangelists
appeared on the podium. Plans to include a New Testament in the wel-
coming kits for delegates were scrapped only at the last minute. In line
with Moral Majority aims, the party platform called for a constitutional
amendment to restrict abortion and for legalization of prayer and religious meetings in public schools, and pledged not to support the Equal
Rights Amendment. Republicans hadn't exactly sold the farm; it was more

a matter of political expediency. As one GOP wag put it, "When you are as distinct a minority as we are, you welcome anything short of the National Order of Child Molesters."[44]

Indirect political influence is often just as important as overt political success. Falwell and Moral Majority can take some credit for the defeat of the Equal Rights Amendment. Reagan consulted Falwell regarding the choice of George Bush as his running mate. When he appointed Sandra Day O'Connor to the Supreme Court, Reagan phoned Falwell to explain his thinking on the matter. Christian lobbying groups on Capitol Hill had more than doubled in number, with evangelicals increasing at more than five times the rate of liberal groups.[45]

The networking was there for future expansion. Twenty-five million Americans were tracked in Falwell's computers.[46] This exceeded the estimated 15 to 20 million fundamentalists in the nation. To this day these people pray for him, write to him, send him money. Christian evangelicals have had their political awareness and political horizons extended. Falwell has convinced them that the political sphere is not something to be eschewed. He has persuaded them to be a part and not apart. They have a formidable war chest. There were years when Falwell's ministries brought in almost $3 million a week.[47] The once-hidden culture had infiltrated the political machine at the grass roots and laid a solid platform for political influence and power in the future.

While his own church ministry is the focus of his life today, Falwell nevertheless remains a preeminent figure in the New Christian Right, lending his support to various Christian political organizations. When Christian Coalition held its Road to Victory conference in September 1998 Falwell was invited and attended. But his political achievements remain in the past.

In the past, yes, but their legacy is with us today. The man who made Lynchburg famous for more than Fleet enema kits and Chap Stick, brought recognition to evangelical and fundamentalist America. Long caricatured, these groups are no longer dismissed or excluded. Falwell can justly count his accomplishments: "Most of the pollsters agree that about 30 percent of the electorate is now composed of these religious conservatives. This is the largest minority voters' bloc in the nation."[48] Because politicians are vote counters first, they must listen. As Professor of Religion and Public Policy with Rice University's Department of Sociology William Martin points out in the distinguished journal *Foreign Policy*, "Anyone who expects to make sense of American politics, domestic or foreign, over the short or long term, must accept that religious conservatives have become an enduring and important part of the social landscape."[49]

Falwell's use of apocalyptic vocabulary—"Armageddon," "apocalypse," "the Rapture"—has not turned people off. If financial revenue is any indication, Falwell is more popular today than he was in his political heyday. He has awakened a sleeping giant. Today there are over two hundred Christian television stations, and over 1,500 Christian radio stations in the United States, the vast majority evangelical or fundamentalist.[50] The once-hidden culture of evangelicalism and fundamentalism has moved into the public square. While it may not be shouted from the rooftops, part of that culture is apocalypticism. It has recently been stated that the "apocalyptic pervades *all* political discourse in the United States. The United States is a movement ... toward the end of the world."[51] Clearly, apocalypticism has come in from the political cold.

10

God's Instrument

If Jerry Falwell and Moral Majority can take credit for helping make Ronald Reagan president, the American people certainly approved of their choice of candidate. In November 1980 in a stampede to the political right not seen since the days of Herbert Hoover, Americans approved of the New Christian Right's man.

Again in 1984, despite the fact that many things he had done during his first term in office undermined the economic interests of the common citizen, Reagan was elected president for a second term. He was even more popular than in 1980. Reagan was re-elected by more Americans than any other president in the nation's history. More votes than Kennedy, more votes than Roosevelt, more votes than Lincoln. Reagan swept every state except Mondale's home state. Even young people voted overwhelmingly for the oldest president in American history. Americans listened to what Reagan said, it seemed, and paid less attention to what he did. And Reagan knew just what to say. He said what Americans wanted to hear. As Speaker Tip O'Neill noted, "With a prepared text he's the best public speaker I've ever seen.... I'm beginning to think that in this respect he dwarfs both Roosevelt and Kennedy."[1]

Even amidst the controversies and scandals of his last years in office, "the teflon president" remained popular. After two terms as president, Reagan left office with the highest public approval rating since Franklin Roosevelt. This was no accident. Back in 1984 White House strategist

Richard Darman wrote a campaign memorandum: "Paint Ronald Reagan as the personification of all that is right with or heroized by America. Leave Mondale [the opposing candidate] in a position where an attack on Reagan is tantamount to an attack on America's idealized image of itself — where a vote against Reagan is in some subliminal sense, a vote against mythic AMERICA."[2]

Mythic America. In 1980 Americans had had too much reality. Vietnam, Watergate, and the recent Iran hostage disaster had greatly undermined the national spirit and self-image. A sour economy had reduced material expectations. Three out of four Americans found the nation in disarray. President Carter had scolded Americans for "malaise," then suggested they lower their thermostats and their aspirations. A nation that defined itself in terms of growth, that prided itself on constantly pushing back new frontiers, did not take to Carter's finger pointing and limit setting.

Reagan capitalized on the disenchantment of Americans. The only thing wrong with America was an administration that had lost its nerve, and lost its way. It was time to rejuvenate America's soul, to bring back her glory days.

Mythic America. The notion of a return to the halcyon days of some imagined past was vintage Reagan. In his inaugural address Reagan said, "And let us renew our faith and hope. We have every right to dream heroic dreams."[3] Sure, Reagan's dreams were of an idealized America which had never existed — he claimed, for example, that America had never known slavery, and that there was no rioting during the Depression — but so what? If Reagan distorted history for his own purposes few realized, and fewer still cared. His dreams were the dreams of ordinary Americans. His dreams — "the world as Reagan sees it: cinematically and imaginatively"[4] — were of a Norman Rockwell America, a mythical past depicted with charm and sentimental conviction.

Because contemporary life in the United States so starkly contrasted the ideal of her mythical past, Reagan gave Americans images, symbols, and ideals. Something to believe in — a mythic America, bathed in the sunshine of unruffled splendor.

Reagan knew his stuff. His finger pressed hard upon the American pulse. His time had come. Television. Here was *the* telegenic president. Television favors persona over the person, image over reality. America was ready for image and tired of reality. A former actor, Reagan was a master of presentation. His career had depended on his ability to project an image. He had forged a career upon all-American good looks and a relaxed reassuring voice. Americans liked the Reagan projected into their living rooms. The television screen showed a man whose immediate and amiable smile betokened an easy rapport with the common citizen and a friendly interest in his or her concerns. Here, surely, was a sincere individual with conventional homespun virtues, a flexible, accommodating, and ingratiating personality who wanted nothing better than to please. The magic of Reagan's down-home charm wooed those in the trance of television's glow.

Mythic America. Ronald Reagan not only imagined a mythic America, he represented a mythic America. Middle America identified with this seemingly ordinary, moderate, and sensible man. In an age which was growing more and more distrustful of career politicians, the idea of the man next door as president had strong appeal. In the movie *Mr. Smith Goes to Washington* (from the era of Reagan's Hollywood heyday) a young man of strong belief and common virtue takes on and defeats the army of powerful interests that have corrupted the national capital and perverted the principles and ideals upon which the United States was founded. Mr. Smith represents the decent citizen-hero dwelling in the soul of all Americans — the silent majority bedrock of democracy. Reagan was America's Mr. Smith in the Oval Office.

If, by chance, Reagan was not really Mr. Smith? Americans, in general, showed little eagerness to know the reality behind the face, the person behind the persona. But it is the task of biographers and journalists to probe beneath the surface. Those who closely followed Reagan's career confess that in the final analysis the man remained a mystery. He was dubbed both "the great communicator" and "the teflon president"— something of a contradiction. "To friends and foes alike Reagan *the man* seemed familiar yet enigmatic — elusive, mysterious, just out of reach," wrote journalists Thomas and Meacham.[5] He was "engaging yet enigmatic" and "eluded even his biographer."[6]

In 1999 Edmund Morris, winner of the Pulitzer Prize for his biography of American president Theodore Roosevelt, completed his 14-year mammoth "authorized" biography of Ronald Reagan, for which he had received a $3 million contract from Random House. He was given complete access to Reagan, his papers, his aides, his friends, and his family. Yet, said Morris about the final product of his efforts, it was "a strange book about a strange man."[7]

Fourteen years, and Edmund Morris remained baffled by his subject. "At times Morris seems to shake his head in wonder," wrote journalists assigned to get the skinny on his new biography.[8] Morris observed, "When you asked him [Reagan] a question about himself, it was like dropping a stone into a well and not hearing a splash."[9] Morris didn't believe Reagan deliberately set out to deceive. Rather, it just "never occurred to him to let anyone in his thought processes." Who was this man whom a Canadian ambassador had called "the most enigmatic character of modern times"?[10]

Morris characterized Reagan as having "a fundamentally religious nature."[11] Biographers in general point out that Reagan was very quiet about his personal religious beliefs. "He's a very private person and he doesn't talk a lot about his faith, at least in a religious way."[12] But for those with eyes to see — the New Christian Right — it was all there, albeit somewhat camouflaged. For Reagan was at the same time *both* the great communicator *and* the teflon president. His words communicated a message to some while others dismissed the president's improbable assertions as mere examples of the Reagan wit.

Just before noon on January 20, 1981, the 40th president of the United States took the oath of office from Chief Justice Warren Burger. On the podium the new president read the words of 2 Chronicles 7:14, his mother's favorite passage from Scripture: "If my people, which are called by my name, shall humble themselves, and pray, and seek my face, and turn from their wicked ways; then will I hear from heaven, and will forgive their sin, and will heal their land."

That the same passage had been the theme of Jerry Falwell's "I love America" tour said something to Jerry Falwell and the rest of the New Christian Right. They were overjoyed that their man was going to occupy the Oval Office — Falwell proclaimed the election of Ronald Reagan "the greatest thing that has happened to our country in my lifetime"[13]— and confident that he would fulfill their agenda. Falwell again: "The President is a man of great faith. He's a man who knows what the Bible has to say. That is why I trust him so implicitly."[14]

Falwell remarked in *The Fundamentalist Phenomenon*, "These are the greatest days of the twentieth century. We have the opportunity to formulate a new beginning for America. For the first time in my lifetime, we have the opportunity to see spiritual revival and political renewal in the United States. We now have a platform to express the concerns of the majority of moral Americans who still love those things for which this country stands. We have the opportunity to rebuild America to the greatness it once had.... The 1980s are certainly a decade of destiny for America."[15] Falwell had the added satisfaction of knowing that he had played a fundamental role in getting Reagan into office. Nineteen years later, Falwell still savored that victory: "Ronald Reagan ... was elected largely on the backs of evangelical voters."[16]

The love affair was not one-sided. Reagan wooed the fundamentalists and evangelicals of the New Christian Right as ardently as they wooed him. The Reagan team hired Reverend Bob Billings from Moral Majority to be their liaison with evangelical Christians. Republican campaign chairman Senator Paul Laxalt sent letters to 45,000 selected ministers and priests urging them to organize registration drives in their churches. In a speech to 15,000 at the Religious Round Table's National Affairs Briefing in Dallas—attended by Jerry Falwell and televangelist Pat Robertson, among others; dispensationalist preacher W. A. Criswell introduced Reagan—Reagan defended "traditional moral values." He promised to keep government out of the schools. A month later he addressed the National Religious Broadcasters Association at Falwell's Liberty Baptist College in Lynchburg, Virginia, and spoke in favor of restoring voluntary prayer in the classroom—God should not be expelled from the schools.

The romance between fundamentalist and evangelical Christians and Ronald Reagan was still publicly evident when Reagan ran for his second term in office. At the 1984 Republican convention Falwell and fundamentalist preacher W. A. Criswell shared the podium with Reagan. During the benediction Falwell heralded Reagan and his running mate as "God's instruments for rebuilding America."[17]

Moreover, this was how Reagan perceived *himself*. God's instrument. Reagan's courtship of the New Christian Right was not mere window dressing. Falwell's assessment of the man in the White House was accurate. Apocalypticists knew more about Reagan than the majority of the public. They had picked up hints and innuendos and Reagan's sly winks to the New Christian Right, missed by most observers—like his words to the National Religious Broadcasters in 1982, which were vigorously applauded: "Maybe it's later than we think."[18] Reagan delighted in sending these subtle hints to the national fundamentalist audience that he was their man. Speaking to the National Religious Broadcasters in 1984 he quoted from Pat Robertson's *Secret Kingdom*. He appeared on Robertson's "The 700 Club."

These subtleties did not always go unnoticed by those who feared Reagan's real intentions: "Reagan has been cautious not to voice his position on biblical prophecy in major public speeches, but he has, at a minimum, confirmed a connection between prophecy and some of his policies to insiders in a casual but direct manner. Moreover, Reagan has openly supported the fundamentalist dispensationalist teachers, like George Otis and Jerry Falwell, who then publicize their special rapport with the President on these matters and leave no doubt that a ballot cast for Reagan is a vote for the right team in the final World Series of these last days."[19]

George Otis was chairman of Christians for Reagan during the 1980 presidential campaign—a group affiliated with Christian Voice, on whose board sat Hal Lindsey and Tim LaHaye. In the 1984 campaign Otis gave a clear read on how Christian apocalypticists viewed Reagan. He stated bluntly that Reagan's re-election "could make a difference in the timing of Jesus' return."[20]

Reagan loved to sprinkle his language with phrases from the Bible and religiously significant wording. A glance through his autobiography reveals a consistent use of such wording. He notes, for example, that inflation was eating away at American savings and paychecks "like a horde of locusts"[21] (a common biblical image). He says his purpose in being elected president was "to bring about a spiritual revival in America."[22] In describing his approach to writing speeches, he notes that "an example is better than a sermon."[23] He "became a kind of preacher. I'd preach in my speeches."[24] He noted that at the end of his term as governor of California he thought he might "hit the road again and try to preach the word."[25] In his negotiations with Gorbachev he cited "chapter and verse"[26] of Soviet misdemeanors. He calls Caspar Weinberger a chief "evangelist"[27] of the Strategic Defense Initiative.

Reagan's belief that he was God's instrument, his feeling of direction, was rooted in his boyhood. Hearing "the word" at the knees of an ambitiously pious mother, he was baptized at an earlier age than others into the church of the Disciples of Christ.

Reagan had always nourished a deep sense of the otherworldly. Spiritual visitations, for example. After his father's funeral he was convinced he heard his father speaking to him. He continued ever after to believe that the sensation had been genuine and not a product of his imagination.[28]

From his early years Reagan's sense of personal identity had been firmly located in God's overall plan: "I've always believed in a divine plan and that God has such a plan for each one of us."[29] Whatever happened was part of God's will and plan. Reagan thought, for example, that his father "was destined by God"[30] to be a salesman. His mother bestowed upon the young Reagan an abiding sense of place and confidence, thoroughly laced with religious overtones. Looking back, Reagan said of his mother, she "had the gift of making you believe that you could change the world."[31]

When, as a young man, he made rapid advances in broadcasting Reagan attributed it to "a miracle."[32] As the years rolled by Reagan more and more saw his life as part of God's plan. The fame he acquired as an actor he attributed to "forces beyond his control."

Then in 1970 Reagan received confirmation concerning the direction in which God's plan for him would unfold. A group of evangelical Christians had gathered at the Reagan home in Sacramento. Harald Bredesen had spoken at some length on how the Bible tells of the Spirit's filling and empowering leaders just before the Second Coming of Jesus Christ. The men agreed they had spent an informative few hours of Christian fellowship. As they prepared to depart it was suggested that they hold hands in prayer. In the words of George Otis of High Adventure Ministries: "The Holy Spirit came upon me and I knew it.... There was this pulsing in my arm. And my hand — the one holding Governor Reagan's hand — was shaking."[33] Bob Slosser notes: "As this was going on, the content of Otis' prayer changed completely. His voice remained essentially the same, although the words came much more steadily and intently. They spoke specifically to Ronald Reagan and referred to him as 'My son.'"[34] This was a son in whom the Lord was well pleased, Slosser points out. Then came Otis's fatal words— understood to be God's words on Otis's lips: "If you walk uprightly before Me, you will reside at 1600 Pennsylvania Avenue."[35] The White House.

Herbert Ellingwood, who had been holding Reagan's other hand during the prayer session, reported afterward that it too had been shaking. Indeed, Ellingwood had felt a "bolt of electricity"[36] as he held Reagan's hand. Otis saw this as a confirmation to Reagan that he was receiving an authentic prophecy from God.

If the spirit had just filled Reagan and he did become president of the United States, then Harald Bredesen's earlier discussion held special significance for all of these men. Christ would soon be coming. The long-awaited Second Coming, and all it entailed. The Rapture. Armageddon.

So, while viewers may have been aghast when in the midst of the 1980 election year Reagan announced on television to TV evangelist Jim Bakker that "we may be the generation that sees Armageddon,"[37] clearly Reagan did not consider it a gamble. Although this statement confirmed the public's worst fears concerning Reagan's militant reputation, and hence risked his chances of winning the election and becoming president, he clearly was not deterred. He already knew he was God's choice as president, part of God's plan. Was not Armageddon also part of God's plan?

As Frank van der Linden observed in his biography, Reagan felt "called" to lead the nation, in the same way that ministers are called to do God's work. With a sense that he somehow always knew what his destiny would be, Reagan said that the White House "had had a mystical, almost religious aura for me since I was a child."[38]

Then came the moment. Reagan describes his swearing-in as president of the United States: "As I took my place, the sun burst through the clouds in an explosion of warmth and light. I felt its heat on my face as I took the oath of office with my hand on my mother's Bible."[39] A shining face is common biblical imagery for God's favor. When Moses came down from Mount Sinai with the Ten Commandments his face was shining from being in God's presence.

Reagan's diary entry for March 30, 1982, noted that a congressman from the Tampico area had brought him a photograph "that is eerie. The day before election day, Nov. 3, 1980, a photo was taken of a rainbow, the end came down exactly on the building where I was born."[40]

Bob Slosser wrote *Reagan Inside Out* to demonstrate that Reagan was God's instrument to fulfill his will on earth. Slosser relates many examples to show that Reagan and his fundamentalist friends were not alone in believing he was God's instrument. Typical was the woman who told Reagan, "I know you're a Christian … and I really believe God has raised you up for such a time as this, and He's going to use you greatly."[41] Reagan's eyes welled up with tears of recognition. It was heartening to see that others believed just as he.

As God's instrument, Reagan must have felt that God would protect him. Reflecting on the attempt on his life, Reagan coyly writes, "God, for some reason, had seen fit to give me his blessing and allow me to live a while longer."[42] New York's Cardinal Cooke clearly knew how to bolster Reagan's sense of calling when he remarked that God's hand was upon him.[43] After leaving the hospital Reagan wrote in his diary, "Whatever happens now I owe my life to God and will try to serve him in every way I can."[44]

Just after receiving the nomination of the Republican Party in 1980, Reagan suggested that those at the convention "begin our crusade"[45] with a moment of silent prayer. Crusade? What did he mean by this word? The thoughts of some must have gone back to his recent statement: "We may be the generation that sees Armageddon." Did Reagan intend to lead the United States on a crusade climaxing in Armageddon? Clearly some Christian apocalypticists thought he did. One should recall George Otis's words: Ronald Reagan "could make a difference in the timing of Jesus' return." Millions would die in Armageddon. Would this thought cause Reagan to hesitate before the crusade God had chosen him to lead, the mission God had chosen him to perform? Reagan's authorized biographer reveals a chilling piece of information concerning the man who held the future of the world's population in his hands: "Even as a teenager, he had taken no personal interest in people. They were, and remained, a faceless audience to his perpetual performance."[46]

Hooked on Armageddon

Late in the afternoon of Sunday, June 7, 1981, eight of Israel's new American-built F-16's took off from Etzion air base in the Sinai. The aircraft were equipped with auxiliary fuel tanks and two 2,000-pound bombs.

In the air the F-16's rendezvoused with six F-15 escorts. Target: the Iraqi Nuclear Research Center at Tuwaitah, 12 miles east of Baghdad. It was a preemptive strike to halt the Iraqis' development of the atomic bomb. Nothing had been left to chance. The 1,800 kilometer round trip would stretch the capacity of the F-16's to the limit, and provision had been made for refueling in the air if necessary.

The force flew east across the Gulf of Aqaba and then close to the border between Saudi Arabia and Jordan, following the blind spots in the radar systems of the various Arab nations. The formation was tight enough to give any radar unit which might pick up a signal the impression of a large commercial aircraft. Military intelligence had determined that American aircraft stationed in Saudi Arabia would be off over the Persian Gulf. Intelligence had also taken account of any possible commercial and training flights in the area. The airspace would be clear.

The planes flew in low over the desert sand to avoid detection. Over the Iraqi border. Past Baghdad. Target ahead. One aircraft buzzed the target to draw off possible antiaircraft fire, while the rest of the contingent gained altitude for the bomb run. Then they flew in with the sun at their backs. The first wave dropped delayed-action bombs that opened gaping holes in the dome's structure. With precision the bombs of the second wave finished the job. Within minutes the Israelis were on their way home. The antiaircraft fire had proved harmless and the ground-to-air missiles hadn't been deployed. The mission could not have been more successful. The pilots looked forward to the long holiday weekend with their families at the beach. Tomorrow would be Shavuot, when Jews remembered the giving of the Ten Commandments to Moses.

When news of the strike reached Ronald Reagan he was not amused. Begin had put him in a tight position by not consulting with him first. In public, therefore, Reagan had no choice but to appear to condemn the attack. Begin had used aircraft supplied by the United States. Reagan noted in his diary, "Under the law I have no choice but to ask Congress to investigate and see if there has been a violation of the law regarding use of American-produced planes for offensive purposes. Frankly, if Congress should decide that, I'll grant a Presidential waiver."[1] Reagan was not about to let Israel and his militant buddy Begin down. As token punishment Reagan *delayed* a shipment of four F-16's to Israel. But he would continue supplying Israel with all the military materiel it desired, no questions asked. In June 1982 Israel invaded Lebanon. A month earlier the Reagan administration had given Israel's defense minister, Ariel Sharon, the green light.

Contrary to the actions of previous administrations, Reagan had been turning a blind eye to the development of nuclear weapons in Iraq. His under secretary of state could not make "any definite conclusions" that the Iraqis were "aiming for a nuclear weapons capability."[2] When questioned, however, he conceded that they would eventually have "a nuclear option" and "the capability to build an atomic weapon." Did Reagan want Iraq to have nuclear arms?

Immediately after the bombing of Iraq Reagan set about arming Saudi Arabia with state-of-the-art F-15's, against strong majorities in both houses of Congress. As his Chief of Staff, James A. Baker, said, "The President would have done almost anything to avoid defeat on this one. He would have made himself available twenty-four hours a day if necessary. He felt that he absolutely had to win."[3] As long as Israel was the only Middle East nation with nuclear weapons the region had some semblance of stability. Why did Reagan want Israel's enemies to have nuclear weapons too? Did he want the Middle East armed to the teeth with nuclear weapons? Was he setting the stage for a nuclear Armageddon? When Begin bombed the nuclear plant Reagan could almost smell the End: "I swear I believe Armageddon is here."[4]

Reagan could have taken a strong leadership role for peace in the Middle East. At a White House dinner Egyptian President Anwar Sadat rose to toast the American president: "You can help this process of reconciliation,

Mr. President, by holding a dialogue with the Palestinians through their representatives.... It would be an act of statesmanship and vision."[5] But not Reagan's vision. The clattering of a dropped clipboard shattered the silence following Sadat's suggestion as baited breaths awaited the president's reply. He let the opportunity pass. In a campaign speech preceding his first term Reagan gave no indication that peace in the Middle East was front and center in his agenda: "While we can help the nations of that area move toward peace, we should not try to force a settlement upon them."[6] Indeed, Reagan's efforts as president seemed headed in the opposite direction. Not only did he arm both sides, he set up the Memorandum of Understanding with Israel which provided for joint training exercises and logistical cooperation. Then when Begin attacked Lebanon his criticism was muted.

The United Nations was founded as a peacekeeping institution. Yet Reagan never hid his contempt for the United Nations. As governor of California he had refused to proclaim United Nations Day. Despite what he might have liked people to believe, Reagan did not support institutions or movements which stood for peace. Instead he blackballed them with the suggestion that they were communist-inspired.

Despite the diligent efforts of professional image-makers, during his reign in the White House peace-loving Americans feared that Reagan's thumb was poised over the nuclear button and that at the slightest pretext he would start a nuclear war. One demonstrator rearranged the letters in "Ronald Wilson Reagan" to spell "insane Anglo warlord."

Even back in 1966 during his campaign for governor of California Reagan was considered "a dangerous extremist beholden to the John Birch Society"—the opposite of the "nice guy" image he worked so hard to project.[7] Reagan knew his reputation. He notes in his autobiography that "demagogues" depicted him "as a shoot-from-the-hip cowboy aching to pull out my nuclear six-shooter and bring on doomsday."[8] Campaigning in 1980 Jimmy Carter said, this election will decide for "peace or war."[9] He depicted Reagan as a dangerous incompetent who could stumble into war[10] and a warmonger who would destroy the world if elected.[11] Former associates in organized labor depicted Reagan as a "strident voice of the right wing lunatic fringe."[12] In Reagan's words, his opponents wanted him to appear as "a combination of Ebenezer Scrooge and the Mad Bomber."[13]

As president, Reagan's reputation remained with him. When he claimed to be trying to end the threat of nuclear war his daughter Patti didn't believe her father.[14] Convinced her father was a warmonger, she marched with the peace movement. When she asked her father to talk with a leader in the nuclear freeze movement, Reagan believed she was the innocent dupe of sinister forces. In her memoir *My Turn* Nancy Reagan defended her husband, painting an unfavorable picture of Patti. Patti, you see, was simply a bad seed. She had had it in for her father from the beginning and just could not be trusted.

Patti knew her father well, though. It was *he* who could not be trusted. Reagan announced on July 16, 1981—35 years, to the day, after the first atomic bomb had been detonated—the need to prevent the spread of nuclear weapons throughout the world: "Further proliferation would pose a severe threat to international peace, regional and global stability, and the security interests of the United States and other countries."[15] Preventing the transfer of nuclear materials, equipment, and technology would be "a fundamental national security and foreign policy objective."[16] Meanwhile Reagan was offering Pakistan a massive five-year aid package totaling $3 billion, including $400 million a year to buy military equipment, along with an unspecified number of state-of-the-art F-16 aircraft. These aircraft would give Pakistan nuclear delivery capability, for Pakistan was thought to have had nuclear weapons since 1979. At that time former President Carter had cut off all aid to Pakistan in accordance with the Symington Amendment to the Foreign Assistance Act which prohibited aid to countries developing nuclear weapons. Reagan moved in the opposite direction.

There was plenty in Reagan's overt actions and in his speeches to substantiate people's worst fears. Back in 1965 Reagan said, "We should declare war on North Vietnam."[17] Senator Barry Goldwater was branded a fanatic for similar ideas. But not Reagan. His aw-shucks manner, down-home charm, and seemingly artless ways disarmed those who might otherwise have been alarmed by his words or disturbed by his philosophy. He simply laughed it off as if he meant it as a joke. Virtually everyone believed him. On November 8, 1984, he announced: "My fellow Americans, I am pleased to tell you today that I have signed legislation that will outlaw Russia forever. We begin bombing in five minutes."[18] Later he claimed he had been testing his microphone and did not intend these words to be broadcast to his radio audience. The "teflon president" went unscathed. The episode passed as another example of Reagan's playful wit. Yet at the same time "the great communicator" communicated his solidarity with the philosophy of the fundamentalist Christians. Such comments garnered hidden winks of approval in the New Christian Right, without arousing general suspicion. As biographer Morris notes, Reagan is "quick, strong, funny—dangerous as hell.... He uses humor to express hate. He smiles and beguiles."[19] The president notorious for "secret agenda," "cover-ups," "covert operations," and a "shadow cabinet" easily hid his true motives and goals. The general public paid too little attention when he began to use the word "Armageddon."

In 1971 Reagan had asked the evangelist Billy Graham to address both houses of the California legislature on the "spiritual state of the State,"[20] a rather bizarre request. Graham knew what his friend wanted. In his address he set communism over against the plan of God found in the Bible. The day was coming when Jesus Christ would return and God would judge humankind and intervene in human history. At the formal luncheon following, Reagan asked the evangelist when Christ would return. He replied that Christ might return at any moment.[21]

Reagan had long been fascinated with the End Time scenario he found in the biblical book of Revelation. Looking back in 1987 the columnist Hunter S. Thompson noted that Reagan "has believed it ... for something like 72 years." "The president is very keen on the Book of Revelation.... Dutch really believes it."[22]

From back in his days as governor of California Reagan had discussed the End Time with his closest evangelical friends. Billy Graham, Pat Boone, and Donn Moomaw, Reagan's pastor, had been influential in encouraging him to study the apocalypticist position on the Second Coming of Christ and the End Time. As Pat Boone put it, "My guess is that there isn't a thoughtful Christian alive who doesn't believe we are living at the end of history.... it gets me pretty excited.... Wow! And the signs that it's about to happen are everywhere."[23]

Reagan took time out from his busy schedule as governor of one of the largest of the United States to give serious study to the details concerning Armageddon, for it was Armageddon that most fascinated him. Lou Cannon, a journalist who had followed Reagan since his California days and has written two detailed biographies on him, notes that Reagan was "hooked on Armageddon."[24]

Reagan never lost his enthusiasm for Armageddon. In 1988, the last year of Reagan's presidency, biographer Morris mentioned the subject during one of his interviews and found himself "rewarded by an animated speech, full of jovial doom, that lasts the rest of the half hour."[25] Reagan points out that the weather has been strange for the past several years—a sign that the End Time may be approaching. Chief of Staff Howard Baker and National Security Adviser Colin Powell arrive for their 30-minute time slot. Morris says he and the president have been talking about Armageddon. Baker and Powell give nervous grins. The President regales them with some prophetic lore. Baker eyes Morris's tape recorder warily. "I tell you, Mr. President, I wish you'd quit talking about that. You upset me!" But the president is not about to stop. This is his favorite topic. He goes on to relate how the Bible prophesied a young nation from the West under the sign of an eagle.

Reagan once told a columnist: "You believed it because you wanted to believe it. There's nothing wrong with that. I do it all the time."[26] Armageddon was clearly something that Reagan wanted to believe in. Armageddon had a particular attraction for Reagan as the essence of muscular Christianity.

Americans liked Reagan's iron-man "tall-in-the-saddle" image. With Reagan in the saddle toting his six-gun, America would be strong again. But Reagan had developed this persona to compensate for memories of his childhood. To boyhood contemporaries Reagan was a "momma's boy."[27] His brother Neil Reagan notes that Ronald associated with "sissies" when he was young.[28] He had been chased home every day after school and beat up until he cried.[29] As a boy Reagan was uncomfortable with his given name "Ronald." It wasn't "rugged enough for a young red-blooded American boy."[30] His choice was "Dutch," a moniker adopted from his father's calling him "the Dutchman." It was a name he would retain in adulthood.

True to form, in religious matters Reagan gravitated toward the he-man militant aspects of the Judeo-Christian tradition. Muscular Christianity. Reagan liked and needed "a manly, sort of Gary Cooper, Western"[31] form of religion. Reagan liked to hear about Armageddon from his rugged pastor, former all–American football player Donn Moomaw. Reagan called God "the man upstairs"[32]—the man who would wage Armageddon.

Reagan's interest in End Times prophecy accelerated with the 1967 Six Day War in which Israel captured Jerusalem. Knowing that the large number of American Christian apocalypticists would be excited by this event he perhaps thought it safe to go public with his beliefs, at least to evangelical audiences. The May 1968 issue of *Christian Life* magazine relates what is possibly the first published evidence of Reagan's fascination with the Last Days. Reagan was in hospital, the lead article says, when he received a visit from Donn Moomaw and Billy Graham. The three men got into a discussion of biblical prophecy and its relation to the present. In Reagan's words: "We got into a conversation about how many of the prophecies concerning the Second Coming seemed to be having their fulfillment at this time. Graham told me how world leaders who are students of the Bible and others who have studied it have come to his same conclusion — that apparently never in history have so many of the prophecies come true in such a relatively short time."[33]

On a 1971 radio program on the subject of "Ronald Reagan and the Prophecy of Armageddon," Reagan's legal secretary Herbert Ellingwood, one of the men present at Pasadena when Reagan received his heavenly anointment and himself a strong believer in Armageddon, pointed out that Reagan had read many popular books on Armageddon, among which was Hal Lindsey's *The Late Great Planet Earth*.[34] Ellingwood said that Reagan "repeatedly discussed" the book's content with him and others, and that in conversations Reagan made reference to the Bible and often quoted it.[35] In a *Newsweek* article Kenneth L. Woodward stated that "Reagan is known to have read and discussed with ... [Jerry] Falwell and singer Pat Boone such pulp versions of Biblical prophecies as Hal Lindsey's best-selling `The Late Great Planet Earth.'"[36] Reagan told Falwell, "I sometimes believe we're heading very fast for Armageddon right now."[37] On one occasion after another he gratuitously broached the subject of Armageddon.

Biographer Cannon notes: "Reagan apparently accepts this [Lindsey's *The Late Great Planet Earth*] version of the Armageddon story."[38] Back in his college days Reagan had scored D's in the Life of Christ. As an adult Reagan would have scored perfect A+'s on the subject of apocalypticism. He followed apocalypticist lore and correlated it with the latest headlines: "*Chernobyl* means `Armageddon' in the Ukrainian Bible, you know," Reagan excitedly revealed to his biographer Edmund Morris.[39] Morris checked. Reagan was close: "Chernobyl" was Ukrainian for "Wormwood"— the great star mentioned in Revelation 8:11.

While Reagan's infatuation with Lindsey's scenario of Armageddon as detailed in *The Late Great Planet Earth* may have been known by a large number of evangelicals, it escaped the attention of the wider public for some time. It was not until 1985, for example, that James Mills reported in *San Diego Magazine* an incident that had occurred in 1971 when Mills was head of the California senate.[40] He had been enjoying Governor Reagan's amusing anecdotes at the head table of a lobbyists' banquet when suddenly the governor turned serious. Reagan asked Mills if he had ever read chapters 38 and 39 of Ezekiel. With "firelit intensity" Reagan noted that it was Ezekiel who had best "foreseen the carnage that would destroy our age." Reagan interpreted Libya's becoming communist as "a sign that the day of Armageddon isn't far off." He then proceeded to lecture Mills "like a preacher to a skeptical college student." As a Bible-believing Baptist, Mills had read Revelation but had misgivings about Reagan's interpretation concerning the End Time. Reagan rebutted Mills's points, and drew special attention to the creation of the state of Israel. "For the first time ever, everything is in place for the battle of Armageddon and the Second Coming of Christ.... Everything is falling into place. It can't be too long now. Ezekiel says that fire and brimstone will be rained upon the enemies of God's people. That must mean that they'll be destroyed by nuclear weapons."

Reagan was attracted to apocalypticism not only psychologically— for its muscular militant aspects— but philosophically. Journalist Laurence I. Barrett proclaimed him "the most overtly ideological President in the nation's history."[41] As an ideologue Reagan liked to "stay the course" with respect to a few strongly held ideas. Apocalypticism was one of these. As his authorized biographer notes, Reagan's "beliefs are as unerasable as the grooves of an LP."[42] "One might as well re-carve Mount Rushmore as seek to change one of Reagan's *idées fixes*."[43] Once Reagan fastened onto an idea he liked — he never gave "any indication that he *thought* about the things he took in"[44] — it was his for life. His authorized biographer Edmund Morris commented, "One gets the uneasy feeling that only the smoothest, most processed grain can be blown into that shallow loft [Reagan's brain], & that once it reaches capacity it will compact & atrophy into something harder than bone."[45]

An apocalypticist needs a vivid imagination — the apocalyptic scenario has a science fiction quality about it. From his youth Reagan had always liked science fiction and other books that indulged the imagination. As a boy Reagan was a loner and a dreamer. He spent hours alone fighting mock battles with his lead soldiers, rather than out with the other boys. He lived in the world of the imagination. Looking back, Reagan confessed that as a teenager he "was a little introverted and probably a little slow in making really close friends,"[46] and he admitted that he had a "reluctance to get close to people."[47] Imagination and fantasy have always played a big part in Reagan's life. Even when Reagan was an old man his biographer Edmund Morris observed that he was "totally interior. He lived inside his head, in the proscenium of his own imagination…. That was where he lived all the time."[48] Evan Thomas and Jon Meacham write, "Reagan lived in the theater of his own mind, where the president created an ideal world that sometimes bore little relation to reality."[49] An old flame recalls, "He had an inability to distinguish between fact and fancy."[50]

As Reagan's authorized biographer, Morris spent a decade and a half around the man. He mentions Reagan's "encyclopedic ignorance"[51] and "intellectual emptiness"[52] and even goes so far as to call him "an apparent airhead."[53] He quotes former French president François Mitterrand on Reagan: "This is a man without ideas and without culture."[54] The youthful Reagan had shown promise while in school. His grades were good — an A in public speaking, many B's. But his lowest grade was in philosophy — a subject which demands looking at new ideas and challenging one's own tightly held ideas. Here's how one couple assessed Reagan: "If we were utterly beguiled by the President's surface charm, we were conscious of inner depletions…. Intellectually, Reagan struck us as a man who had been living off capital for so long that he had finally exhausted his resources."[55]

Reagan's most cherished ideas — like apocalypticism — went untested by the acids of critical, analytical thought. He was well known for saying, "Do not disturb me with the facts."[56] He avoided reading anything which would challenge his pet ideas. It has been said that Reagan was the first president to own more horses than books.[57] He was notorious for getting his information from *Reader's Digest*.[58] Biographer Morris notes that Reagan regarded this magazine "as the sum of all human wisdom."[59] He liked "its braying religiosity" and "muscular Christianity." In her memoirs Nancy Reagan tried desperately to deny the fact that her husband read little, but she could come up with nothing of substance that he *had* read. Out for a little president-baiting, reporters asked Reagan what books he was reading. There was a long pause, after which he said that during vacation at the beach he had been reading a book Nancy had given him, but he couldn't remember the title.[60]

What Reagan did read was usually consistent with already held ideas. In 1985 he read *Air Force One Is Haunted*.[61] In this novel the ghost of Franklin Roosevelt advises a decent but confused president on how to save the United States from Soviet attack by using an umbrella defense system. Did this book influence Reagan's determination to push his Strategic Defense Initiative ("Star Wars") despite almost unanimous resistance from the scientific and technological community?

Robert Scheer claims Reagan fleshed out his nuclear ideology with details from Laurence Beilenson's *Survival and Peace in the Nuclear Age*.[62] Beilenson had been a friend of Reagan since the latter's acting days, and the two were often in close touch during Reagan's tenure of office. Beilenson's books were published by small right-wing publishing houses because he was known to be both an ideologue and an amateur in matters of nuclear policy and technology. Lou Cannon asserts that Reagan patterned the details of his foreign policy almost solely on Beilenson's 1969 book, *The Treaty Trap*.[63]

Thomas and Meacham write, "That Reagan was able to make the real world more like his imagined one is a testament to his will and his manipulative powers."[64] An effort to bend reality into religiously inspired contours was evident. Once ensconced in the Oval Office, Reagan lost no time surrounding himself with those who thought as he did. It was said that hiring practice during the Reagan administration was based on the slogan "get Born Again or get out."[65] Herbert Ellingwood, who was present at the prophecy of Reagan's presidency and was a firm believer in Armageddon, played a key role in the selection process. Perhaps this was part of the reason French President Mitterrand believed Reagan was a theocrat: "Il est dans ses pensées un théocrate."[66] Biographer Morris confirms Mitterrand's suspicions: Reagan "really did dream of a godly government staffed by semi-clerical believers."[67]

Secretary of Defense Caspar Weinberger was quick to confess, "I have read the Book of Revelation and, yes, I believe the world is going to end — by an act of God, I hope — but every day I think that time is running out."[68]

Edwin Meese III was Attorney General, and Reagan's right-hand man to such a degree that he earned the soubriquets "Prime Minister" and "the deputy president." Both the National Security Council and the Office of Policy Development reported to him. He had a say in recommending the appointment of important personnel. By Reagan's side since his days as governor of California when he was chief of staff, it was Meese's job to translate Reagan's ideas into policy. No one, it seemed, was closer to Reagan — except, of course, Nancy. It has been said that the two men worked so well together because they were so alike. Meese even shared Reagan's skewed sense of humor. In the midst of antinuclear rallies he asked why the MX missile was like a Hallmark greeting card. Television cameras zoomed in. The answer: Because if we go to war we want to send the very best.

Meese seriously believed that "the White House and State Department are inhabited by evil ghosts and demons whose goal is to cause harm to Israel and prevent Armageddon from taking place."[69] He attended 24-hour prayer vigils against the "demonic and satanic spirits [which] occupied key offices"[70] in the United States government. One witness reports that Meese would pray all night at the Washington headquarters of the American Christian Trust for Israel, clutching a stone from the hills of Jerusalem. He would pray "for the fulfillment of prophecy by the quick arrival of Armageddon."[71] Sometimes Meese would be joined by President Reagan.

Environmentalists called Interior Secretary James G. Watt's tenure of office "a disaster a day."[72] Petitions against his policies garnered millions of signatures. Asked why he had no long-range policy for the environment, he quipped, "I don't know how many future generations we can count on until the Lord returns."[73] Watt was a cocky, self-styled, unrepentant, self-righteous, and vociferous fundamentalist. A religious fanatic, he sent his son and daughter to Oral Roberts University, "the finest Christian school there is."[74] For Watt if you were religiously liberal you were not an American. As Guy Martin, an erstwhile assistant secretary for land and water resources, remarked, "The most striking element of the new leaders at Interior is their almost evangelical confidence in their ideology."[75] Like Meese, Watt also believed that "demonic and satanic spirits occupied key offices"[76] in the United States government.

During Reagan's years in the White House Hal Lindsey was introduced to the corridors of power. It wasn't just that Reagan had read *The Late Great Planet Earth*; Lindsey was a vociferous Reagan booster. Historian Paul Boyer says of Lindsey's *Countdown to Armageddon*, "A book more in tune with the beefed-up military spending and anti–Soviet rhetoric of the early Reagan presidency is hard to imagine."[77] Passages in this 1980 book read like election campaign material promoting Ronald Reagan for president: "If you are a Christian reading this book, then it is up to you to get involved.... the Bible's morality in government.... courage to make the tough decisions.... stand up to communist expansion.... a strong military....."[78] On the Strategic Arms Limitation Treaty (SALT) it is as if Reagan were dictating what Lindsey should write: The Russians are preparing for a first strike. The United States must increase, not reduce, its stockpile of nuclear weapons. Lindsey, like Reagan, ignores the most important point—America's vast superiority in nuclear submarines, the most singularly effective weapon.

Such public adulation paid off. President Reagan, along with several members of the United States Congress and the Pentagon, became clients of Lindsey's consulting business.[79] Lindsey's role as ambassador-at-large for military apocalypticism had gotten started several years earlier when a prominent attorney active in the government of Jamaica had distributed 1,500 copies of *The Late Great Planet Earth* to select friends and government officials. They were so impressed that they wanted Lindsey to come to Jamaica "to tell them what they should do next."[80] Soon Lindsey was invited to speak to the American Air War College, an Air Force school that teaches air warfare strategy to military commanders. Attendance was voluntary, but virtually the whole school turned out, including many of the officers' wives. Lindsey's topic?—the military aspects of biblical prophecy with reference to the Middle East and World War III. The audience responded "with an enthusiastic ovation."[81]

Lindsey tells about an invitation to speak to a private gathering in an exclusive suburb of Los Angeles. He spoke on "the detailed accounts of how the final world war would develop, as recorded in Daniel, chapter 11, verses 40-45."[82] He discussed the nature of the forces involved, details of troop movements and ensuing battles, and how the war would spread to the rest of the world. Lindsey says that up to this point he had no idea who his audience was. He then learned that they were "part of an elite group"[83]—Lindsey could not reveal who they worked for—whose assignment was to gather intelligence on every nation's war-making potential and then to predict the final outcome of conflict by using sophisticated computer programs.

Hal Lindsey informs us that Reagan had him address the Pentagon on the subject of nuclear war with the Soviet Union.[84] Lindsey says the room was packed to capacity. Others were "outside ... trying to crowd in."[85] The "response was overwhelming."[86] Pentagon officials had independently come to the "same conclusions"[87] as had Lindsey using biblical prophecy. This is not surprising since Lindsey was a careful student and advocate of Reagan's military policies.

Hal Lindsey was by no means the only apocalypticist Reagan invited to discuss high level military matters. Reagan asked Jerry Falwell to attend National Security Council briefings and to discuss with top officials plans for nuclear war with Russia.[88] Falwell had the president's ear on such foreign policy matters as aid to the Contras in Nicaragua and the Strategic Defense Initiative ("Star Wars").[89] Leaders of the Religious Right were invited to meetings of the National Security Council and to Pentagon strategy sessions[90] and White House meetings with generals and admirals;[91] for war with the Soviet Union and other communist regimes was, for Reagan, no mere political endeavor. Reagan's "crusade" was not about political boundaries. War, for Reagan, was holy war. War was fought in a religious context. For this reason Reagan gathered religious men — Christian fundamentalists, apocalypticists — to advise the military. Military leaders needed to be imbued with the correct ideology.

Hal Lindsey was a guest at many important functions in Washington. The Reagan administration regularly conducted briefings and seminars for its supporters from the New Christian Right, especially in connection with Israel and the Middle East. In a letter to President Reagan Mike Evans mentions "the last meeting in the White House when you invited over 90 distinguished evangelical leaders to meet with your top advisors on the Middle East."[92] He thanks the president "for your most recent card and for the gracious time you afforded me in the White House." At one of the occasions to which Lindsey was invited over 150 Christian fundamentalist leaders — including televangelist Pat Robertson and Tim LaHaye — met with like-minded Jewish American Zionists for a reception and briefing at the White House.[93] Featured participants included Americans for a Safe Israel and the American Israel Political Affairs Committee (AIPAC), both strong supporters of Begin's aggressively militaristic Likud Party. Four top Reagan spokesmen in the State Department addressed the gathering, including Undersecretary of Defense Fred Ikle and national security chief and chief Middle East negotiator Robert McFarlane. Such meetings demonstrated the administration's support for Israel, introduced like-minded Christians and Jews to one another, and showed the New Christian Right how it might better support Israel's territorial goals.

Reagan well knew the importance of Israel in the apocalyptic scenario as detailed by Hal Lindsey and others. The Dome of the Rock played a key role in this scenario. In an interview with Lou Cannon, Reagan mentioned the significance of the Dome of the Rock in relation to Armageddon.[94] The fact that Israel was in possession of Temple Mount was a sure sign, Reagan insisted, that Armageddon was imminent.[95] In 1983 Reagan told AIPAC's executive director, Tom Dine, "You know, I turn back to your ancient prophets in the Old Testament and the signs foretelling

Armageddon, and I find myself wondering if we're the generation that is going to see that come about. I don't know if you've noted any of those prophecies lately, but believe me, they certainly describe the times we're going through."[96] These words were widely distributed by the Associated Press and published in the *Jerusalem Post*.

Reagan knew Israel must maintain occupation of Jerusalem and the surrounding territory if the End Time events were to take place. Back in 1976 during the election campaign George Otis, who had been present at the Sacramento incident which prophesied Reagan's presidency, interviewed Reagan on television. Otis followed the Lindsey scenario for the End Time — that an Arab-Israeli war will pull in Russia and then the United States for the final war, in which the United States will be effectively the hand of God. He knew that Reagan also was a close follower of the Lindsey line. He asked Reagan what the United States should do if Israel were attacked. "Well, here again we have a relationship," Reagan replied. We have "a destiny."[97] It was all part of "God's plan" for the United States, which Reagan had often spoken about.

In his memoirs Reagan asserts: "No conviction I've ever held has been stronger than my belief that the United States must ensure the survival of Israel."[98] He writes, "We [meaning Reagan] had an irreversible commitment to the survival and territorial integrity of Israel."[99] As one who has studied evangelical support for Israel, Donald Wagner notes, "Reagan himself was a committed Christian Zionist.... His support for Israel derived from both strategic political concerns and a vague dispensationalist perspective."[100] Reagan never retreated from his pro-Israel position. Even after he was out of office his presidential seal continued to bear a configuration of stars in the shape of the Star of David.

Jews were well aware of Reagan's support of Israel right from the beginning. The 1980 United States election results witnessed an interesting anomaly. For the first time since 1928 the majority of American Jews did not vote Democratic.[101] The swing was more severe in New York — Orthodox Jews voted 76 percent for Reagan.[102]

A short time into his first term as president, while lobbying Congress for surveillance aircraft for the Middle East, Reagan got into a discussion about biblical prophecy with Senator Howell Hefflin. They talked about how Armageddon would start in the Middle East. Hefflin told reporters, the president "interprets the Bible and Armageddon to mean that Russia is going to get involved in it."[103]

In Hal Lindsey's *The Late Great Planet Earth* Armageddon is the titanic and cosmic struggle between good and evil. Earthly armies are merely representative of the supernatural powers. Reagan regarded the struggle with the Soviet Union as part of the cosmic struggle between good and evil, and the United States as God's chosen nation. One should recall his inaugural, his mother's Bible open to the passage: "If my people ... [shall] turn from their wicked ways ... [I] will heal their land." The real enemy of the United States is Satan, represented on earth by the Soviet Union. "We are at war with the most dangerous enemy ever known to man."[104] Reagan eagerly followed Lindsey's argument that Ezekiel's "Gog" was Russia. Russia was one of the "powers of darkness against Israel."[105] "Atheistic"[106] Russia had "set itself against God."[107]

Reagan called the Soviet Union "an evil empire"[108] and talked about "communism's attempt to make man stand alone without God."[109] This was no battle between mere mortals. It was nothing less than "the struggle between right and wrong and good and evil."[110] In an interview with journalist Robert Scheer, Reagan depicted the Russians as almost subhuman: "The reason for the godlessness with regard to Communism — here is a direct teaching of the child from the beginning of its life that it is a human being whose only importance is its contribution to the state ... and that there is no God, they are just an accident of nature. The result is, this is why they have no respect for human life."[111] Reagan had asked rhetorically some years earlier, "How do you compromise between good and evil? How do you say to this enemy that we can compromise our belief in God.... How do you compromise with men who say we have no soul, there is no hereafter, there is no God?"[112]

From the beginning of his presidency Reagan knew that winning a nuclear war with the Soviet Union would mean a loss of 150 million American lives.[113] But this was not going to hinder or put an end to his "program." In Reagan's words, "I had come to Washington with my mind set on a program and I was anxious to get started on it."[114] In his March 8, 1983, address to the National Association of Evangelicals Reagan explained his "program." The Soviets "must be made to understand we will never compromise our principles and standards.... We will never abandon our belief in God."[115] He went on to tell about a father who had said, "I would rather see my little girls die now, still believing in God, than have them grow up under communism and one day die no longer believing in God."[116] Reagan strongly approved of "the profound truth in what he [this father] had said with regard to the physical and the soul and what was truly important."[117] In a manifesto which became known as the "Reagan Doctrine" he sent "out a signal that the United States intended to support people fighting for their freedom against Communism wherever they were."[118] Soviet leader Leonid Brezhnev believed Reagan was looking for an excuse to provoke war. In 1982 Brezhnev declared that Reagan's rhetoric threatened "to push the world into the flames of nuclear war."[119]

The President discussed with Jerry Falwell Christ's Second Coming and the role Russia would play. Journalist Robert Scheer prodded Falwell: "The whole question of prophecy? Does he agree with you?" Falwell replied in the affirmative, noting the president's ofttimes quoted words: "Jerry, I sometimes believe we're heading very fast for Armageddon right now."[120] Reagan's longtime friend and constant companion Billy Graham proclaimed: "Judgment is coming.... It seems that all the signs are pointing to Armageddon. The storm clouds are gathering, the lightning is flashing, the thunder is roaring."[121] Did he know something concerning his friend's plans?

In 1980 Colin Gray and Keith Payne published an article in the periodical *Foreign Policy* which stated that "American strategic forces do not exist solely for the purpose of deterring a Soviet nuclear threat or attack against the United States itself. Instead, they are intended to support U.S. foreign policy .... [which] requires American strategic forces that would enable a president to initiate strategic nuclear use."[122] This article took on new meaning when Ronald Reagan entered office.

The new president and many of his close associates had come from the Committee on the Present Danger, an unofficial, voluntary organization of determined militants. The committee, replete with Yale and Harvard intellectuals, gave Reagan's nuclear theology the guise of intellectual respectability. Charles Tyroler, the director of the Committee on the Present Danger, was impressed with Reagan's seriousness compared with other politicians over the previous 30 or 40 years.[123] Reagan would give committee meetings—which often lasted five hours—his rapt and enthusiastic attention. This was in stark contrast to his reputation for dozing at meetings on other matters. Reagan had nodded off even while meeting with the Pope. Biographer Edmund Morris found Reagan "vacuous." "After three or four meetings, I realized that culturally he was a yahoo."[124] But the topic of nuclear weapons and Armageddon was another matter.

Contrary to his public declaration that nuclear war was unthinkable and suicidal, Reagan was secretly planning for its prosecution. Indeed, less than a year after taking office Reagan approved a secret plan for nuclear war — the National Security Decision Document.[125] Eugene Rostow, ironically Reagan's director of the Arms Control and Disarmament Agency, bluntly asserted that we were living in "pre-war" times.

The envisioned war did not follow the usual grim picture. It was not a matter of instant annihilation for both sides. It would be a protracted war in which the United States would force the Soviet Union to surrender. There would be a winner and a loser. Nuclear weapons would be used much like conventional weapons of past wars. Or so the plan was, anyway. But nuclear experts agree that Reagan was far less informed about all aspects of nuclear weapons than any other president since the beginning of the atomic era. Indeed, his ignorance in this area was positively astounding. He was unaware of even the most rudimentary and untechnical facts.[126] To make matters worse he had removed from office knowledgeable military personnel he deemed might object and get in the way of his "program."

Outside the inner circle there was a clamoring for disarmament. But Reagan had no intention of disarming. As he said in his first major foreign policy speech: "The argument, if there is any, will be over which weapons, not whether we should forsake weaponry for treaties and agreements.... No nation that placed its faith in parchment or paper, while at the same time it gave up its protective hardware, ever lasted long enough to write many pages in history."[127] Reagan backed his words with action. He was barely in office when he ordered production of new nuclear warheads equal to half the number already existing, the highest rate of production in more than two decades,[128] and appropriated $1.46 trillion for military hardware. "Defense is not a budget issue. You spend what you need,"[129] said a president notorious for chopping the welfare budget. His security chief, Robert McFarlane, noted, "Reagan's interest in antimissile defense was the product of his interest in Armageddon."[130]

Nuclear weapons were traditionally considered a protection *against* war. This theory of "deterrence" assumed that neither side would initiate a first strike because the retaliative strike would destroy them as well. But when Caspar Weinberger and others raised the subject of nuclear deterrence Reagan lectured them about Armageddon.

Reagan knew that the Soviet Union was no longer a military threat. He wrote in his autobiography that the Soviet economy was in a horrendous state when he took over the presidency: "The Soviet economy was being held together with baling wire; it was a basket case.... It seemed clear to me that in time Communism would collapse of its own weight."[131] A year later the Soviet economy was worse. Reagan wrote in his diary, "They are in very bad shape and if we can cut off their credit they'll have to yell 'Uncle' or starve."[132] Looking back, Reagan remarked that the Soviet situation had deteriorated to the degree that, if the Western nations cooperated in cutting off credit, "we could bring it [the Soviet Union] to its knees."[133] Clearly there existed no frenzied need to arm the United States against the Soviet Union.

Over and over Reagan indicated that he knew the Soviet Union was no threat to the United States. In a 1982 address to the British Parliament he said that "the decay of the Soviet experiment should come as no surprise to us."[134] "Time was on the side of the democracies."[135] Communism "could no longer bottle up the energy of the human spirit and man's innate drive to be free, and its collapse was imminent."[136] Reagan noted "the simple but overwhelming" fact that "of all the millions of refugees we've seen in the modern world, their flight is always away from, not toward, the Communist world."[137] Yet Reagan continued to stay the course with his program.

Many had feared Reagan's militant spirit from the moment he entered office. But the existence and significance of his Armageddon theology was a subject known in most cases by only his fellow apocalypticists. Nevertheless, as time passed his beliefs in Armageddon leaked to a wider audience. The American public grew increasingly nervous. There were antinuclear marches. Just experiencing the first hint of real political power, Jerry Falwell deemed it prudent to back off on the apocalypticist rhetoric. He hedged. He made qualifications. By 1983 he began to suggest that imminent nuclear holocaust might not be inevitable. It might come *after* the millennium. He offered what he hoped would be words of assurance: "We don't need to go to bed at night wondering if someone's going to push the button and destroy the planet between now and sunrise."[138]

Nevertheless people continued to worry, and with good reason. With Reagan, and Falwell still, apocalypticism was taking on threatening overtones. The *New York Times* bruited the concern that "Armageddonist" advisors might influence nuclear policy. A lead article in the *Washington Post* for Sunday, April 18, 1984, asked, "Does Reagan expect a nuclear Armageddon?" Even the evangelical magazine *Sojourners* reiterated the alarm: "The linking of 'our' weapons and 'God's' plan became a part of presidential rhetoric, and frighteningly it has provided the one thing our military planners have always lacked — a religious justification for nuclear weapons."[139]

It was not surprising, then, that in the 1984 election campaign during the television debates between Reagan and Walter Mondale, Marvin Kalb asked Reagan about Armageddon. Off camera Nancy Reagan groaned. "Oh, no." She dreaded what her husband might reveal. Reagan looked rather uncomfortable and then acknowledged a "philosophical" interest in Armageddon: "A number of theologians" believe "the prophecies are coming together that portend that [Armageddon]." But no one knows whether "Armageddon is 1,000 years away or the day after tomorrow."[140]

One waited with bated breath for the fireworks to begin, for Mondale to jump in, for further questions on the subject. But there was nothing. Nothing. Once again the president's teflon shield was working. Nor did the Democrats make Reagan's interest in Armageddon an issue during the days which followed.

Nonetheless, the word "Armageddon" was now before the public. Shortly after the television debate a coalition of 100 prominent liberal Jewish and mainline Christian leaders warned that the president might be unduly influenced in foreign affairs by a "theology of nuclear Armageddon."[141] They urged Reagan to disavow the idea that nuclear holocaust was prophesied in the Bible, for it might lead to "historical fatalism" and become self-fulfilling. Concerned writers remarked, "More than any other American president in recent history, Ronald Reagan has displayed a keen interest in biblical prophecy. His interest is evidently more than academic, for he has linked a number of political decisions to a biblical prophetic scenario familiar to fundamentalist dispensationalism."[142] They concluded their article fearfully. "We hope that the presidential election in 1984 does not become a mandate to experimentally test the dispensationalist hypothesis with a war of our own making."[143] Daniel Wojcik summed up public fear: "Reagan's interest in biblical prophecies about the last days and his relationships with Christian theologians who had expressed apocalyptic views (Jerry Falwell, Billy Graham, Jimmy Swaggert, Pat Robertson, Jim Bakker, and Hal Lindsey) caused fearful speculation about the possibility of an apocalyptic religious coalition influencing foreign policy and initiating what they believed would be a divinely sanctioned nuclear war."[144]

Near the conclusion of his earlier autobiography, *My Early Life*, Reagan writes: "It may come as a surprise ... but the fact is— we will all die.... What makes the difference in the matter is what we die for.... It is not war-mongering to say that some things are worth dying for."[145] A few lines later Reagan quotes from Macaulay's "Horatio at the Bridge": "And how can man die better than ... [for] the temples of his gods?"[146]

It is unlikely that Reagan would ever have shied away from nuclear war. He seemed appalled at former President Lyndon Johnson's fears: "He [Johnson] made a remark that I never forgot.... 'When Richard Nixon took the oath,' he said, 'I had the greatest burden lifted from me that I ever carried in my life.' He said, 'There was never a day that went by that I wasn't scared that I might be the man who started World War III.' Well, how *can* you be scared?.... As if that's something that comes on you, and you don't have anything to do with it! If such a war became necessary, through no choice of our own (in our country, we've never started the wars), you ... you have to accept that. That's part of what this job is all about! How could he have sat there, living in fear that somehow he might trigger a war?"[147]

Twenty-four hours a day, seven days a week, 52 weeks a year, for every year of his term in office, four military officers stayed as close as possible to President Reagan, allowing due respect for privacy. They were not bodyguards. Their assignment was to watch over "the football," a thick black leather briefcase containing the codes and mechanisms that initiate the sequence of events resulting in nuclear war. The infamous "button." Even as Reagan's motorcade swept up Pennsylvania Avenue on the way to his second inaugural the football was there.

In Reagan's words, "The decision to launch the weapons was mine alone to make."[148] In his first foreign policy address as president, Reagan remarked, "It takes no crystal ball to perceive that a nuclear war is likely sooner or later."[149] The religious certainty of the man whose finger loomed over the button bordered on fatalism: "If it's to be, it will be."[150]

Reagan was fond of saying that it is alright to make small mistakes in the pursuit of a "larger truth."[151] In his autobiography he speaks of the decision "whether to unleash Armageddon."[152] It is little wonder that after studying the man for over a decade his official biographer could write concerning Reagan, "Perhaps that's what we all privately fear: not godless Communism but Practical Christianity, that blind belief in belief which Dutch acquired at age eleven, & has never so much as questioned since."[153]

Reagan took every detail of the apocalypticist scenario with the greatest seriousness. After his tenure as president he changed the number of his new residence from 666 — the mark of the Satanic beast in the biblical book of Revelation, the Antichrist, a key figure in the events of the End Time.[154] Nonetheless, some close followers of Revelation have noted that counting the letters in "Ronald Wilson Reagan" yields the number 666.

12

"The Time Has Come"

Jerry Falwell and Moral Majority had brought Christian fundamentalism out of the political cold and laid the groundwork for future political inroads. Ronald Reagan had espoused the Christian Right position and left office as one of the most popular presidents in the history of the nation. In the 1988 United States presidential election televangelist Pat Robertson attempted to build on this platform, to capitalize on what had been accomplished so far. Certainly his chances seemed good, considering the successes of previous years. As Jeffrey K. Hadden and Anson Shupe emphatically state, "There is no question that even the *consideration* of a Robertson candidacy would have been impossible without Falwell's efforts among conservative Christians in America."[1]

However, after surprising several media pundits by his success in the early rounds, Robertson dropped out of the race in May of that year. A great many Americans breathed a sigh of relief. They found Robertson a very frightening man. They feared that if he became president he would institute a theocracy — a dictatorial and totalitarian mix of religion and politics. Planned Parenthood's Al Ross, for example, in a conference on the New Religious Political Right held in Sweden argued in his presentation that Robertson is out to create a "theocratic fascist state" and that he has allied himself with neo–Nazis and the KKK.[2] Behind "his seemingly permanent grin"[3] some discerned a "sinister persona."[4] Journalist Tom Junod found that television image and reality conflicted. On TV Robertson's "jug ears ... make him look as if he could be a former child actor who rose to fame capturing the innocence of hillbilly life."[5] Face to face Junod found Robertson to be a "virile old dog, making a show of his own virility. Thicker in person; darker, more formidable — not as funny-looking as he is on TV, not as goofy."[6] In summary, "pretty scary."[7] Journalist and editor Christopher Hitchens writes that Robertson is "smarmy and crinkly-eyed and sinister."[8]

Several years earlier some feared that Jerry Falwell was becoming a threat to the religious freedom of Americans. But even during his day in the national political sun, Falwell was always, and to this day remains, a local Lynchburg pastor. His television exposure, while viewed by Americans across the nation, is little more than an abbreviated version of his Sunday church service. Yes, he is still an apocalypticist. In the month of August 1998 alone he preached three separate sermons on the coming of the year 2000. But this aside, Falwell was, and remains, what he always said he was — a pastor concerned about what he sees as the moral decline of America. Pat Robertson, however, is a horse of a different color.

Pat Robertson is a man of consuming religiosity and limitless ambition. He compares himself not to Jerry Falwell, but to Ronald Reagan. Robertson had always admired Reagan. Reagan's 1980 election was "a direct answer to prayers to God."[9] Robertson actively promoted Reagan in the 1984 election. Later he loudly proclaimed, "There isn't a dime's worth of difference between me and Ronald Reagan."[10]

Robertson's comparison rings true. Both men had learned television's power to make images and how to groom the best possible image. Like Reagan, Robertson vehemently opposed any Soviet-American nuclear arms reduction. "Pacifism is not biblical."[11] He has constantly urged that the "atheistic enemies of the Lord" in Afghanistan, Nicaragua, and Angola be defeated. With Reagan it had been the "godless" communists. Their rhetoric entails a belief in the cosmic war between good and evil, for both men are apocalypticists.

Not that Robertson's apocalypticism is paid much attention by the news media. Journalists focus on more dazzling lights. Religious figures are generally unnewsworthy unless they engage in scandal — something to excite the lubricious imagination of the public, with all the ingredients of a live soap opera (sex, money, more sex). But Robertson has always been careful to keep his hand out of the cookie jar and the honey pot, so the nonevangelical news media have tended to give him minimal play.

Yet as Tim Stafford has observed, "As much as anybody, he [Robertson] has put his stamp on American Christianity as it approaches the third millennium."[12] He has effectively spread his apocalyptic message. He is a recognized figure to the larger public. In the evangelical community he is next to God. For he has long cultivated and wooed these his people, the people he hoped would elect him president. He has infiltrated their homes. Television.

Robertson has the numbers. He has clout. Speak of television empires and his name springs to mind. Family Channel is America's seventh most popular cable channel,[13] reaching 60 million American homes.[14] It was Robertson's until he sold it to media mogul Rupert Murdoch in 1997 for $1.9 billion.[15] MGM Enterprises, owner of many of the most popular TV sitcoms and adventures, is Robertson's. Mary Tyler Moore Entertainment is his. His "The 700 Club" was broadcast on over 100 stations when he threw his hat into the political ring. Since that time the figure has doubled. The program has a daily audience of one million viewers.[16]

Robertson had the first religious television station and the first religious network. His Christian Broadcasting Network (CBN) has been the second-largest satellite-to-cable service in the United States for almost a decade; it is viewed by one American in three,[17] and pumped into 110 million homes via cable.[18] The largest syndicator of satellite programs in the nation, CBN promises someday to be the fourth national network. But Robertson doesn't limit his message to the United States. CBN's signal beams to 90 nations in 40 languages.[19]

Nothing has been spared to get the best. Gerard Straub, for several years producer of "The 700 Club," and before that a producer or executive with CBS, ABC, and NBC, says CBN's studios "are crammed with the latest state-of-the-art technical equipment. Beyond a doubt, the television facilities are the best in the world and are the envy of every television operations manager in the country.... The place is a technological marvel."[20]

It should be. The money is there. Members of CBN's Christian financial planning department are paid by a bonus system for money they raise. The system works. Over $1 billion has been raised in potential bequests.[21] CBN brings in between $75 and $97 million a year, tax-free.[22] Despite Robertson's claim that CBN's "financial affairs have been completely open and on the record,"[23] CBN has failed to meet Better Business Bureau's standards for nonprofit organizations. Until 1995 CBN refused to join the Evangelical Council for Financial Accountability, an organization which monitors evangelical ministries for fraud. It finally capitulated only because National Religious Broadcasters threatened to expel members that were not accredited by ECFA. By that time Robertson had managed to spin off from CBN most of his more profitable businesses, so it really didn't matter anymore.

In 1981 CBN dropped all religious broadcasting except "The 700 Club." Robertson was responding to studies which showed that televangelists were preaching to the converted. Robertson wanted to entice those outside the religious ghetto. He hoped to hook viewers with secular programming, gradually weaning them over to "The 700 Club" and his religious viewpoint. He filled CBN's time slots with reruns that had proven track records. CBN produced its own "positive, godly soap opera," but "Another Life" failed to attract sponsorship adequate to offset production costs.

Despite his other efforts the jewel in Robertson's crown, the center of his focus, has always been "The 700 Club." What began as an openly religious program has become a mouthpiece for apocalypticist propaganda masquerading in news magazine format. The talk-show format is popular. Robertson's guests are often of marquee billing. They range from actresses and professional athletes to foreign heads of state, senators, and former presidents. Topics cover anything from how to lose weight and marital problems to issues of national and international significance: unemployment, budget deficits, terrorism.

There is always the religious message, though. The lecture, the subtle preaching. A viewer naïvely tunes in after Thanksgiving, hoping to learn how to trim off those recently gained unwanted pounds. But surprise. The attractive singer on the screen doesn't mention diets. She attributes her great figure to the Lord. After she had become born again, God took away her craving for food. On another show a celebrity frankly confesses that, yes, he had long been a closet homosexual. But that was before he came to know the Lord. Pat turns soulfully to his home audience. Glory be!

Interspersed among homier tidbits are hard-hitting straightforwardly religious issues and interviews with religious and political figures with a fundamentalist and apocalypticist slant. Ronald Reagan. Edwin Meese. Evangelical theologian Francis Schaffer. Harald Bredesen. Oral Roberts, Robert Schuller, Billy Graham. Israeli Defense Minister Shimon Peres. Hal Lindsey. Topics ranging from religious liberty for evangelical schools and colleges and church-state relations to the imminent End Time and Israel's enemies in the Middle East.

One of Robertson's guests on "The 700 Club" has been Gershon Salomon, founder of Israel's Temple Mount Faithful. Since 1967, Salomon has been pushing the idea of "liberating" Temple Mount of its Islamic mosques and rebuilding the Temple. It's an idea Robertson fully supports. Rebuilding the Temple on Temple Mount is one of the steps along the road to Armageddon and the Second Coming. Introducing Salomon on the show as the leader of a group fighting for the liberation of Temple Mount, Robertson remarked, "We will never have peace until the Mount of the House of the Lord is restored."[24]

As Robertson's guest in 1991 Salomon stayed in the governor's suite of CBN's five-star hotel. Because Salomon's name appeared above Meir Kahane's (the noted Israeli anti–Arab racist) on a PLO hit list, Robertson assigned five armed bodyguards to shadow him night and day.

There is one gaping hole in Robertson's religious programming, however. There is no unbiased discussion of the problems and issues confronting the mainline Christian church. Why not? Because Robertson considers mainline Christianity liberal and Satanic: "You say you're supposed to be nice to the Episcopalians and the Presbyterians and the Methodists and this, that, and the other thing. Nonsense! I don't have to be nice to the spirit of the Antichrist."[25] Robertson says that more than half of all Protestants attending church, even those who go every Sunday, are not really Christians. He spares no words—they are quite simply "going to hell [and he means literally] if they don't get born again!"[26]

Some people mistakenly feared that Jerry Falwell might transform the United States into "a Christian nation." Pat Robertson *does* intend to transform the United States into "a Christian nation." But this nation would not emphasize social justice, equality, and charity to one's fellow human beings—that is the liberal's definition of Christianity. Like all apocalypticists Robertson defines "Christian" in a very peculiar and narrow sense, meant to include himself and others like him while excluding "the so-called mainstream churches [he names the Episcopal, Presbyterian, and Lutheran churches, but means to include the rest].... I think they're peripheral these days."[27]

Ben Kinchlow has long been Robertson's cohost on "The 700 Club." A graying, dignified figure of a man, Kinchlow radiates warmth and sincerity. It would be difficult not to like him. And he is black, which has obvious advantages. It helps defuse the belief that Robertson is a racist, and it is a step in the outreach to a growing black evangelical community.

For several years Robertson and Kinchlow were joined by Danuta Soderman. If Kinchlow had seemed too acquiescent, nodding too readily at every word from the master's lips, Soderman added an edge, put some zip into a staid format. The dialogue was just as scripted as before—Robertson insists on total control at all times—but it had the appearance of spontaneous disputation, a semblance of intellectual thrust and parry. Soderman was the perfect foil. She asked what appeared difficult questions, seeming to put Robertson on the spot. But, of course, Robertson always emerged victorious. Everything had been carefully rehearsed. Nothing had been left to chance.

Robertson calls "The 700 Club" "advocacy journalism." It is his aim to present "journalism with a different spirit," "news from a Christian perspective." He effectively Christianizes the news. His biased commentary is the bottom line. When Robertson reached out to acquire United Press

International in 1992 a wave of fear spread through the news media. This vaunted press service had been relied upon for a value-free approach to the news. Would Robertson give it an Orwellian Big Brother bias?

On "The 700 Club" Robertson insidiously introduces his own particular brand of belief into American homes—delivered with his characteristic "humorless hilarity," his "odd conflation of grim assurance and chuckling alarm."[28] He knows how to manipulate his viewers' fear, their anxiety, their frustration, their alienation, their anger, to his purposes. His style is slick, his execution professional. He constantly pounds away on a single theme. He pounds and he pounds and he pounds and he pounds.... Every news event, every issue, eventually comes around to one theme. We are living in a time of chaos. Pat loves to supply the evidence—film clips, charts, interviews. Terrorists have free rein. The environment is strangling in toxins. There is famine and disease and violence. Governments seem powerless in the face of economic mayhem. They have no answers regarding the growing epidemic of crime and drugs. The End is near.

Then, just when the picture seems absolutely hopeless, Robertson offers hope. Our hope lies with the Lord. He will execute to the letter his eternal plan—the End Time events, including Armageddon. But Christians—Robertson's brand of "Christians"—need not fear. For the Lord will protect his own from "the tribulation." "We're going to see stuff crashing around us, and it won't come nigh us. God is going to protect us, I am convinced of it. I am convinced of it. That's why He's saying do not fear."[29]

Yet in an interview with *Christianity Today* Robertson said, "And the Christians of America unfortunately have been lulled to sleep with this doctrine of an imminent Rapture that says if anything bad happens in America, we get pulled out of it. That's utter nonsense. It doesn't correspond to anything the Bible says. And it gives a false sense of security."[30] Is Robertson denying the Rapture here? If he is, what does his above phrase "God is going to protect us" mean?

In a February/March 1980 newsletter Robertson finds no trouble with the Rapture. In that issue of "Pat Robertson's Perspective: A Special Report to Members of the 700 Club" with the title "Special Issue: Prophetic Insights for the 'Decade of Destiny'" and signed by Robertson he writes, *"Then Christ will lift His saints both dead and living to be with Him (the 'Rapture')* [emphasis in original]."[31]

Does Robertson believe in the Rapture, or doesn't he? Journalists have always had trouble pinning Robertson down, getting him to commit to something hard and fast. He'll deny he said what he said. He'll claim he's been misquoted, that he's been misinterpreted. As Joe Conn of Americans United for Separation of Church and State notes, Robertson shapes his message to his audience: "He doesn't talk about these things [Satanists, the Illuminati, the new order under Lucifer] when he's addressing the general public."[32]

He does in his books, though. In his 1992 publication *The New World Order* he links all sorts of organizations in a perceived conspiracy to take over the world: the press,[33] the United Nations,[34] the Trilateral Commission,[35] "the international financial coterie,"[36] "secular humanism, radical communism, the human sexuality movement, and New Age religion,"[37] "secret societies and the occult,"[38] the Council on Foreign Relations,[39]... The list goes on.

Robertson cannot draw definitive links joining all these groups together into a tight logical whole. Nor can he prove that any such conspiracy exists. But it is Robertson's "firm belief that the events of public policy are not the accidents and coincidences we are generally led to believe. They are planned."[40] There are "enough unexplained phenomena in the past two hundred years that clearly points [*sic*] to a hidden plan intended to establish the new world order.... I believe we can then trust reason and intuition to bridge the gaps."[41]

Robertson cannot believe that "normal men and women ... spend a lifetime to form the world into a unified whole."[42] "Impulses of that sort do not spring from the human heart," Robertson contends. "They spring, instead, from the depth of something that is evil." The "goal" of this "tightly knit cabal ... is nothing less than a new order for the human race under the domination of Lucifer and his followers."[43] Behind all of these human machinations is "a single source of evil identified by the Bible as Satan,"[44] "a supernatural force ... contrary to God and opposed to whatever He does."[45]

Robertson counts himself among those "who realize the invisible spiritual dimension of the struggle to overthrow the existing world order and its Christian roots."[46] What leads him to be so perceptive? Simply that he believes "in Jesus Christ, and I do not think that a man-made new world order is His will for mankind."[47]

Robertson has convinced many of his readers. When the FBI began Project Megiddo it closely watched those who were paranoid concerning "the new world order." These people were easy to trace. One place to start was the Internet. Here could be found networks of individuals who mirrored Robertson's belief in a giant conspiracy.

The phrase "new world order" had been used by American President George Bush. Libya's Muammar Qadhafi thought Bush meant Christians and Jews putting an end to Islam. Whole books in Arabic have been devoted to the subject, almost a mirror-image of Robertson's *The New World Order*. Some Israelis believe the Vatican is behind a Christian effort to absorb Israel into a similar world order.

On January 1, 1980, Robertson had something special to tell his employees gathered at CBN for the annual New Year's Day prayer meeting. It was the first day in a new decade. Years ending in zero have an irresistible attraction for apocalypticists; Robertson is no exception. As with all his formal talks, his words that day were recorded on tape. Former staff member Gerard Straub has disclosed the contents of the tape. Here is how he described Robertson's talk: "It was long — more than an hour — rambling, paranoid, almost incoherent talk that mixed many Old Testament quotations about an avenging God with direct messages from God, which Pat had written down on lined, legal-sized yellow pads, and a lengthy lesson on the Middle East...."[48]

Robertson told how in 1982 the Soviet Union would invade the Middle East, and seize the oil reserves, plunging the western world into economic chaos — shortages, bread lines, starvation, unemployment, riots, revolution. Europe would fall in 90 days. Then it would be the turn of the United States. It was all unfolding according to prophecy. Robertson has always maintained that when Israel gained control of Jerusalem during the Six Day War of 1967 it fulfilled biblical prophecy and started to move events toward the End Time: "When that event took place a clock began to tick that signaled the downfall of the great Gentile powers, the last and greatest of which is the United States of America."[49] A major war would devastate the Middle East — the "Middle East is going to explode"[50] — and usher in the beginning of the Last Days. All the signs were there. Earthquakes. Divorce. Godless communism. Moral collapse. Threats against Israel. As Robertson prophesied, "The time has come...."[51]

With respect to his own people Robertson demonstrated a strange "twofold approach to the coming Armageddon plot: Don't worry, and get ready."[52] This practical schizophrenia is common among apocalypticists. They claim the Lord will take care of them, yet, taking no chances, they busily go about taking care of themselves. Robertson's "Christians" at CBN must ready themselves. They must learn to become independent. In the Last Days the economic system would collapse and money would be useless. Robertson urged that a barter system be designed. One Christian would exchange goods or services with another. Unused land on CBN premises would be turned over to the staff for growing vegetables. When the world's food supply started to run short Robertson's people could survive on soy beans.

As it turned out, the events Robertson predicted for the year 1982 didn't materialize. So, when 1982 had come and gone, Robertson revised the date to 1984. But he kept the scenario.

Concerning Robertson's talk on that New Year's Day in 1980 Straub observes that it was "a hell of a way to spend New Year's Day.... 'God so loved the world that he made up his mind to damn a large majority of the human race,' accurately sums up Robertson's manifesto from heaven."[53] As Straub notes, "because there were no cameras and he was speaking to the most faithful of his followers, Robertson was able to rip off his mask of reasonableness and reveal his true identity: a mad, modern day version of an Old Testament prophet of doom, whose God merely mirrored his own human frailty."[54] Straub summarized Robertson's talk as "a despicable message of fantasy, horror, and hate."[55]

As Straub observed: "None of the more than five hundred people who listened to that dreary message thought it was odd or off the wall. Pat was on speaking terms with God, and we simply followed where God led Pat. The insanity of the Jonestown mass suicides has become more understandable to me. Nobody thought Robertson was headed for the loony bin. Now Pat's got them believing that God is leading him down the road to the White House."[56] "It is incomprehensible to me that any person who had delivered such a deranged, absurd, cruel message could one day sit in the Oval Office."[57]

13

The Chosen One

For all of his Spirit-filled utterances and actions, Pat Robertson is far from the image of the Bible-thumping, country-bumpkin, give-'em-hell preacher his critics might wish him to be. He is an astute businessman. His business endeavors, including his television empire and other enterprises such as Ice Capades, bring in about half a billion dollars annually. He owns $50 million in stocks, and as executive of CBN earns a salary of half a million dollars—which, he likes to point out, is low for a broadcast executive.[1]

Robertson enjoys the fruits of his material success. He lives in a brick mansion on the grounds of CBN in Virginia Beach, Virginia. The building of this mansion was financed by the proceeds of his book sales. The Arabian horses he collects graze in the adjoining paddock.

Robertson's mansion is surrounded by a brick wall. The brick wall is in turn surrounded by a wooden fence. The wooden fence is in turn surrounded by an electronic fence, which if breached summons a guard. The mansion is linked to CBN by an underground tunnel so that Robertson need not be exposed if particular risk is anticipated.

When journalist Morley Safer went to CBN he was surprised by the polished sophistication of the man. Indeed, Robertson has all the refined, self-possessed confidence one would expect in the son of a Virginia senator. His social charm, his grace, his wit, he learned in the private educational institutions of that class. His culture he acquired during extended holidays in Europe.

Robertson was to the manor bred. "The Little Lord Fauntleroy of Lexington,"[2] Virginia, was well insulated from the harsh realities of the Depression. Robertson denies that he grew up with the proverbial silver spoon in his mouth. Despite the fact that it was a fortune in those days, he calls his father's salary of "no more than $10,000" a year[3] "a modest sum."[4] This when they paid the family cook $7 a week and the family maid $5 a week.

Robertson's parents—first cousins—were of genteel upbringing and distinguished pedigree. Their proud family lineage could count one signer of the Declaration of Independence, two United States presidents, and the renowned Churchill family of Britain. Robertson's father had a long and successful career in the House and the Senate of the United States. His mother, a cultured woman known for her sparkling dinner parties, loved to travel and gather lavish furnishings for her home.

Robertson himself was a prize-winning student at a prep school which educated the male heirs of the South's finest families. Thence he proceeded to Yale to study law. Life in the East was splendid: a summer job with the Senate Appropriations Committee, for which he received a note of commendation; many pleasant hours in his father's senatorial office; a position as management trainee with a world-class conglomerate. The young Robertson wanted nothing more than to make his fortune, and to make it quickly. His parents had certainly given him the right start. His background assured every prospect of realizing his goal. The road lay open before him.

As a student at Yale, however, Robertson found himself outclassed intellectually. The rigorous scholarly reality proved too much for a mama's boy who had, until this time, had everything his own way. His grades slid. He avoided academic halls where he was unable to compete successfully, and spent time where his reputation was more certain—playing poker. More disillusionment was in the offing. Robertson failed the New York bar examination.

However, fortune smiled on Robertson in the form of a beautiful, intelligent, and gracious wife. Children soon followed, and although Robertson's get-rich-quick schemes backfired to the point where the young family had to depend upon his parents' financial support, they lived in a modish Staten Island apartment and enjoyed a comfortable life. But Robertson was too restless and ambitious to find contentment in family pleasures. These might suffice for the average man, but he was special. Or so his mother had always assured him.

Robertson had grown up under the guiding influence of his mother. He saw little of a father who had to spend most of his time in Washington. His father's generous financial support allowed Robertson's mother the freedom to indulge in flights of spiritual fantasy, which she did, abundantly.

Although formally a member of the Southern Baptist church, she began to strike up an acquaintanceship with several local fundamentalist preachers. There were long telephone conversations about matters of the spirit. She gave them money. She handed out their tracts. As time passed she became more and more a religious recluse. She declined invitations to the White House. She missed gala events. She refused to travel with her husband unless he promised to take her to an evangelist's crusade en route.

When Robertson's bubble began to burst, his mother's prayers became more fervent and more frequent and the number of tracts that came in the mail increased. She turned to her fundamentalist friends, and one agreed to meet with Pat. The next thing Robertson's loving wife knew, her husband was leaving for a Christian summer camp.

It was at this Christian summer camp that Robertson encountered dispensationalist apocalypticism. He became like a man on drugs. He was hooked. And he has never looked back. The change must have been shattering for his faithful young wife — she has accused him of being a "religious nut" with "schizoid tendencies"[5] — but she hung tough and remained loyal.

Robertson was next directed to the Biblical Seminary of New York which, in the tradition of fundamentalist Bible institutes, insisted that all theological truth was to be found in Scripture. It was during this period that he met Harald Bredesen at a banquet — the same man who later witnessed the prophecy at Pasadena that Ronald Reagan would become president.

It has been said that Pat Robertson has "a way of making the ordinary seem spectacular." The story of how he met Bredesen and learned about baptism in the Spirit he describes in his autobiography: "On the way to the banquet, he [Bredesen] had asked, `Lord, you must have some reason for taking me to this dinner. What is it?' The moment he walked into the room and saw me [Robertson], it was as if God said, `This man is the reason I have brought you here. He is open to the baptism in my Spirit.'"[6] Shortly thereafter Bredesen baptized Robertson. As Bredesen recollects, "the glory of the Lord came down on me,"[7] and he began to babble in tongues. The two took a church together, and soon Robertson was also speaking in tongues.

Bredesen was to be a part of Robertson's life thereafter. He served on the first board of directors of CBN and has remained on the board ever since. Only he, and Pat and his wife have held their positions so long. Guided by his spiritual mentor, Robertson understands the founding and growth of CBN in terms of a New Pentecost immediately preceding the End Time.

Bredesen's spiritual influence at CBN has been overwhelming. Robertson has never been one to give ear to others' opinions, but Bob Slosser points out that "on spiritual matters Pat pays more attention to Harald than anybody else."[8] As Harrell says in his biography, Bredesen "looms Rasputin-like behind the spiritual scenes."[9] Robertson has always had tremendous respect for the elder man's prophetic gifts. In one of Bredesen's visions he sees himself [Bredesen] in the White House at a "very critical time," joining the president in "beseeching God."[10]

Robertson as president? Robertson's mother had considered her son the scion of kingly heritage. She had diligently traced the family history back to the Norman conquest and had discovered a trail sprinkled with kings. Pat Robertson has absorbed the maternal message. Everything about him smacks of the divine right of kings: his supercilious smile, the haughty lift of the nostril. He bristles when his will is challenged.

For Robertson sees his will as tantamount to God's. He is the one chosen to carry out God's will, God's plan for the End Time. Had not Harald Bredesen prophesied as much back in 1968 during a dedication ceremony for Robertson's expanding broadcast facilities? "The days of your [Robertson's] beginning seem small in your eyes in light of where I [God] have taken you, but, yea, this day shall seem small in light of where I am going to take you ... for I have chosen you to usher in the coming of my son."[11] A chilling prophecy. The chosen one.

Gerard Straub states that "way back in 1979, during private moments in his dressing room before the taping of 'The 700 Club,' Pat shared with me his presidential fantasy and his firm belief that he was the one person uniquely qualified to lead this nation."[12] The one person. The chosen one.

Some years later, announcing his decision to seek the presidency, Robertson said, "I have made this decision in response to the clear and distinct prompting of the Lord's spirit.... I know this is His will for my life."[13] Gerard Straub, who was very close to Robertson for several years, says that Robertson is on a mission "to bring the kingdom of God into existence."[14] Straub elaborates: "Robertson wants his brand of Christianity to gain control of the nation so that the government can be put back into God's hands and then can properly exercise its responsibility to punish evil-doers—both the evil individuals within the country and entire countries that are considered evil. The government of the fundamentalist would function mainly as God's swift sword of retribution."[15] Robertson likes the Old Testament God of hard justice. On "The 700 Club" he lingered lovingly over an Old Testament passage in which God commanded the Israelites to destroy the Midianites: "And God said, 'Kill 'em all.' ... that would be ten thousand people who probably would go to Hell. But if they stayed and reproduced...."[16]

Straub goes on to say that "the job Pat believes God has chosen for him is not just to be the leader of the greatest country on earth; it is also to help to usher in the return of Jesus to earth."[17] How will the evildoers the world over be done away with? "Summing up President Robertson's foreign policy can be reduced to one word: Armageddon."[18] Straub knew Robertson well and was concerned: "The possibility of Pat Robertson's finger being near that button really worries me, and it should worry you, too."[19]

Sympathetic biographer David Edwin Harrell Jr. could not deny that there was concern about Robertson's apocalypticism. He notes that "critics were particularly mindful of Robertson's comments about the inevitability of nuclear war. Would, indeed, a dispensational premillennialist be more apt to instigate a nuclear war?"[20] Surely the key question.

Robertson is no fool. Throughout his biography Harrell stresses Robertson's pragmatism. Pragmatism would be the operative word for the upcoming campaign, Robertson told his staff at CBN. The campaign would be guided by "pragmatic decisions that should be made through compromise." What counted was victory in the voting booth.

He knew his apocalypticism would be a problem. Because "The 700 Club" showcased his apocalypticist viewpoint, he had to take a sabbatical from the program during his presidential bid. He had to distance the presidential candidate Pat Robertson from the ardent apocalypticist Pat Robertson. He dropped the title "Reverend" and resigned his ordination as Christian minister. Although he was the first religious leader to be a serious candidate for president of the United States he would have to clip "God" out of his vocabulary and speak instead of "traditional values" and "basic moral principles."[21] History was rewritten. The new edition of his autobiography no longer mentioned that God had once told him not to go into politics. His more damning utterances were denied. As Harrell notes: "Until his presidential ambitions surfaced, his insights were likely to be framed in the language of dispensational premillennialism. But by the mid-1980s his prophetic dogmatism had waned…. by the 1980s radical eschatology had disappeared from his rhetoric, if not from his religious faith."[22]

Harrell quotes Bob Slosser: "'As a close friend,' said Bob Slosser, 'I'd be hard pressed to say exactly what he believes regarding premillennial philosophy…. He wrote some brilliant things and he wrote some things that I wish he hadn't written.'"[23] Slosser is more than just a "close friend." Slosser has ghostwritten many of Robertson's books. He has been an executive of CBN, and on its board of directors, which consists of only three persons other than Robertson and his wife. He has been president of Robertson's Regent University and a professor of journalism there.

The news media were certainly not fooled. To protect himself during his campaign Robertson was at times evasive and even downright surly in response to journalistic prodding. Yet CBS's Dan Rather treated Robertson respectfully and ABC's Peter Jennings was the perfect gentleman. They refrained from asking the difficult questions. Not so, NBC's Tom Brokaw. The day of the Iowa caucus, on the "Nightly News" telecast Brokaw referred to Robertson as a televangelist and asked if he got his advice from God on specific political decisions. The implication was obvious—that Robertson would be acting under God's orders if he made it to the White House. Clearly agitated, Robertson snapped back, "I'd like to point out to you, if you don't mind, I think it's the last time I want to be called a television evangelist.... I really believe that henceforth the religious bigotry that question of yours implies is going to be a dead issue. I don't like it."[24]

As a talk-show host Robertson was used to controlling the interview situation. Now the tables were turned. Robertson was no longer in control. He hated it. In this age of audio- and videotape it was impossible to escape skeletons from the past, and the news media always seemed to find those skeletons. The smooth veteran of television became so flustered when *Newsweek* called him a televangelist that his grammar suffered: "It is this incredible arrogance of the liberal media and guys like you who come around from your high horse, label me contrary to my desires."[25]

The religious Robertson kept sneaking up to haunt him. In February 1988 a *Newsweek* article dredged up Robertson's words from "The 700 Club," October 29, 1982: "We ought to close Halloween down. Do you want your children to dress up like witches? They are acting out satanic rituals."[26] Robertson found himself constantly defending the claim that he had prayed away a hurricane that had threatened the eastern seaboard. He could not shake questions concerning his speaking with God. If he denied this he would risk losing the evangelical vote, which some had estimated to be as large as 80 million.

Robertson obligingly kept furnishing the news media with tempting morsels. [He claimed to journalists at the *Washington Post* found that he was not a member of the board of directors of the United Virginia Bank,] but had only served on a community advisory board. The *Dallas Morning News* noted that Robertson's IQ kept changing—159, 139, 137—making him a genius, and that his claim in his book *America's Dates with Destiny* to be a tax lawyer was an exaggeration; he had never passed the bar.

His résumé fudged the facts—something sure to make a journalist's antennae quiver. Robertson said he had been educated in Europe. In fact, he had had only one summer as a student of fine arts at the University of London, and most of this "education" occurred outside the covers of any book—living the fine life of a carefree, well-to-do young playboy, traveling through France and Italy. His résumé also stated that he had been a combat officer in Korea. But Robertson had never engaged in combat, nor had he ever been in any danger from combat. Former GOP congressman for California Pete McCloskey had served with Robertson in the same unit. According to McCloskey, Robertson had boasted that his father's influence had gotten him out of combat duty. Instead, Robertson served as a division liquor officer, flying supplies in from Japan. Robertson was so furious with the charge he sued McCloskey and Indiana Democratic Representative Andy Jabobs for $35 million.[27] That proved to be a mistake. More dirty laundry got aired. In a sworn deposition an emeritus professor at Tulane, who had also served with Robertson in Korea, not only confirmed McCloskey's statements but said he heard that Robertson had "messed around with prostitutes" while serving in Korea[28] and had sexually harassed a young Korean girl who cleaned the barracks.[29]

Robertson made politically fatal remarks about his competition. On one occasion he accused George Bush of maneuvering events in the world of televangelism — particularly with respect to Jimmy Swaggart — in order to cast Robertson in a bad light.[30] Meanwhile, Robertson's troops were busy launching a whispering campaign alleging that the daughter of another competitor in the political ring had had an abortion.[31]

Despite all these troubles Robertson had one big plus as a campaigner. His television experience. He had years in front of the television camera — enough to dwarf other potential candidates for the highest office in the land. In this day when few people take the time to read, television has become the arbiter of public opinion, the image-maker par excellence. Ronald Reagan had known this, and used it to his great advantage. Mastery of this medium confers power, and Robertson had mastered television. He had long provided reassurance to lonely thousands huddled before the glow of their televisions. They had come to trust his smiling electronic face, his calming voice.

He could be sure of the evangelical vote. Well before publicly declaring his political intentions, Robertson told the audience of "The 700 Club" that "We have enough votes to run the country…. And when the people say 'we've had enough,' we are going to take over the country."[32] Triumphing in his stunning success in the Michigan caucus in 1986 Robertson proclaimed, "The Christians have won!… What a breakthrough for the Kingdom."[33]

His influence with the evangelical world and his gargantuan mailing lists allowed Robertson to tap into a well of funds. When he announced his candidacy he had already raised $11 billion, second only to George Bush.[34] At that time Democratic National Committee Chairman Paul G. Kirk, Jr. stated that "Pat Robertson has the most powerful political organization in America."[35] He was right. It has since been discovered that as early as the latter part of Reagan's first term in office Robertson had already begun to accumulate a war chest. From 1984 to 1986, he had channeled $8.5 million in CBN funds to his Freedom Council.[36] Although Freedom Council had been set up in 1981 to encourage conservative Christians to participate in the political process and to educate charismatics in local political tactics, it had evolved into a de facto Robertson-for-president organization. When the IRS began investigations on charges of misappropriation of funds, Robertson disbanded Freedom Council.

Robertson left the race for the White House in 1988. However, almost exactly two years earlier God had spoken to him: "I have chosen you to usher in the coming of My Son."[37] Robertson remembered these words. His days in politics were far from over.

Virus

No, Robertson was not finished with politics. Quite the contrary. Since his presidential campaign Robertson's political activities have increased in size and effectiveness. David Harrell's appraisal of Robertson as "an extraordinarily sophisticated leader"[1] has proven true.

At the Republican convention of 1992 Robertson had over 300 delegates—2½ times as many as he had for his presidential quest four years earlier. It wasn't so much that Robertson had risen from the political grave, as that he had never died. As one writer remarked, "The national media missed what was possibly the biggest political story of 1992."[2]

The secular press failed to grasp the politics of the New Christian Right, and to appreciate its power. In reporting on the campaigns of Jerry Falwell and Pat Robertson the *Washington Post* had described their evangelical followers as "largely poor, uneducated, and easy to command."[3] An obsolete stereotype. As Joe Conason observed in the *Columbia Journalism Review*, the level of knowledge and mastery of current political technology among the leadership of the religious right is generally far higher than that of the journalists who regard them as hicks."[4]

The '88 campaign propelled Robertson into a political future. It gave him a list of three million petition signers[5] and a core of dedicated activists. There are many strong political organizations in the New Christian Right but, as those who study this trend observe, Robertson "is the most powerful of the lot and the first to build a truly effective, nationwide, political machine."[6]

As a virus changes its configuration in order to fool the body's defenses, Robertson's political organizations drop old names and adopt new ones to keep their opponents confused. When Freedom Council was disbanded, up popped the Christian Coalition — a group founded to "mobilize and train Christians for effective political action."[7]

As a virus creeps up on the body to catch it unawares, Robertson's foot soldiers keep a low profile. They use direct mail and phone trees. Freedom Council distributed an instruction sheet to its workers in Minnesota warning that "experience has shown it is best not to say you are entering politics because of your Christian beliefs."[8] In Iowa Freedom Council's instruction sheet suggested, "Give the impression that you are there to work for the party, not to push an ideology.... Try not to let on that a close group of friends are becoming active in the party together.... Hide your strength."[9] The Christian Coalition had originally aimed to take control of the Republican Party, but it didn't want this fact shouted from the rooftops. A handbook designed for those running for political office in Pennsylvania warned, "In Republican circles, never mention the name Christian Coalition."[10] In local and state elections all over the country the Christian Coalition ran "stealth candidates" who talked of secular issues like budgets and taxes while keeping secret their religious agenda. As with other New Christian Right organizations, it hides its activities under the "profamily" banner. Subterfuge and misdirection were the ploy. Get pro-choicers to vote against their candidate by focusing on some other local issue — like traffic — to keep them off the scent.

From the beginning the Christian Coalition's executive director said, "We're flying below radar."[11] His troops came to be known as "the invisible army." Robertson's then right-hand man in the organization, Ralph Reed, liked to brag about "stealth" tactics and "guerrilla warfare"[12] until he found it prudent to moderate such language. In a 1991 interview with *Virginian-Pilot* regarding the Christian Coalition's stealth tactics Reed said, "I want to be invisible. I paint my face and travel at night. You don't know it's over until you're in a body bag. You don't know until election night."[13]

So well did the Christian Coalition hide its doings, as late as 1992 the *Christian Century* could report that the development of the Coalition as a political force was "largely ignored by media."[14] As Joe Conn of Americans United for Separation of Church and State remarked, "The press has been mistaken in thinking that when Moral Majority died the Christian Right died."[15]

The Christian Coalition has over two million members and 2,000 local chapters spread over all 50 states.[16] Its goals are longterm, its ambitions unlimited — a "Christian in the White House" (Robertson's kind of "Christian").[17] On September 13, 1997, Robertson told 100 coalition activists that he wanted "a winner" in the next presidential election: "There are 175,000 precincts in the country, and we want ten trained workers in each of them. That's about [enough] to ... take the nation."[18] The Christian Coalition hasn't gotten one of its own into the White House yet, but as a large grass-roots political machine it has little comparable competition and plenty of time.

The key to its hegemony has been Robertson's grass-roots approach. The organization has gotten its people in at the local level. Just as a virus attacks the human body at the cell level, Robertson's troops seek to change society precinct by precinct. They have grown the movement from the ground up. Members don't need to worry about the presidency right away; the presidency will follow in due course. It's a matter of activism, organization, process, tactics, strategy.

Realizing that only a fraction of registered voters ever exercise their democratic franchise,[19] members of the Christian Coalition concentrate on getting "the bodies" into the voting booth. How did the Christian Coalition know whom to target, so that their efforts would prove most efficient? One strategist suggested setting up a phony polling firm which would ask loaded questions about abortion, school prayer, gays. On election day it was a simple matter of calling those who had offered right-wing responses and reminding them to vote. The telephones at the Christian Coalition are never idle. People's concerns and voting patterns are canvassed in detail and the results stored in computer data banks. Tested in the Virginia Beach area, this method resulted in seven of nine state senate races going to conservative Republicans.

The organization must aim to fill the gaps in the political system. As former field director of the Christian Coalition Guy Rodgers told delegates to an organizational meeting, members don't need to convince the majority of Americans that they're right. Voter turnout is so low that getting the right people away from their television sets and out to vote is all that matters. Members can get those delegate slots at conventions. They can elect their people to school boards, municipal councils, GOP state committees. They should register churchgoers. Only a fraction of eligible voters are registered and elections are decided by merely 6 or 7 percent of eligible voters in city council, state legislature, and county commission elections, and by just 15 percent in presidential elections.[20] In some local elections for school board, for example, 3 or 4 percent of eligible voters would ensure victory. Electing precinct delegates to state conventions was a joke. Often only one person filed, and in one case one third of 12,700 precincts went begging.[21]

When it came to county conventions the trick was to outlast the competition. One document advised the Robertson people to ask for a vote on every item that came up to drag things out. When the time came at the end for the important votes many people would have left. The coalition's members would now be a larger fraction of the total present — 30 out of 50, instead of 30 out of 100 — and would win those critical votes. The next day people would be surprised to learn that the usual favorite got ousted as county chairperson.

Members are advised to see their first efforts as a dry run, a chance to gain some experience, to learn from mistakes. They are told to build on this. Robertson never tires of pounding home the necessity of hard work at the local level. It was because he insisted that the cumbersome and intricate procedures in every electoral precinct be mastered, that he was able to glean some early political success. In the 1992 election the Christian Coalition contacted 40 million voters, and distributed literature at 40,000 churches.[22] Its efforts paid off. A survey by People for the American Way showed that the coalition won 40 percent of 500 selected representative elections.[23]

Specific areas have been targeted in the invasion plan. One is indirect political pressure. The goal here is to keep after anyone who has won an election, to influence the platform of the Republican National Committee, and eventually to control this body. The nominee should be made to dance to Robertson's tune, and the convention held hostage to his extremist views. As a result of his surprising showing in 1988, Robertson demanded, and got, a chance to address the Republican convention in prime time.

It has been standard coalition practice during elections to send out "score cards" which indicate how the several candidates have voted on various issues. Another standard practice is to write and distribute "voter guides" which list the various candidates' positions on issues of coalition concern. In the 1998 election 45 million of these guides were distributed,[24] often through sympathetic churches, even though two years earlier the Federal Election Commission had filed suit against the Christian Coalition, charging it with illegally influencing elections in favor of the Republicans. FEC lawyers had come across one letter from Ralph Reed to George Bush containing the incriminating statement, "If you want our votes, put some of us in charge."[25]

For ten years the Internal Revenue Service had been pondering the tax-exempt status of the coalition. In 1999 it came to a decision. The Christian Coalition would not be tax-exempt. Its voter guides were little short of electioneering for the Republican Party. But the coalition got around this. The national body became the Christian Coalition International. It would outright endorse candidates and contribute election funds. Meanwhile, the Texas affiliate, which was tax-exempt, would move into the

Virginia head offices and become the Christian Coalition of America. In reality it would take over the role of the erstwhile national Christian Coalition. It would continue the policy of distributing voter guides, but on a national rather than state scale. Not deterred, the Christian Coalition of America planned to distribute score cards and 75 million voter guides[26] through 70,000 churches[27] for the 2,000 election. To recruit voters $21 million was set aside.[28]

Robertson claims the Christian Coalition is nonpartisan. Yet right from the beginning its GOP bias was obvious. Robertson credits the Rev. Billy McCormack with urging him to form the Christian Coalition. McCormack's record as an operative for the New Christian Right was solid. He had led a successful effort within Louisiana's GOP to block a denunciation of Klansman and neo–Nazi David Duke and an investigation into his alleged distribution of hate literature from his office as a state legislator.

Nonpartisan? The Christian Coalition took credit for the Republican Party's sweeping gains in the 1994 midterm elections. They claimed that participation by born-again evangelicals had vastly increased, accounting for 28 of 48 new members of Congress. The day after the election Ralph Reed appeared on "The 700 Club" with the good news: "If the Republican candidate won with less than 53 percent of the vote, these voters [evangelicals wooed by the Christian Coalition] provided the margin of victory."[29] The Republican Party had taken both Houses for the first time since 1952. Political scientists assert that "the 1994 election was an 'earthquake' that transformed the political landscape," and note that "Christian conservatism was an important force in producing the 1994 earthquake."[30] Others wrote that those in the New Christian Right "spearheaded the Republican triumph in the 1994 congressional elections and remain a powerful force in American politics — indeed, they form a base of the Republican Party."[31] The Christian Coalition is the leading light of the New Christian Right.

Nonpartisan? In 1995 the Christian Coalition held a "Road to Victory" conference. Every major Republican presidential contender except Arlen Specter spoke from the podium. All pledged loyalty to the coalition's goals. Speaker of the House Newt Gingrich and other prominent Republicans also addressed the conference. The coalition's 1998 Road to Victory conference (not a presidential election event) attracted the House majority leader and the Senate majority leader, among other notables.

In 1995 Americans United for Separation of Church and State in concert with Interfaith Alliance Foundation undertook a survey. They found that nearly 200 of the 535 members of Congress voted in line with the Christian Coalition's goals at least 83 percent of the time, many 100 percent of the time.[32] When Michael Kinsley, senior editor with *The New*

Republic, wrote that Robertson is "the most important person in the most powerful faction within the Republican Party"[33] he clearly knew what he was talking about.

Nonpartisan? Robertson's minions control the Republican Party in 18 states and have a significant voice in it in 13 others.[34] So much do Robertson's Christian Coalition and other Christian Right groups influence Republican politics, American business executives and Wall Streeters have begun to feel left out. They have accused the Republican Congress of "being in the pocket of Christian conservatives."[35]

In the 1998 congressional election the Republicans lost ground. Some wrongly interpreted this to mean that the Christian Right was also losing ground. If nothing else this faulty inference demonstrates how closely associated in public perception the Christian Right and the Republican Party have become. Political scientists have pointed out that, although there was some slippage in the 1998 election, it "did not crack the foundation of Religious Right influence."[36] Most of the Christian Right stalwarts were reelected.

Political scientists believe that conservative Christians such as those who belong to the Christian Coalition are so important that the Republican Party "must have their support to succeed."[37] In the '98 election the GOP failed to get that wholehearted endorsement from the Christian Right. Evangelicals and fundamentalists came out to the polls. Twenty-four percent of those who voted in the '98 election were religious conservatives.[38] This is consistent with voter registration. Twenty-five percent of registered voters are white evangelical Protestants.[39] Evangelicals were voting. They just were not voting for the Republicans. An exit poll conducted by the Christian Coalition showed that "conservative" Christian support for the Republicans had dropped to 54 percent — down from 66 percent in 1994.[40] Randy Tate of the Christian Coalition thought he knew why. The Republicans had no clear agenda, no vision, as they approached the election. Sociologist Christian Smith pointed out that "evangelicals are cynical about the GOP and have reason to be"[41] — the GOP did not push Christian Right issues through Congress.

Yes, the Christian Coalition and the rest of the Christian Right are still alive and vigorously healthy. Although Ralph Reed has relinquished his executive role in the Christian Coalition he remains as vigorously involved with the Christian Right as ever: "We [the Christian Right] are going to stay and stay and stay"[42] — until they achieve all their goals. The Republican Party is their domain of operation. The liberal northeastern press has never been overly sympathetic to the Christian Right. Nevertheless, facts are facts. Writes columnist John Ellis of the *Boston Globe,* Religious conservatives are "the soul of the Republican Party ... the GOP's most important ... constituency."[43] In the 2000 presidential election one of those threw his hat into the ring — Gary Bauer, a key advisor to former president, Ronald Reagan.

Since 1987 when he joined the staff of Americans United for Separation of Church and State, Robert Boston has been keeping close tabs on Pat Robertson. Boston has since become an assistant director in the organization and an assistant editor of its periodical *Church & State*. He has used the mammoth files of the organization for his book *The Most Dangerous Man in America? Pat Robertson and the Rise of the Christian Coalition*. He describes his book as "a fire alarm, ringing loudly and warning of immediate danger — that an intolerant extremist now comes perilously close to holding the reins of American politics."[44]

If one asks Boston whether Pat Robertson and his Christian Coalition are nonpartisan, his answer is an emphatic "no." "The organization already holds the GOP in a virtual headlock, and serious contenders for the presidency are forced to kowtow to Robertson and Reed."[45]

Robertson has come a long way since his failed campaign for the presidency in 1988. At that time he was considered to be on the margins of the political sphere, not to be taken too seriously. "Today," writes Robert Boston, "he has top leaders of the Republican Party hanging on his every word,"[46] despite the fact that his "views are extreme, dangerous and, frankly, often bizarre."[47]

In a fundraising letter during his campaign against the Equal Rights Amendment Robertson wrote, "The feminist agenda is not about equal rights for women. It is about a socialist, anti-family political movement that encourages women to leave their husbands, kill their children, practice witchcraft, destroy capitalism and become lesbians."[48]

Many persons in the political rightwing may be embarrassed, even outraged, by Robertson's bald assertions against women, Jews, and others. But they hold their tongues. Why? Robert Boston says it is because Robertson controls a powerful bloc of votes. Robertson's influence is smothering. This "extremist TV preacher is on the verge of seizing control of the country's dominant political party, rapidly putting himself in the position of having enough political power to make or break presidents."[49] For this reason many are willing to put politics above principle and remain silent in the face of Robertson's unsavory assertions. However, their very silence only reinforces Robertson's position. Boston observes that Robertson's "political movement is so influential in the GOP that he has in effect become untouchable."[50]

Others have aspired to his influence. Twenty leaders of a dozen rightwing evangelical organizations who, like Robertson, would be kingmakers were quick off the starting blocks regarding the next presidential election. They summoned potential candidates to Washington in February 1999 to take the "Christian" litmus test.

Meanwhile, Robertson's viruses are busy stealthily undermining the future health of the body politic. He has his own university — Regent University (formerly CBN University). Its endowment is in the top 100 among universities in the United States.[51] It trains 1,700 graduate students[52] in law, education, business, theology, and communications—all areas of key influence. The School of Communication, which offers a doctoral program, embraces radio, television, drama, film, public relations, media management, journalism, and advertising. Clearly, no gaps are left unfilled.

This is what the author of Robertson's "authorized" biography has to say about the philosophy behind the founding of Regent university: "The goal was [and still is] gradually to infiltrate secular society with committed Christians who were at least as well prepared as their uncommitted colleagues and thereby to permeate the local fabric with biblical values." Infiltrate. Permeate. Gradually. Robertson is building for the future, for the long term. An extension campus in Washington, D.C. is in the works. He confidently predicts that Regent University will survive Armageddon, and become the center for a flowering new "Christian" society. As Pat Buchanan stated from the podium at the 1992 Republican convention, "There is a religious war going on in this country ... critical to the kind of nation we shall be."[53]

15

The War of Good
Versus Evil

Robertson is a charismatic. Charismatics believe themselves to have received from God Pentecostal gifts— speaking in tongues, working miracles, hearing God's voice. Those who claim to hear God's voice are called "Pentecostals" or "charismatics." The difference is formal, not material: the former belong to Pentecostal denominations; the latter do not. With respect to religious style and ethos they can be considered identical. A 1980 Gallup poll estimated that 29 million adult Americans counted themselves among these two groups.[1] Such a surge in Pentecostalism is considered a sure sign that the End is not far off. Pentecostals and charismatics await the imminent Second Coming of Christ, and yearn for signs of the outpouring of the Holy Spirit in our time.

The charismatic movement is institutionally diverse. Some charismatics are found in mainline denominations; others in an assortment of small independent churches. Then there's Robertson. A member of Freemason Street Baptist Church, he has not attended in years. "It is boring. I didn't enjoy going there. How about that?" he tossed at his interviewer.[2] He had stopped attending church as a teenager when he left home to go to military prep school because he found church "primarily social, not spiritual."[3]

Nor does Robertson pastor a church. In fact Robertson isn't a pastor and, unlike Jerry Falwell whose life revolves around his pastorate, has never pastored a church. The Southern Baptist Convention maintains that charismatic gifts such as speaking in tongues and faith healing are theologically invalid.

Despite this Robertson has become a focal point and the most visible leader of America's charismatic movement. Indeed, Robertson is one of the pioneers of the modern movement as it has manifested itself within traditional churches. His entry into politics hasn't changed things. In September 1995 he held an old-fashioned tent revival on the lawn in front of CBN headquarters featuring Pentecostal preachers.

Robertson believes he is several cuts above the average charismatic. Unlike most born-agains, he has been specially baptized in the Holy Spirit. This designates those who are "empower[ed] for service,"[4] and is demonstrated by speaking in tongues. In his early television days Robertson spoke in tongues on camera.

Robertson has asserted that he can tap into the Holy Spirit for other powers. In August 1995 Hurricane Felix had moved dangerously close to the American east coast. Then suddenly, almost miraculously, it turned from its pathway and headed out to sea where its ferocity dissipated. Shortly afterward Robertson announced on "The 700 Club" that the prayers he had led on that program a few days before — "Lord, take the sting out of this Hurricane Felix!"[5] — had caused the hurricane's about-face. But no one ought to have been surprised. Robertson had diverted Hurricane Gloria from Virginia Beach ten years earlier. As he himself pointed out on "The 700 Club," since he began warding off hurricanes through prayer none had dared approach Virginia Beach. But the same Hurricane Gloria that Robertson kept from Virginia Beach devastated Long Island and Connecticut, killing 16 people and causing $47 million in damage.[6] Two months after Robertson had warded off Hurricane Felix another hurricane smashed into Florida, killing and destroying.

Just as he believes in the Holy Spirit, Robertson believes also in the very real presence of the demonic. A 1993 CBN pamphlet titled "Freedom from Demon Bondage" asserts that many mental afflictions— split personalities, anxiety, paranoia (!)— may result from demon possession. On television he divulged the belief that his adversaries were "laying witchcraft curses on us and on my children."[7] "I got so mad ... that I commanded the spirit of witchcraft to *leave my household*; to go right back where it came from."[8] Robertson recalls when his son was in hospital with a staph infection: "I turned to that seemingly empty room and I said in a tone of command, 'Virus, in the name of Jesus Christ of Nazareth, I take authority over you. Get out of here.'"[9]

When he first took up his abode in the Virginia Tidewater area he was certain that it was in "the grip of demon power."[10] Why that particular location? The evil influence had been attracted by the presence of the Edgar Cayce Association for Research and Enlightenment. Robertson had chosen to found his empire in the midst of Satan's own. It was the beginning of his cosmic battle against evil which would end only with Armageddon.

As the one chosen to lead the forces of good against those of evil, Robertson receives his instructions straight from God: "God talks to me."[11] Sometimes God speaks to him in "the silence of his inner thoughts,"[12] and sometimes he actually hears a voice. Robertson admits that "some people might find this spooky."[13] It is because God talks to him that Robertson can be so sure in his actions and in his judgments. Sometimes these judgments may seem harsh and self-righteous to outsiders. When Robertson's father was nearing the end of his political career Robertson chose not to help him win one more election. It says in Robertson's "authorized" biography that "Pat had a premonition that his father's pride was something that probably needed to be pruned."[14]

Robertson's actions throughout his life demonstrate that as far as he is concerned his will is consistent with God's. When his wife's pregnancy had almost reached term, Robertson announced that he was going into the Canadian wilds to be alone with the Lord. He left his wife to care for their small child and to oversee a move to a new home. She begged him to stay, and wrote letters entreating his speedy return after he had gone: "I need you desperately." Robertson prayed. What do I do, God? He opened his Bible at random and found his answer. Or so he interpreted it. He was to remain in the wilds. "God will take care of you," he wrote his wife.[15] He was acting on instructions from God.

How could Robertson be sure he was not simply acting from personal motives, and that God had nothing to do with his decision? *U.S. News & World Report* asked Robertson how he distinguishes between his own ideas and God's. Robertson replied: "Nobody knows for sure; it's [like] an intimacy that develops between a man and a wife over the years: You just begin to sense each other's moods and feelings, and you believe you know what it is that your partner for life desires."[16]

Notice Robertson's wording: "you believe you know." But is believing you know, and actually knowing, the same thing? If Robertson cannot be sure that he knows what his wife desires, how can he be sure that he knows what God desires? As he says, nobody knows for sure.

From the beginning, Christians have realized the danger of inner voices. It was partly to counter the negative influence of those who claimed to hear new words from God that early Christians decreed the Bible to be the only authoritative Word of God. Today many fundamentalists, like Jerry Falwell, fear that the voice heard may be the devil's. Was this why Falwell supported Bush in 1988, and not Robertson?

In one of his books Robertson tells about a time he came under demonic influence. All of a sudden he was sure that everyone was against him. On the verge of suicide, he realized what was happening and cast the devil from his presence. Satan has long been considered the ultimate deceiver. What better way to deceive than to make someone think that they have heard the words of the Lord? *Time* magazine reports an incident where Robertson was not sure of his sources: "Was God telling me to go home or was it Satan?"[17] Robertson has admitted that "there is a percentage of error"[18]—some advice that appears to come from God is really from Satan in disguise.

Who told Robertson about the "guaranteed" 1982 Tribulation? Who told Robertson on New Year's Day of 1980 that war in the Middle East was imminent—"The Maximum peril is in the next two years"[19]—and would be closely followed by Armageddon and the End?

If Robertson someday realizes his ambition to be president, he will also be commander-in-chief of the military forces of the United States: he will be in charge of the "football"; his thumb will be poised over the nuclear button. Could he be sure that the voice he is following is not that of the Great Deceiver?

In Robertson's "authorized" biography his son states that Robertson is "a very, very determined guy. If he has to get something done, he'll go in there and get it done. A lot of people don't have his sense of urgency, but if he has a need to get something done, he'll do it right then. He's not a procrastinator and he doesn't sit around and analyze a problem eighty-five different ways."[20]

Before he openly indicated his political ambitions Robertson felt no compulsion to hide the fullness of his religious beliefs. Out of political pragmatism he was forced to stifle his most ardent views. But the Robertson of today is the Robertson of old. His beliefs have not changed. It was, in fact, his religious position which motivated his presidential aspirations. Robertson was, and remains, an apocalypticist through and through. As the new millennium approached he held a "Preparing for Y2K" conference at Founder's Inn, his luxurious Christian resort in Virginia Beach. Robertson's CBN was considered one of the best sources for Y2K information.[21]

Apocalypticists have always imagined conspiracies; for instance, Monte Kim Miller and the black helicopters. Paranoia about black helicopters runs high in some chapters of Robertson's Christian Coalition. The forces of the Dark One under guise of the United Nations—they've seen them "right here in Lake County."[22]

One of Robertson's favorite imagined conspiracies is David Rockefeller and the Chase Manhattan Bank. According to Robertson, these servants of Satan are bent on taking over the world. They are only one of many groups which appear to act independently, but which Robertson insists are part of a calculated plot orchestrated by Satan: "The abortionists, the drug addicts, the homosexuals, the promiscuous, the financial spoilers, the Marxists, the humanists will make an all out assault on God's people."[23] In recent years Robertson has focused particular venom on People for the American Way. Directed by an ordained Southern Baptist minister and founded for the purpose of protecting "pluralism, individuality, freedom of thought, expression and religion, a sense of community, and tolerance and compassion for others,"[24] this organization is thought by Robertson to be comprised of "anti–Christian atheists."[25]

Paranoia — endemic among apocalypticists — is front and center in Robertson's book *The New World Order*. In his *Wall Street Journal* review Joe Queenan commented, "*The New World Order* is a predictable compendium of the lunatic fringe's greatest hits."[26] Queenan has nothing but scorn for its author, a "paranoid pinhead with a deep distrust of democracy" and a "permanent village idiot's grin." Queenan labeled the book "crackpot." Robert Boston observed that it "quickly earned a spot as a classic of crackpot literature."[27]

Robertson finds signs everywhere that the Last Days are imminent. In Robertson's eyes the economy is always on the edge of disaster. Hyperinflation, depression, debt collapse are just around the corner. The time to prepare for the Last Days, for the ultimate war between the forces of good and evil — Armageddon — has come. Satanic forces are behind every rock and tree. They must be countered. Robertson favors "a massive military buildup"[28] to thwart the ubiquitous forces of evil. The evangelical *Sojourners* magazine charges that CBN helped fund the Contras, a revolutionary army in Nicaragua which Robertson calls "the army of God."[29]

Gerard Straub who worked closely with Robertson for years and came to know him well warns that Pat Robertson "is a threat to all free-thinking, freedom-loving Americans who respect the dignity of humanity and who desire to live in peace and harmony with each other and the world."[30] Straub is clearly correct. In his book *The New World Order* Robertson writes, "All over this country [the United States], children are being indoctrinated as world citizens, with reverence for the earth, the environment, the animals, and for people of all ethnic, religious, and sexual orientations."[31] Is there anything wrong with this? Robertson asserts there is, and calls it "thought control," "brainwashing," "Orwellian." He is adamantly against "programs ... on ecological concerns, on hunger and the politics of food distribution."[32] He castigates those who engage in "antiwar and antinuclear activism" or concern themselves with "ecology and environmental protection."[33] He criticizes one who "takes the realization of values (peacefulness, economic well-being, social and political justice, ecological balance, and humane governance), rather than materialistic and technological gains, as the decisive criterion of progress in human affairs."[34] He thinks us "gullible" who "so desperately want to live in a peaceful world."[35]

Straub continues: "He is dangerous. Robertson's secret agenda for transforming America into a 'holy' nation, as well as his hope for a world-wide physical manifestation of a secret spiritual kingdom needs to be exposed."[36]

Even if Robertson never attains the presidency or any other position of great power nationally, his efforts have dangerous implications internationally. Like Jerry Falwell, Pat Robertson is a major booster of everything Israeli. He once told close associates that he "swore a vow to the Lord that despite the opposition to Israel on many sides, we would stand with Israel, come what may."[37]

Robertson has always been pro–Israel. One of his first guests on "The 700 Club" was Yitzhak Rabin, prime minister of Israel. Through the years the program has featured news from the Middle East and interviews with Israeli leaders. In January 1998 Robertson interviewed Israel's Prime Minister Benjamin Netanyahu, leader of the militaristically aggressive Likud Party. "What would you like our audience to do?" Robertson asked his guest.[38] They should continue to do what they had been doing, Netanyahu replied. They should write letters to editors; they should communicate with their political representatives, urging them to support Israel.

As a dispensationalist apocalypticist Robertson's support of Israel comes naturally. But while dispensationalists are enthusiastic supporters of Israel, they can be rabidly anti–Semitic. In his lengthy review in *New York Review of Books* Michael Lind drew attention to the fact that Robertson's *The New World Order* (a book *The New Republic* editor Leon Wieseltier termed "deranged historiography"[39]) was based on "a laundry list of anti–Semitic sources."[40] Lind furnished ample documentation. However, Robertson constantly and vociferously denies that he is anti–Semitic, although the charge gets repeated over and over again. He finds himself waging continual battle with the press, not just in the United States but abroad: "The press in Great Britain, in alliance with certain radical elements of society, have launched a campaign of unprecedented bigotry against me because of my deeply held Christian beliefs."[41]

The charge of anti–Semitism is serious.[42] Had anyone else said what Robertson said in *The New World Order* he would have been publicly denounced by liberals, moderates, and conservatives. But not Robertson. Robertson has considerable political power and influence. Even some Jews have argued on Robertson's behalf. Norman Podhoretz, for 35 years the editor-in-chief of *Commentary*, admits to "Robertson's crackpot theories" but insists that "there has been an evolution in his thinking."[43] In a lengthy article he castigates his fellow Jews—the liberal ones, those who attack Robertson: Sure, many of Robertson's ideas are "demented" and he is subject to "paranoid historical fantasies,"[44] but when a report by the Anti-Defamation League (*The Religious Right: The Assault on Tolerance and Pluralism in America*) finds him anti–Semitic?... Podhoretz says no. How can these liberal Jews be so ungrateful? Hasn't Robertson always been one of Israel's staunchest supporters? Doesn't Robertson send truckloads of money in Israel's direction? To the argument that "Pat can't possibly be anti–Semitic, because he's such a staunch friend of Israel," *The Nation* editor, Christopher Hitchens, simply states, "Any fool ought to be able to see through this."[45]

It is indicative of his overriding interest that one of Robertson's very few news bureaus is located in the Middle East. The Middle East has been the locus of his most ambitious overseas work, and into this region he has extended the tentacles of his media empire. Acquisition of the Middle East Television (MET) "Star of Hope" station was hailed by Robertson as "the greatest day in CBN history."[46] The station was a gift from his friend George Otis.

Otis could afford the gift; he had made his money as an executive in climate control systems for Minute Man missiles. Otis came to the Middle East in 1973 to cover the October War from the apocalypticist viewpoint. In the resulting book, *The Ghost of Hagar*, he stated, "We Christians believe in fighting for God's people, the Jews."[47] "If we can hold steady we will see the salvation of the Lord!"[48] Otis wanted Israel to completely smash the Arab forces once it was on a roll. Henry Kissinger's peace efforts annoyed Otis. Perhaps, he suggested, Kissinger was the Antichrist.

Otis, too, had a radio station which began broadcasting in the Middle East in 1980. During the Lebanon war he offered his "Voice of Hope" radio station to born-again Lebanese Major Saad Haddad. Haddad made use of the opportunity to threaten PLO sympathizers and to announce the shelling of civilian villages. The U.S. State Department urged Otis to stop these venomous "gospel" messages, but to no avail. Eventually the other side put an end to the hate propaganda by destroying the station.

Two months before Israel invaded Lebanon in 1982, Robertson's Middle East Television (MET) "Star of Hope" station began beaming anti–Arab, anti–Muslim propaganda from its southern Lebanon location.[49] The station was bombed twice before he relocated inside the compound of the Israeli military forces. From this vantage point reporters in bullet-proof vests continued to broadcast the "news."

Robertson's missionary message is insensitive, offensive, and insulting to Christian Arabs. Gabriel Habib, General Secretary of the Middle East Council of Churches, finds such fundamentalist preachers patronizing with respect to Arab Christians: "Most of them, if they do not ignore our very existence, tend to consider us 'not Christian enough' or 'insufficiently biblical' or not 'Christ-centered.'"[50] Habib says such fundamentalist Christian witness is considered "inappropriate by local or national churches," and "provokes strong reactions from other [non–Christian] religious communities."[51] Bishop Aram Kishishian, a theologian of the Armenian Orthodox Church and a president of the World Council of Churches finds the fundamentalist missionary thrust ignorant and disrespectful: "If you hear people call the Middle East a mission field, remind them that it is the birth place of our faith."[52]

Robertson's anti–Arab propaganda embarrasses Christian Arabs. Muslim Arabs who have traditionally lived at peace with Christian Arabs have, as a result of such broadcasting, begun to scoff at their fellow Arabs, asking how they can remain Christian after hearing such tirades. Christian Arabs comprise a sizeable fraction of the Palestinian population. By alienating them Robertson and other fundamentalists could push them toward the rising tide of Muslim fundamentalism.

In addition Robertson's Christian fundamentalist propaganda irritates Muslims, further polarizing the already volatile religious situation in the Middle East. Jordan's late King Hussein remarked on this: "These fundamentalist Christians are gaining considerable attention in Jerusalem, and the Israelis broadcast these images throughout the area. Our people see them in the press or on Israeli television and hear their opinions. It is very disturbing. We do not have any problems between our [nonfundamentalist] Christian and Muslim communities in Jordan, but we are concerned that these Christian fundamentalists could stir up unnecessary tensions, even here in Jordan."[53] But this is what Robertson wants. It would help precipitate Armageddon.

Robertson is quoted in a *Washington Post* article: "The chances are that the U.S. will come in as a defender of Israel. It looks like everything is shaping up."[54] Robertson and others like him believe that if a major war involving Israel can be initiated the United States will blow it up into something of great magnitude. Robertson eagerly awaits the final war in the Middle East. Examining prophecies in the book of Ezekiel during an episode of "The 700 Club" in 1980, he concluded with these ominous words: "The coming Middle East war is an absolute certainty."[55]

An absolute certainty. It is little wonder that People for the American

Way warns, "Armageddon theology clearly has political implications.... The greatest danger it presents is a disdain for peace, particularly in the Middle East."[56]

Letters are constantly sent to viewers of "The 700 Club" requesting donations. One circular asked for "$100 or more over and above your regular giving"[57] to support CBN in a broadcast of a cartoon version of the Easter story for children. At the bottom of the letter — in fine print — were the words: "All funds are used for designated projects and for the worldwide ministry of CBN in accordance with Ezra 7:17-18."[58] The biblical book of Ezra tells how the Temple was rebuilt after the Jews returned to Israel following their captivity in Babylon. Money collected was to be used "for the house of their God which is in Jerusalem, that thou mayest buy speedily with this money bullocks, rams, lambs, with their meat offerings and their drink offerings, and offer them upon the altar of the house of your God which is in Jerusalem. And whatsoever shall seem good to thee, and to thy brethren, to do with the rest of the silver and the gold, that do after the will of your God." Now the Jews have again returned to Jerusalem, and today some religious Jews seek to rebuild yet another Temple and are making preparations for the day when sacrifices will be offered on its altar. On Temple Mount. All of which, of course, requires financing. In a letter to the editor of *Commentary* Barry A. Solomon muses, "I wonder what might happen if Robertson were to become impatient for apocalypse ... and used his influence and money accordingly."[59]

Robertson is dedicated to Israel. His words: "On Christmas Day 1974 ... I interviewed then Israeli Prime Minister Yitzhak Rabin in his office in Jerusalem. That night, while looking out on the Temple Mount.... I vowed to God that whatever happened, however unpopular the task, I and the organization I controlled would stand with Israel and the Jewish people."[60] "While looking out on Temple Mount...."

As journalist Tom Junod notes of Robertson, "He's a pretty scary guy."[61] When Robertson is gone there will be someone to take his place. Pat Robertson's minions are toiling long and hard in the apocalypticist vineyard. Apocalypticists are dead serious. Peter Gardella speaks of "the deadly serious, egoistic particularism of American apocalyptic"[62] and "the destructiveness of an apocalyptic culture."[63] Apocalypticists are on a deadly crusade. Arthur P. Mendel writes, "Robertson, or someone sharing his worldview, could be the white-horse savior who pushes the Armageddon button."[64]

16

The Jerusalem Connection

Both Jerry Falwell and Pat Robertson, along with several other leading apocalypticists, including Ralph Reed, signed an April 10, 1997, *New York Times* ad titled "Christians Call for a United Jerusalem."[1] The ad included dispensationalist themes and citations of Scripture to back Israel's claim to land in the Middle East. The ad asked that Israel "not be pressured to concede on issues of Jerusalem in the final status negotiations with the Palestinians."[2] Readers of the ad were urged to support the Israeli government's position on sovereignty over Jerusalem.

While Jerry Falwell vows his support for the state of Israel, and Pat Robertson proclaims his love for the Jews and for Israel, these two figures are merely representative of a trend among Christian fundamentalists. They are just the tip of the iceberg. As church historian Timothy P. Weber observed, "The State of Israel has no better friends than American evangelicals."[3] Former Israeli Prime Minister Menachem Begin knew that. In 1981 he was questioned on American television about an F-16 mission into Iraq he had ordered. Was he not concerned that he might lose American support? No, he replied. Israel has many American friends — 40 million fundamentalist Christians. Grace Halsell, a former White House staffer was stunned: "I began to research Christian Zionism. And I became convinced that Begin was right: Christian support of Israel is more important than Jewish support to the Zionist state. There may be six million American Jews who support Israel, but there are about 40 million Christians who do."[4]

One of these is, once again, apocalypticist W. A. Criswell. In 1978 Israel's then Prime Minister Menachem Begin recognized Criswell's enthusiastic support of Israel by awarding him the Israeli Humanitarian Award. He was the first Christian minister to be honored in this way. A year earlier he was one of 15 signatories—along with Pat Boone and John F. Walvoord, the president of Dallas Theological Seminary—to an ad in the *Chicago Sun-Times* titled "Evangelicals' Concern for Israel." "The time has come," said the ad, "for Evangelical Christians to affirm their belief in biblical prophecy and Israel's Divine Right to the Land by speaking out now."[5] It went on to assert that a "lasting peace cannot be achieved" until all nations accept the fact that the Jewish people have an "unalienable right" to exist as a nation "within the boundaries of their ancient homeland." Criswell found a position in his church for Rabbi Yechiel Eckstein, employed by the Anti-Defamation League to monitor and build links with the Christian evangelical community.

Another of the 40 million is American evangelist Mike Evans. Evans eagerly anticipates a final war so terrible that blood will "flow down the Jordan River Valley, down the length of the Dead Sea, and thence ... the entire length of the Negev."[6] His ministry is focused on getting the American government and people to give full support to Israel. If the United States does not do this, Evans contends, it will lose God's blessing. Here Evans mouths a constantly repeated apocalypticist mantra. Hal Lindsey, Jerry Falwell—they all use it. In the words of Pat Robertson, "The future of this Nation may be at stake, because God will bless those that bless Israel. And God will curse those that curse Israel."[7] In a letter to the president of the United States Evans writes, "We, as evangelical Christians, consider the Word of God to be non-negotiable! For the sake of this great nation, please do not endeavor to frustrate God's prophetic plan."[8]

"Non-negotiable," "unalienable"—these are words used over and over by Christian fundamentalists to express Israel's right to Jerusalem and all the land within the biblical boundaries of ancient Israel,[9] land which would include the Occupied Territories (the West Bank, Gaza, and the Golan Heights), land which is internationally not recognized as belonging to Israel. These Christian apocalypticists are not overly concerned with what the Israelis themselves want. When a Jew rose during the first Christian Zionist Conference to point out that according to a recent poll taken in Israel a large portion of the population would be willing to trade land occupied since 1967 for peace with the Palestinians, a Christian leader shouted,

"We don't care what the Israelis vote! We care what God says! And God gave the land to the Jews!"[10]

Large-scale evangelical involvement with Israel began shortly after the Six Day War in 1967. Evangelicals organized Christians Concerned for Israel but this organization soon changed its name to the National Christian Leadership Conference for Israel. It opposed any attempt to trade land Israel had confiscated in the West Bank, for peace. It opposed efforts to internationalize Jerusalem. It defended Israel's invasion of Lebanon in 1982. It held a pro–Israel rally at the White House, and strives to educate the American public in the political and religious significance of close ties with Israel. It has worked closely with the offices of the Israeli embassy in Washington and has strong links with other powerful Christian fundamentalist Zionist organizations, most notably the Jerusalem Temple Foundation and International Christian Embassy.

From the time it was first published in 1970 Hal Lindsey's *The Late Great Planet Earth* did much to link the aspirations of fundamentalist Christians and fundamentalist Jews. His focus on the events of 1967 helped conservative Christians in America make an identification between Israel, God's will, and the military. Lindsey's book became a common vehicle for Christian fundamentalists and religious Jewish Zionists alike. It is no mean accomplishment to get a Christian book published in Israel, yet *The Late Great Planet Earth* was translated into Hebrew and published. It became an immediate success with Israeli military men and government officials. They understood that successful aggression would be forgiven by fundamentalist Christians as the working out of God's will.

In May 1977 Menachem Begin's Likud Party defeated the secular Labor Party at the polls. It was part of a trend toward religiosity in Israel. Fundamentalist Jews and settler organizations were strong supporters of the new government. Likud called the West Bank by its biblical name, "Judea and Samaria." Hard-line militarists, Likud used religious arguments to justify the confiscation and settlement of Arab lands. As expected, American Christian fundamentalists and evangelicals gave strong endorsement to this new power in Israel and the settlement of the Occupied Territories.

Two months before Likud came to power in Israel American President Jimmy Carter announced his support of the Palestinians' right to a homeland. The United Nations was proposing a Middle East Peace Conference. Neither of these developments pleased the new Israeli government. Likud was determined to strip Carter of his evangelical political base and to drum up support for its opposition to the U.N. proposal.

The result was an advertising campaign which Donald Wagner, director of the Center for Middle Eastern Studies at North Park University in

Chicago and director of Evangelicals for Middle East Understanding, has called "one of the first public signs of Likud-evangelical alliance."[11] A full-page ad was placed in major American newspapers: "We affirm as evangelicals our belief in the promised land to the Jewish people.... We would view with grave concern any effort to carve out of the Jewish homeland another nation or political entity."[12] Soviet involvement in the proposed U.N. peace conference was also targeted.

The ad was financed by Jerusalem's Institute for Holy Land Studies, an evangelical Christian Zionist group. It was signed by Kenneth Kantzer of *Christianity Today* (an evangelical periodical) and Trinity Evangelical Divinity School, by Reagan's pal, the singer Pat Boone, and by dispensationalist theologian, president of Dallas Theological Seminary and former teacher of Hal Lindsey, John Walvoord. Jerry Strober, a former employee of the American Jewish Committee who coordinated the advertising campaign, had strong praise for his Christian counterparts: "The real source of strength the Jews have in this country is from the evangelicals."[13] So successful was this endeavor, when Israel invaded Lebanon in 1982 full-page ads requesting evangelical support once again appeared in the leading newspapers throughout the United States.

In *The 1980's: Countdown to Armageddon* Hal Lindsey claims that the United States has been allowed to remain a free nation because it has stood behind the Jews in their times of need when no one else has. He points out that in Genesis 12:3 and 27:29 God promised to bless those who bless the descendants of Abraham and to curse those who curse them. Lindsey believes that if the United States should ever turn its back on Israel its days as a nation would be numbered. "Don't take this lightly,"[14] he warns; the rise and fall of empires has been directly related to their treatment of the Jews. In effect, Lindsey's thinking, and that of other apocalypticists, offers Israel carte blanche. It is little wonder he is so enthusiastically received by Israel's militant religious right wing.

Historian Weber notes that the close tie between Christian evangelicals and Israel has shaped popular opinion in the United States and influenced American foreign policy.[15] The United States has poured money into Israel. What Reagan started, Bush continued — $4 billion annual aid to Israel, a nation of only 3.2 million people.[16] In addition the Bush administration guaranteed a $475 million loan for new immigrant housing in Israel.[17] Despite promises to the contrary, Israeli Housing Minister Ariel Sharon announced plans to build 15,000 apartments in Arab East Jerusalem. Israel went on to spend more than $3 billion on settlement expansion in the Occupied Territories in just a year and a half,[18] and spent 75 percent of the Housing Ministry's budget for the year in these territories.[19] Certain that the United States will never turn off the money tap,

Israel's leaders go ahead and spend the money however they desire, defying the wishes, and the political prudence, of Israel's major ally.

The beat goes on. Israel's Bureau of Statistics records that in 1998 more than 4,000 new housing units were started in the West Bank and Gaza alone, excluding Jerusalem and the Golan Heights.[20] This represented nine percent of all residential construction in Israel. American money. Ehud Barak defeated the Netanyahu government and pledged he would not support any new settlement projects. Yet one day later ground was broken in an Arab neighborhood of Jerusalem for a 132-unit housing project. A wealthy American had paid the tab.

Many Zionist American Jews are keenly aware that today's fundamentalist Christians are their allies. When they voted for Reagan in droves this was no accident. Harry Hurwitz spent three years at the Israeli embassy in Washington and advised Israel's prime minister on how to deal with American Christians. His advice: "Go up to the Hill [Capitol Hill] with these Christians to lobby for Israel — because the fundamentalists are the most powerful Christian element in America."[21] Observes Rabbi Marc Tannenbaum of the American Jewish Committee, "The evangelical community is the largest and fastest-growing bloc of pro–Jewish sentiment in this country."[22] Both the American Israel Political Affairs Committee (AIPAC — a lobbying organization)[23] and the Anti-Defamation League look to the growing population of Christian evangelicals and fundamentalists for support. Both groups have added staff specifically for the purpose of developing closer relationships with dispensationalist Christians.

Thanks to the work of Zionist American Jews and Christian fundamentalists, Israelis have begun to ardently pay court from their side. The Israeli Ministry of Tourism has made a practice of bringing evangelical pastors to Israel, all expenses paid. The idea is to have them return to Israel with tour groups of their own. These tourists provide a steady and substantial source of income for the small nation, and the tours allow the Israeli government an opportunity to educate Americans on their position vis-à-vis the Palestinians. In January 1998 Israel invited a large group of American evangelical seminary presidents and deans to the Holy Land and paid their expenses. In all of these efforts Israel hopes to increase the ties with Americans, which should result in augmented funding from the United States and her individual citizens in the evangelical community.

Christian apocalypticism has become so well known in Israel that Israeli tourist officials made a special effort to attract Christians to Megiddo (Hebrew for Armageddon) in the year 2000. Israeli National Parks Authority approved a multimedia reconstruction of Megiddo on the site of the ancient city's ruins. High-tech prayer booths showed the final battle in virtual reality.

During his years as Israel's representative at the United Nations Benjamin Netanyahu spoke regularly on the New Christian Right's "Prayer Breakfast for Israel" circuit. Within a few months of becoming Israel's prime minister in 1996 and returning the Likud to government, he convened the Israel Christian Advocacy Council. Seventeen American evangelical leaders were flown to the Holy Land for a tour and conference. Among their number were Don Argue (president of the National Association of Evangelicals) and Brandt Gustavson (president of National Religious Broadcasters, which oversees 90 percent of Christian radio and television broadcasting in North America). The assembled group signed a pledge expressing the hope that "America never, never desert Israel."[24]

Netanyahu continued to vigorously woo the American evangelical community while he was in office. In April 1998, for example, he addressed the Voices United for Israel Conference in Washington. Most of the 3,000 in attendance were evangelicals. Among the notables was Ralph Reed. Jerry Falwell and Pat Robertson were not present but supported the conference. Netanyahu laid on the praise: "We have no greater friends and allies than the people sitting in this room."[25] During the same visit to the United States Netanyahu went on to address the National Unity Coalition for Israel.

Reformed and Conservative Jews in the United States had always been generous contributors to the Jewish National Fund and other agencies which support Israel. But this flow of money slowed as Orthodox Judaism gained increasing influence with Netanyahu's government. The International Fellowship of Christians and Jews, led by Rabbi Yechiel Eckstein of Chicago (Criswell's pal), stepped up to fill the gap. They raised $5 million, almost all from Christian evangelicals and fundamentalists.[26]

In many cases contributions result from individual efforts. John Hagee was the pastor of Cornerstone Church in San Antonio, Texas, but, like many Christian apocalypticists, Hagee found pastoring a church was not enough. So he broadcast the message nationally on radio and television. He also wrote books. In his best-selling *Beginning of the End: The Assassination of Yitzhak Rabin and the Coming Antichrist* he said that Rabin's assassination and recent attempts to design a peace accord in the Middle East have "launched Bible prophecy onto the fast track."[27] Peace, ironically, would be the sign that Armageddon was close at hand, for the Antichrist would be a key figure in peace agreements. Hagee was among the fundamentalist leaders invited by Jerry Falwell to meet with Netanyahu in January 1998. A month later Hagee announced that his congregation had given over one million dollars to Israel to help settle immigrant Jews in the West Bank and Jerusalem: "We feel like the coming of Soviet Jews to Israel is a fulfillment of biblical prophecy."[28] When asked if he realized that the Likud government he was supporting was acting contrary to the policies of the United States government and that by contributing he may have been acting illegally, he replied, "I am a Bible scholar and a theologian and from my perspective the law of God transcends the law of the United States government and the U.S. State Department."[29]

As historian Weber observes, "The real story in the last 20 years is the founding of scores of small, grassroots, pro–Israel organizations that rarely get into the headlines."[30] They send funds to Israel, they educate the public, they form links, and they network over the Internet.

Voices United for Israel is one of these dynamic groups. It was formed by two friends—Jew Esther Levens and Christian Allen Mothersill—in reaction to the Bush administration's making loans to Israel contingent upon there being no new Israeli settlement of the West Bank. The group has networked with 200 other organizations (two thirds of which are evangelical) to sponsor conferences with Israel's Netanyahu as speaker, to consult with the Israeli government concerning promotional and educational materials, to sponsor a speakers bureau, and to fax information to the public. Ira Nosenchuk attended one of their conferences: "Sometimes I feel like there are more supporters for Israel among evangelicals than among Jews."[31]

International Christian Embassy in Jerusalem acts as an umbrella organization for many of these groups and tries to coordinate their efforts. It was established by apocalypticists and its literature mentions Armageddon. In the face of the Israeli government's nervousness about Temple Mount, a chief spokesman for Christian Embassy said that the Muslims are usurpers and that Temple Mount should be returned to the Jews "even if it means Armageddon."[32] Literature from Christian Embassy states that "Judea and Samaria (inaccurately termed 'the West Bank') are, and by biblical right ... ought to be, a part of Israel."[33] Christian Embassy took over the major operations of the Voice of Hope radio station in southern Lebanon, and broadcasts fundamentalist programming.

The Israeli government knows that Christian fundamentalist organizations like Christian Embassy are a strong source of political and economic support in the West, particularly in the United States. Christian Embassy lobbies the United States government on behalf of Israel. It raised several million dollars to fly 35 planeloads of Soviet Jews to Israel and assist in their settlement, often in areas which violated international law. Christian Embassy testified before the United States House of Representatives' Foreign Affairs Committee in 1984 in favor of moving the United States Embassy from Tel Aviv to Jerusalem. Then Prime Minister Yitzhak Shamir addressed the Second Christian Zion Conference (organized by Christian Embassy), praising Christian Embassy as "true friends of Israel."[34]

Christian Embassy annually participates in the Jewish Feast of Tabernacles. Several thousand march down from the Mount of Olives and through the streets of Jerusalem. On one such occasion then Prime Minister Menachem Begin addressed the marchers: "Your decision to establish your embassy in Jerusalem at a time when we were being abandoned because of our faith was an act of courage and a symbol of the closeness between us."[35] Chief Rabbi Shlomo Goren added his words of praise: "Your sympathy, solidarity, and belief in the future of Israel, this to us is tremendous. Your presence here will always remain a golden page in the book of heaven. May the Lord bless you out of Zion."[36]

Christian Embassy is reputed to have an annual budget of $1 million, and many suspect that some of this money comes from a grateful Israel — but this cannot be confirmed, as Christian Embassy's sources of income are a tight secret.[37] When the director of Israeli Religious Affairs was asked, "How can you in the government continue to support a movement that believes Jews must ultimately be converted to Christianity or face a cosmic holocaust at the battle of Armageddon?" he responded, "We need support from wherever we can find it, but we keep these people on a very short leash."[38] Israel is happy to woo the evangelical purse but it doesn't want its people converted to Christianity. Attempts to proselytize the Jews are punishable by up to five years in prison and a stiff fine.

Israeli sentiment regarding the barely hidden anti–Semitism of Christian apocalypticism is surprisingly muted. The former editor of a liberal American Jewish publication observes that when Israelis woo Christian fundamentalists it is strictly a "self-interested move," but the Israelis are not unaware: "They operated under the assumption that when you scratch the surface of these guys, there is a lot of latent anti–Semitism."[39] Late director of the Anti-Defamation League of B'nai B'rith Nathan Perlmutter encapsulated this tough-nosed pragmatism with the words, "Praise God and pass the ammunition."[40]

Late in 1997 Christian Zionist organizations, like International Christian Embassy, cooperated with Netanyahu's public relations specialists in the office of David Bar-Ilan to exaggerate accounts of persecution of Christians by Yasser Arafat's Palestinian National Authority. When this "news" broke, Republican Congressman J. C. Watts of Oklahoma called America's grants to the Palestinian National Authority into question. Sure, grants to the Palestinians were less than one tenth of the amounts given to Israel, but consider the atrocities. Fourteen persons from Evangelicals for Middle East Understanding and Open Doors International were dispatched to the Holy Land to investigate. They interviewed many Christians but could find no evidence of the alleged persecution and little in the way of discrimination. The Palestinian National Authority was exonerated.

Director of Evangelicals for Middle East Understanding Donald Wagner made the following remark after observing at close hand the religious and political climate in Israel: "The Christian Right's alliance with Likud may in the end serve as a self-fulfilling prophecy ... leading to a new round of conflict in the Holy Land, which the Christian Zionists will readily interpret as 'the final battle.'"[41] Those who wish to hasten this "final battle"— Armageddon — are found on both sides of the Atlantic. They are both Christian and Jew. Christian and Jew working together with one goal — to bring on the End. One fundamentalist prepared a paper for Israeli leaders which listed 250 pro–Israel Christian evangelical organizations which might be helpful to their cause.[42]

Christian fundamentalists in the United States have helped fund Gershon Salomon's Temple Mount and Land of Israel Faithful Movement — noted for pushing End Time theology and actions— in Israel.[43] There are Christian chapters of the Temple Mount Faithful in New York, Texas, Florida, and California. Says Salomon, "God is waiting for us to move the mosques and rebuild [the Temple]. The Jews may not be ready, but the Christians are."[44] Salomon stokes the fire by leading American born-again tour groups in Israel and by visiting fundamentalist groups in the United States. Since 1990 when he led an act of provocation on Temple Mount he has had frequent invitations to lecture "Bible-believing" Christians. When he tours the American Bible Belt fundamentalists implore him to get on with building the Temple. During a typical visit, to a fundamentalist Baptist church in Florida in 1999, he collected money and jewelry worth $3,500 toward rebuilding the Temple.[45] But at many American synagogues he is *persona non grata*. They want nothing to do with him. But Salomon just shrugs, "The prophets said ... that when the people of Israel return to the Land of Israel in the End of Days, the gentiles will carry them as a mother carries her child."[46]

The American Christian Trust is an umbrella agency for many major evangelical and fundamentalist Christian groups, collecting funds and transferring the money to Israel. Much of the money — tens of millions of dollars— goes to Jewish settlements in the West Bank, an area the United Nations has consistently refused to recognize as part of Israel. The founder and director of the American Christian Trust is Bobi Hromas, the wife of an executive in the defense contracting business, and the daughter of an Assemblies of God Pentecostal preacher from Dallas whose ministry takes her around the world. Bobi Hromas is proud of her close connections with Jerry Falwell, Pat Robertson, and Ronald Reagan's born-again friends: Edwin Meese, James Watt, and Herb Ellingwood.[47]

Part of Hromas's work involves a round-the-clock prayer chapel for those who wish to pray that Israel will successfully drive all of the Palestinians out of the Holy Land. The chapel is conveniently located across from the Israeli embassy in Washington, D. C. It has a private door for members of the United States Senate, Congress, and Joint Chiefs of Staff. Ronald Reagan was warmly welcomed. His name adorns the chapel's guestbook, as do the names of members of Israel's Knesset. Visitors to the chapel hear a 45-minute tape in which Hromas makes an emotional plea, explaining how Palestine must be exclusively in Jewish hands before the Second Coming of Christ. Visitors to the chapel take responsibility for a prayer "watch"— a three-hour stint. Of course, one can commit to more than one watch at a time. In her tape Hromas makes it clear that the purpose of this continuous chain of watches "is to give the Lord no rest, until He answers these prayers. That's praying."[48] (Edwin Meese and Ronald Reagan are two of the many who have frequented the chapel and given the Lord no rest.[49])

Another Christian organization supporting questionable activities in Israel is the Jerusalem Temple Foundation. Stanley Goldfoot was one of the founders of Salomon's Temple Mount Faithful, but gradually came to feel that they had "lost their way."[50] He found their methods too slow and peaceful. He knew that American Christian apocalypticists favored rebuilding the Temple, so he decided to approach some influential Christian fundamentalists and set up his own organization. As a result he, along with Terry Risenhoover and Douglas Krieger, formed the Jerusalem Temple Foundation, established for the purpose of funding Jewish terrorists intent on destroying the Dome of the Rock and the al-Aqsa Mosque.

Terry Risenhoover is an Oklahoma oil and gas millionaire. Among other ventures he and Douglas Krieger, a lay minister from Colorado, drill in search of oil deposits in the West Bank. He and Krieger have also teamed up to form Temple Mount Foundation based in Los Angeles, an affiliate of the parent organization Jerusalem Temple Foundation.

In a third endeavor Risenhoover and Krieger helped organize the American Forum for Jewish-Christian Cooperation to insure that wealthy Americans could help Israel tax-free. American Forum also brings like-minded Jewish and Christian leaders together. In 1980 the president of American Forum chaired the religious committee for Ronald Reagan's inauguration. During Reagan's presidency in 1984 when Risenhoover was president of American Forum, he helped organize a White House reception where Jewish Zionists could meet Christian fundamentalists. Invitations were sent on State Department stationery and signed by J. William Middendorf, the United States representative to the Organization of American States. Not a single Roman Catholic or mainline Protestant Christian was invited. In attendance were over 150 Christian fundamentalist leaders, the founder of AIPAC, and the leading figures in major Zionist Jewish American organizations. Hal Lindsey was there. So was apocalypticist author and political strategist Tim LaHaye. Four top Reagan spokesmen in the State Department addressed the gathering. As Risenhoover was a featured soloist at White House gatherings of right-wing Christians during Reagan's administration,[51] he was the evening's entertainer.

A friend of Reagan, Risenhoover chaired the 1985 National Prayer Breakfast in Honor of Israel, an annual event which began in Reagan's term in office and is sponsored by National Religious Broadcasters. Like Reagan he is committed to Israel. Although not a Jew, he has dual citizenship in the United States and Israel. At times he can raise even Stanley Goldfoot's eyebrows. Accompanying Goldfoot to Temple Mount one day, he said, "I am Nehemiah."[52] Nehemiah was the restorer of the Temple in ancient times and according to Jewish legend is to be the herald of the coming Messiah.

Krieger too has served as executive director of the National Prayer Breakfast in Honor of Israel. Prominently displayed in the convention hall where the breakfast was held was a scale model of the rebuilt Temple. This, among other things, led some American Jews to worry that Krieger intended to "blow up the mosques." Krieger's words do not reassure them. He says it is "preordained" that the Dome of the Rock Mosque will be destroyed and the Third Temple arise in its place. He believes that nuclear war involving Israel is imminent, but is reticent about joint Jewish-Christian apocalypticist efforts to realize their common goals: "It's all hush-hush.... We don't want to embarrass our friends in Israel" [such as Goldfoot] where work is proceeding "underground."[53]

Five of the six directors of the Jerusalem Temple Foundation are American fundamentalists.[54] In addition to Risenhoover and Krieger these include Jim DeLoach, a Houston, Texas, pastor. DeLoach admits to once being anti–Semitic, but says he is now "pro–Israel." He sports a diamond ring that combines the star of David with the cross. On his lapel is a double flag — the United States and Israel.

The annual yearly funding goal for the Jerusalem Temple Foundation is $100 million.[55] Where does the money go? One of the foundation's projects is helping fund Yeshiva Ateret Cohanim where young men study the priestly Temple rites. This yeshiva is also active in the purchase of Arab real estate near Temple Mount. Ten million dollars was collected to donate to West Bank settlements and to buy Arab land in the Occupied Territories.[56] But the important money is earmarked to assist the real activists — the Temple Mount terrorists.

On March 10, 1983, 45 yeshiva students were arrested in Jerusalem while trying to break into Temple Mount with explosives. Three weeks later a full-page ad appeared in the *Jerusalem Post* and several other Israeli papers calling for their release as "earnest, faithful sons of Israel" whose arrest was "biblically unconscionable."[57] The ad was placed by the Committee of Concerned Evangelicals for Freedom of Worship on the Temple Mount. The three cochairmen of the committee? Terry Risenhoover, Douglas Krieger, and Jim DeLoach. Shortly after, a Jerusalem judge threw the case out of court, saying the students were "amateurs" who had no serious intention of blowing up the mosques. Krieger claimed that Goldfoot had received $50,000 from wealthy evangelical bankers in Texas to help pay the students' legal fees.[58]

Lambert Dolphin was another Christian fundamentalist on the board of directors of the Jerusalem Temple Foundation. He headed the radiophysics department of the prestigious Stanford Research Institute in Menlo Park, California, among whose principal clients is the U.S. government. His interest in Temple Mount had apocalypticist motivation. Others had spent considerable time and money trying to prove conclusively that the Jews' ancient Temple had been located on Temple Mount, but all attempts to date had failed. Archaeological digs were out of the question — the Muslims forbade them. But Dolphin had access to state-of-the-art technology. Aerial photography and infrared imagery in combination with ground penetration radar and seismic sounding might ascertain the existence of foundations or storerooms or archaeological artifacts. Goldfoot secured an Israeli Army helicopter and other assistance with some help from Ariel Sharon in the Israeli government. But when the team began photographing Temple Mount the Muslims became suspicious. There was rioting. Formal objections were launched. Even some Jews disapproved. Dolphin headed back home to California.

As a Jew Stanley Goldfoot is the kingpin in the organization. He has links with Gush Emunim and Kach, extremist religious organizations in Israel. Risenhoover calls Goldfoot "a very solid, legitimate terrorist."[59] Indeed, Goldfoot is a charter member among Israeli terrorists. He was jailed in 1948 by the new state of Israel for murdering a United Nations envoy. He served with the notorious Israeli Stern Gang, denounced by Israel's first prime minister, David Ben-Gurion, as Nazis, and outlawed. The Stern Gang earned its reputation by murdering women and children and blowing up hotels.

Goldfoot does not believe in God, yet he justifies his activities by pointing out that God gave Palestine to Abraham and Jacob. His Christian friends are deterred neither by this flagrant inconsistency, nor by his atheism. Goldfoot is a regular guest speaker in fundamentalist churches and on evangelical radio and television. He cheats a bit — he doesn't draw attention to the fact that two of Islam's most important mosques are now on the site where he proposes rebuilding the Temple.

Chuck Smith, a Baptist pastor in Costa Mesa, California, was an associate of board members of the Jerusalem Temple Foundation. Smith was sold on Goldfoot. In an interview he said, "Do you want a real radical? Try Stanley Goldfoot. He's a wonder. His plan for the Temple Mount is to take sticks of dynamite and some M-16s, and blow up the Dome of the Rock and al-Aqsa Mosque, and just lay claim to the site."[60]

A recent poll by the Israeli newspaper *Ha'aretz* had found that 18.3 percent of Israelis wanted construction of the Third Temple to begin immediately. Smith had an idea. His Calvary Chapel had a lavish 3,000-seat auditorium. He would hold a fundraiser for Stanley Goldfoot.

Smith sent a Cadillac equipped with bar and telephone to pick Goldfoot up at the airport. It was to be champagne treatment all the way. The auditorium was packed to overflowing. The applause was deafening. They loved Goldfoot in Costa Mesa.

Goldfoot's rabid apocalypticism easily rises to the surface. Here is an excerpt from one of his letters: "We should be running a worldwide propaganda campaign and using clever promotions (like Machiavelli) and preparing public opinion for the day we drop a nuclear device on Damascus — we will have to do it — and time it possibly with another on Libya. The prescription is in *Tanach* [the Bible]: 'Behold, Damascus is taken away from being a city, and it shall be a ruinous heap.'"[61]

It is no secret to the Muslims that Jewish extremists have plans for Temple Mount, and that fundamentalist Christians are behind them financially. Ekrima Sabri, the Mufti of Jerusalem (a Muslim religious leader appointed by Arafat's Palestinian Authority), says, "We know the Jew is planning on destroying the Haram. The Jew will get the Christian to do his work for him. This is the way of the Jews. This is the way Satan manifests himself. The majority of the Jews want to destroy the mosque. They are preparing as we speak [1999]."[62] Had he heard the rumor that all the stones for the new Temple have been cut and are ready for assembly on Temple Mount ... as soon as the mosques are destroyed?

Hassan Haddad and Donald Wagner are keen observers of the Middle East and have studied the effects of the insertion of Christian fundamentalism into what was an already volatile situation. Here is how they sum things up: "It is our contention ... that the resulting politics of contemporary Biblical fundamentalism are not only hermeneutically unsound, but are so dangerous that they encourage the very international and interracial confrontation they prophesy: a nuclear Armageddon."[63]

17

The Red Heifer

"And the Lord spake unto Moses and unto Aaron, saying, This is the ordinance of the law which the Lord hath commanded, saying, Speak unto the children of Israel, that they bring thee a red heifer without spot, wherein is no blemish, and upon which never came yoke."

Pentecostal preacher Clyde Lott continued reading. The 19th chapter of the book of Numbers in Lott's Old Testament went on to tell in great detail how the high priest was to kill and burn the heifer and use the ashes in the "water of separation" used to purify Jews. "And it shall be unto the children of Israel, and unto the stranger that sojourneth among them, for a statute for ever."

Forever. So this law still holds, Lott thought to himself. As one of the leading cattle breeders in the American Southeast (his office is jammed with ribbons, plaques, and trophies) he was reading passages in the Bible which deal with cattle, when he came upon this startling passage which mentioned the requirement of a red heifer in the purification of those administering rites in the Temple.

A Christian fundamentalist, Lott eagerly awaited the second coming of his Lord Jesus. He was well versed in the End Time scenario—Armageddon, the Rapture, the whole bit. He knew the significance of Israel's capturing of the Old City of Jerusalem in 1967, and that the next step was the rebuilding of the Temple and the reinstatement of sacrificial rites. Then Christ would return. But the red heifer was a necessary step. Without its

131

ashes the priest and those who would help him serve in the Temple would be unclean. The rites could not proceed. Lott would come to learn much more about the significance of the red heifer and all that surrounded it in the coming months.

One day Lott felt guided by the hand of God to visit the director of international trade for the Mississippi Department of Agriculture and Commerce. He prevailed upon this individual to write to the person in the American embassy in Athens who was in charge of agricultural exports to the Middle East, saying that Red Angus cattle raised in the United States might be suitable for Jewish purification rites as described in the Old Testament. The letter bounced around for a few months before ending up on the desk of Rabbi Chaim Richman at the Temple Institute in Jerusalem.

Jews the world over constantly pray for the rebuilding of the Temple. Each Jewish wedding ceremony ends with the breaking of glass, as a reminder of the destruction of the last Temple. However, these prayers and ceremonies are just that — ritual, to be understood figuratively, not literally. So it is for most Jews. But there are those who take the idea of rebuilding the Temple literally and seriously. The Temple Institute is a group of such Jews — dedicated to rebuilding the Temple, and to reinstating the priestly castes and clerical rule and animal sacrifice. As its director Zev Golan states, "Our task is to advance the cause of the Temple and to prepare for its establishment, not just talk about it. Sooner or later it will be done. And we will be ready for it."[1]

Rabbis at the Institute were struck by the coincidence of names. This Lott and the Lot of the Old Testament. Both gentiles, and both capable cattle breeders. Surely this was a sign of good things to come. This Lott must be invited for a visit.

So Clyde Lott came to Jerusalem. He got to meet Rabbi Chaim Richman who took him to a basement in the Jewish quarter of the Old City. Here Richman operates a small museum housing the artifacts which will be used in rites at the rebuilt Temple. How thrilled Lott was to actually see the clothes and utensils which he had previously only read about in the Bible. Richman has studied Jewish law and asserts that Judaism as practiced today is not as God intended. Lott had been directed to the right man. Richman has written a book, *The Mystery of the Red Heifer: Divine Promise of Purity*.

Those at the Temple Institute regaled Lott with details of Judaic lore concerning the red heifer, the Temple, and the coming of the Messiah.

Temple Mount is holy ground. How holy? At one time El Al Airlines advertised a special feature — its flights from South Africa flew over Temple Mount at low altitude, allowing passengers a magnificent view of the holy site. That was until rabbis and religious parties campaigned against this practice. Apparently not only is the ground holy but so is the air space above Temple Mount, extending infinitely upwards. El Al was given strict orders to cease flying in this holy air space. It complied.

Because Temple Mount is sacred, any Jew must be purified before stepping upon it. Anyone who has had contact with, or been in the presence of the dead is ritually unclean. This means all Jews, because the ground is in contact with the dead and everyone has walked on the ground. This is where the red heifer and the act of purification come in. A red heifer in its third year is totally burned opposite the site of the Temple and the remaining ashes along with the ashes of the wood upon which the heifer is burned are added to water from the pool of Siloam. If this mixture is sprinkled upon a Jew he is purified. The mixture can be extended almost indefinitely. As Rabbi David Yosef Elboim notes, one speck of ash in millions of tons of water will suffice.[2]

The water of purification must be made to last in this way because of the scarcity of red heifers. There have only been nine red heifers so sacrificed in all of Jewish history. Judaica scholars claim that no red heifer was born in Israel since the destruction of the Second Temple by the Romans in 70 A.D.[3] At least, not until 1996.

Born at a farm in northern Israel, "Melody" bore the weight of the eons upon her shoulders. If she tested out to be a truly pure red heifer, depending on one's viewpoint it could be a good or a bad thing. Some welcomed the prospect as the wondrous portent of the coming messianic age — the Mishnah said that the tenth red heifer would usher in the coming of the Messiah. Others viewed Melody as a serious threat to peace in the Middle East: religious extremists might step up plans to destroy the Dome of the Rock and al-Aqsa. Gershon Salomon, for example, considered Melody "another sign that we are very close to the rebuilding of the Temple. This will [allow] big crowds of Orthodox Jews to join us in our campaign to liberate the Temple Mount."[4] Concerned about such consequences, David Landau wrote in the Israeli newspaper *Ha'aretz*, "The potential harm from this heifer is far greater than the destructive properties of a regular terrorist bomb."[5] He suggested it be killed immediately.

Hold it! Not so fast. Local Rabbi Shmaria Shore points to a pair of white hairs on Melody's tail. And look, white whiskers on her snout, eyelashes red only on one end. Melody has failed the test. She is not a pure red heifer without blemish. Jewish ritual law is very specific. Even the heifer's nose and horns must be red. Nor can it have carried a burden; if anyone has so much as leaned on the heifer it is ineligible. Because a truly red heifer is so rare, geneticists have been engaged to see if one can be produced using the latest in scientific techniques. Perhaps it is a good thing that Jewish tradition is so strict about these things, say those who yearn for peace in the Middle East. Besides, was Melody really red? Or brown, as some say?

The crisis, however, is far from over. Melody has given new momentum to the several groups in Israel who are making preparations for the rebuilding of the Temple. Plans have been drawn. Jacob Yehuda of Safad, an old recluse considered a genius by many, spent his whole life researching the construction of the Third Temple. Building materials are being kept in a hidden place.

Back in 1978 eight young Orthodox Jews led by Matityahu Dan set up a yeshiva in the Muslim Quarter of the Old City a few hundred meters from Temple Mount. They named it Ateret Cohanim ("the Priestly Crown"). Part of the function of the yeshiva was to extend the settlement crusade of Gush Emunim into East Jerusalem, to "redeem" Arab property—one way or another. The other function of the yeshiva was to study the works of the younger Kook (a highly revered founder of Israeli Jewish fundamentalism) and his contemporary Hafetz Haim on the priestly rites and duties pertaining to the Temple. Kook had encouraged Dan to devote himself to the question of how the Third Temple should function once it was in existence, so that all would be in readiness for the big day. It was all very well to have that rare red heifer, but how exactly should it be slaughtered? How should its ashes be prepared? All these things were of great importance. Yeshiva Ateret Cohanim rabbis instruct 25 young men on how to make animal sacrifice. While some students pore over these problems others practice weaving the sacred garments to be worn by the high priests. Still others mix squid and snail extracts, trying to obtain the purple-blue dye used in these robes.

It isn't all bookwork and labwork, however. These are young men, after all, with young men's spirits of adventure. Back in 1982 students from the yeshiva began to tunnel under Temple Mount in search of a chamber where King Solomon is thought to have hidden gold vessels used in the First Temple. But Arab guards heard the digging and a riot ensued. The tunnel was sealed and the students returned to their books and looms.

Not all the preparatory work is done by this one yeshiva. For example, Rabbi David Yosef Elboim formed the Movement for Establishment of the Temple (Tnua Lechinun Hamikdash). Some of his workshops are devoted to making the artifacts and sacred vessels of worship. Others are busy weaving the pure linen for the priests' garments. The Torah is followed strictly—no needles are used for specific pieces. At three other yeshivot, students learn the details of temple service. The project assigned one group is to find a red heifer.

Melody has gotten people thinking. Suppose she had passed the strict tests. What then? It isn't enough simply to have a red heifer. The heifer must be slaughtered by a priest who is without blemish and ritually pure. But where do you find such a priest? It's that old chicken-egg thing.

The solution is to raise babies who are not exposed to contact with the ground (and hence the dead). In the days of the Second Temple (the one destroyed by the Romans) priests were raised in compounds of solid bedrock, out of range of possible grave sites. A group of rabbis is locating families among the Cohanim (Jewish priestly caste) who would be willing to submit their male babies for isolation. It is important to get started on this because the priests must have passed bar-mitzvah. This means at least 13 years must elapse before a red heifer can be slaughtered, if available. So Melody, had she been the real thing, would have been of no use. At least 19 babies must be found because the priest must be without blemish, and in 13 years a lot can happen to a boy's physical condition (there are 70 types of blemish which would disqualify a boy from being chosen as priest).

Rabbi Nahman Kahane of Jerusalem has created a database of all Jews descended from Aaron, from which could be selected those to serve in the rebuilt Temple. Rabbi Elboim has been assigned the task of signing up expectant mothers willing to dedicate their babies to the future priestly caste. He has located a group of people settled in the hills surrounding Jerusalem who have expressed an interest in erecting a building to house the boys as they grow to age 13. The building would be elevated from the ground by an air space. The boys could be visited, even kissed. But only after the visitor has been immersed in a ritual bath (mikvah), and the visitor cannot wear or hold a finished object. The latter eliminates many types of clothing, shoes, and utensils.

Those at the Temple Institute told Clyde Lott about a strange coincidence. He had used precisely the same words as had another gentile over 2,500 years earlier in his dealings with the Israelites concerning Temple artifacts. At that time the Israelites involved had prayed that from his gentile lineage might come the producer of a red heifer. And behold, here before them was that gentile descendant!

Lott's trip to Jerusalem was followed by Rabbi Richman's visit to Mississippi. Born American, Richman had moved to Israel in 1982. He grew up in Massachusetts, but the Deep South would be a new experience. He was aware that its culture would seem as foreign to him as that of another country.

Lott had booked the local community center and it was filled to capacity — over 300 persons occupied every seat and lined the walls. They had come to see this Jew from Jerusalem who would speak about the red heifer and its significance in Jewish beliefs, about the rebuilding of the Temple and the coming of the Messiah. Richman looked every bit the part. Dark curly beard, rose-tinted oval glasses. From the hem of his suit jacket hung the blue fringe of the zizith. On his head a kipa. What was that for? asked a man in the audience. Was that to hide his horns? The man appeared not to be joking, or in any way to intend insult.[6] Indeed, Richman was impressed with the candor, the warmth, and the desire to learn evidenced by this crowd of apparent bumpkins. They certainly knew their Bible, especially those parts pertaining to the Temple.

This turned out to be the first of many such gatherings. Soon Lott and Richman were barnstorming the Deep South, informing fundamentalist Christians of the work concerning preparations for the Temple, and collecting contributions to that end.

Lott has made an observation which he discloses with marked embarrassment. "The very people that are advocating this [rebuilding the Temple] are the ones that are very anti–Semitic in their feelings."[7] Those Christians who aid fundamentalist Israelis in their endeavors, he maintains, do so only to speed up the coming of the Rapture, not out of any altruistic motives. They do so knowing full well that this will leave the world in chaos and flames.

Isn't there some inconsistency, then, between this knowledge and Lott's endeavors? Well … Lott does believe, along with other Christian fundamentalists, that God favors those who help Israel. While he doesn't think it is right to *force* the coming of the End, he sees nothing wrong in acting in ways that might *lead* in this direction. It is then up to God to choose whether or not to affirm these human actions by allowing events to unfold in that same direction.

In the meantime Lott is doing his part. With their tour of the Southeast completed, Lott and Richman set about more concrete plans. By 1997 they had located a group of West Bank settlers who agreed to raise red cattle with the object of breeding the pure red heifer required by Judaic law. To get things started Lott would see to the raising of red cattle in Nebraska. Five hundred pregnant red cows would then be shipped to Israel.

18

Mesirut Hanefesh

Professor of Islamic Studies at Hebrew University Emmanuel Sivan notes, "The fact is that until '67 the national religious camp [in Israel] was a very moderate Zionist movement. It has turned extremist because of this apocalyptic vision. Jewish fundamentalism of the nationalist branch is mostly the product of the Six Day War."[1]

This outburst of religious fanaticism was found originally only among the minority of Israel's population. Israel was founded as a secular nation, and until recently only one Israeli in five defined himself or herself as "religious." What does that term mean, however? "Religious" compared to what? Judaism as practiced in Israel is primarily Orthodox, and hence far less liberal than much of North American Judaism. Religious authorities of the Conservative and Reform movements are not officially recognized by the state. As professor of sociology at Ben Gurion University Stephen Sharot observes, Orthodox Judaism can be considered the "official" religion in Israel.[2] Hence, within Judaism as a whole Israel can be considered on the right of the spectrum.

However, things have been changing in recent years. Shlomo Deshen, professor of anthropology at Tel-Aviv University finds "a significant, salient and general shift of the orthodox strategy, away from isolation, centrism and leftism — towards the right-wing pole."[3] He notes that even if the religious parties falter at the polls Orthodox Judaism provides "the main ideological bolster of the hawkish position" and is "the essential powerhouse of the right wing."[4]

The trend to the religious right has not been without soul-searching and violence within Israel. Since the religious renewal after 1967 a nervous Israeli McCarthyism has asked what it is to be a Jew. Ehud Sprinzak has documented Israel's internal troubles in a study of the violence of Jew against Jew, appropriately titled *Brother Against Brother*. He concludes his study with the observation that "the deep ideological cleavage between the Israeli right and left over the question of Eretz Israel [a major tenet of the new religious right] produced the largest amount of domestic violence in Israeli history."[5]

The Six Day War was the most significant factor in a general movement toward the religious right. Other factors have contributed to this trend, however; demographics, for example. The first waves of immigration to Israel were mainly western in origin (Ashkenazim). When Israel became a state in 1948 only 10 to 15 percent of the population was of eastern origin (Sephardim). Today the Sephardim constitute about one half of the Jewish population in Israel.[6] Studies have determined that almost one half of European Jews could be classified as essentially secular, compared to less than one fifth of Asian and North African Jews.[7] Sephardic Jews were more likely to espouse Zionism and to see their own immigration in a messianic context. The more conservative beliefs of a growing portion of the population shift the balance to the religious right. Michael Walzer, a member of the faculty of the Institute for Advanced Studies at Princeton, says that if things continue to head toward the religious right to the degree that the rabbinate comes to power in Israel "the country would become like Iran under the ayatollahs."[8]

The right-wing position of Orthodoxy in recent years is something new, as Deshen points out. When Zionism arose a century ago most Orthodox rabbis and their people were apathetic. Indeed, a large and vocal minority were strongly opposed. Zionism was viewed as heretical. As the Zionist movement became increasingly dominated by nonpracticing Jews and took on a secular hue Orthodox Jews found it even more objectionable.

Ultra-Orthodox Neturei Karta Jews to this day refuse to recognize the state of Israel because the true nation of the Jews can only be established by the Messiah himself, not by the force of human armor. They condemn Zionism and the state of Israel as blasphemous abominations. Yet despite their theology most ultra–Orthodox Jews support the militant Likud Party and espouse a hawkish right-wing stance.[9]

Traditional Judaism holds that some day a Messiah will come to the Jews, and that his coming will be the crowning act of the "Redemption" of Israel. Israel has been in the religious doghouse for almost 2,000 years. To some Jews it has seemed almost that God is dead. He seems to have turned his back on his people. But Redemption is God's reclamation of his people. Their sins as a people will be forgiven and Israel will once again live in the bosom of her Lord. God's eternal promises to his people will be fulfilled.

Traditional Judaism maintains that the coming of the Messiah and the Redemption of Israel cannot be hastened by human action. By contrast, Rabbi Avraham Yitzhak ha-Cohen Kook, writing in the 1920s and 1930s, claimed that the Zionists—even nonreligious Zionists—were the unknowing agents of the messianic age. Human beings and human activity were already setting the stage for the Messiah's coming. It had started with the Balfour Declaration and the recent influx of Jews into Israel. Kook's theology had no revolutionary political implications. It was in full support of the status quo—the slow progress of secular Zionism toward a Jewish homeland. The Redemption of the Jewish people had begun.

Ehud Sprinzak is a political scientist at Hebrew University of Jerusalem and other renowned institutions of learning and has been a fellow at the Center for International Development and Conflict Management at the University of Maryland. He writes, "Kook's interpretation of redemption was original and daring. It signified an immense deviation from the traditional Jewish belief that the messiah could only come through the single meta-historical appearance of an individual redeemer."[10] "There were clearly some elements of heresy in the new interpretation."[11] Because his views were considered heretical Kook, even though he was the first chief rabbi of the Jewish community in Palestine, was castigated by ultra–Orthodox Jews.

Kook has been called a fundamentalist. "Fundamentalist" was a term originally applied to a minority Christian group but it has come to designate extremists of any religious tradition. Israeli Zionist fundamentalists resemble their Christian counterparts in many ways. For one thing, they are both innovative, yet claim to be offering the true original interpretation of their respective religious traditions. Jewish fundamentalism developed its theology in the 20th century. Kook was its spiritual father.

His son Rabbi Zvi Yehuda Kook continued where the father left off. He presided over Yeshivat Merkaz ha-Rav. The yeshiva is a quasi-monastic community where young men can live separate from regular family and social life and indulge in the study of traditional Judaic texts and religious law. The younger Kook said that his would be the generation which would see the dawning of the messianic age. Moreover, as the kingdom of heaven on earth, the state of Israel would some day encompass Eretz Yisrael. "Eretz Yisrael" is a theological term referring to the religious community of Jews which dwells in all of the land given by God to Abraham — generally considered to be that between the Nile and the Euphrates rivers, a much larger chunk of land than the new nation has possessed in its short history.

On the eve of Independence Day in May 1967 at an alumni reunion at Yeshivat Merkaz ha-Rav the younger Kook, as was his custom, was delivering a festive sermon to the graduates. Suddenly his normally quiet voice lifted to lament the partition of sacred Eretz Yisrael. It was intolerable that Jews had not returned to the holy cities of Nablus and Hebron. This must be rectified. "God had determined, once and forever, that ... this is a holy land and this is a holy people," Kook asserted. "Is it our right to concede even one millimeter of it?"[12] Kook also observed that the Temple would be rebuilt: "That great and glorious day is drawing nigh."[13]

Just three weeks later the Six Day War broke out, and some of Kook's students, now soldiers, touched the Western Wall. Kook himself was driven by jeep to the site. Accompanied by the crackling of gunfire he proclaimed: "We announce to all of Israel, and to all of the world, that by divine command, we have returned to our home, to our holy city. From this day forth, we shall never budge from here. We have come home."[14] These youthful soldiers were convinced that they alone realized what was really happening. The graduates of Yeshivat Merkaz ha-Rav had been intellectually and spiritually prepared for this moment. They could put the conquest of Jerusalem and the taking of Temple Mount into the context of all they had learned and had come to expect. What was a shock of victory for the general public was a "burst of light,"[15] of revelation, for the youthful students of Yeshivat Merkaz ha-Rav. They saw the events of those few days within an already developed theological context. The events confirmed the theology, as the theology gave significance to the events.

Many of the young Kookists testified that they felt as if "possessed."[16] The spirit of their newly enhanced beliefs strengthened their will on the field of battle. "With the taking of the Temple Mount," wrote one, "...divine and spiritual force ... cascaded onto us from heaven."[17] As part of the new "messianic philosophy of history,"[18] 1967 was declared the year zero in the era of Redemption. Just as 1967 was given priority over 1948, Jerusalem Day—the day Temple Mount was liberated during the Six Day War—was given precedence over Independence Day.

The results of the war were interpreted as a miracle, the "victory of the Sons of Light over the Sons of Darkness."[19] There had been, in the words of Uriel Tal, a "metaphysical shift" to a "transcendent political reality."[20] The newly Occupied Territories now embraced the two holy cities Kook had mentioned in his sermon. Those who had heard Kook's sermon such a short while before were convinced that the spirit of prophecy had come over their rabbi on that day. Kook became revered as a prophet.

As spiritual leader of this new fundamentalist messianic movement the younger Kook elaborated its theology. Israel was no longer considered to be simply a secular state. It had been transformed under Kook's theological wand into "the Kingdom of Heaven on Earth."[21] Every grain of its soil was holy ground. Israel's army was a holy army; its people, a holy people. Its government must be ruled by the ancient laws given to the people by God — the Torah.

The new Occupied Territories were an integral part of this holy land. The Jews had no right to forsake their claim here. Their right to this land was a matter of divine will. To surrender even one inch of this holy land would be to defy God's will. Furthermore, before national salvation could be completed, territory in Jordan, Syria, and Iraq would have to be annexed to the extent of the biblical boundaries. Not to seize this land would be to go against God's will. It would mean forfeiting the Redemption of the Jewish people. Land was not a matter of politics or security. This land had eternal, supernatural significance. It was holy land for a holy people. In addition, although Kook himself never actually called for a crusade of conquest during his lifetime, if necessary it would be won through Holy War.

Kook's students were filled with unshakable conviction in the authority of the new theology, convinced that God was sanctioning their cause. Every event had theological significance. Surely recent events had opened the eyes of a greater portion of the wider Israeli public to a messianic and eschatological interpretation of their times. The students and graduates of Yeshivat Merkaz ha-Rav would soon be joined by thousands of their fellow Israelis. In a crusading missionary spirit these young men would lead by example. They would show the way. It would be their mission to enlighten the wider Israeli community. They had a cause — to realize the eschatological Eretz Yisrael.

As time passed, however, this early enthusiasm was dampened. The secular government did not share the new messianic convictions. It did not govern according to the Torah. Judea and Samaria were not annexed.

In 1973 the Yom Kippur War yielded another incredible victory. But it was a wasted victory. The Israeli government was granting territorial concessions in the Sinai Peninsula, land it had won in battle.

Something had to be done. In March 1974 at a kibbutz in the West Bank the founding meeting of a new organization took place. Gush Emunim (Bloc of the Faithful) was the result of earlier discussions led by students of the younger Kook. It began as a faction of the National Religious Party. This party was a partner in the Labor coalition government, but when the government's actions proved so disappointing Gush Emunim parted ways with the party and became an independent pressure group. It protested government actions, staged demonstrations in Judea and Samaria, and began illicit settlements in the Occupied Territories, what Robert I. Friedman has described as "the militant mystical-messianic settler crusade of the fanatically religious."[22]

Menachem Friedman of Bar-Ilan University in Israel calls Gush Emunim "innovative fundamentalism,"[23] and considers it "religious radicalism"[24] and "revolutionary."[25] It offers idealistic young people a meaningful religious existence in the state of Israel. It provides to youthful Israelis what young people everywhere crave — an idealistic cause, and action. It is activist, not passive. It is Redemption, not exile. Friedman notes that Gush Emunim represents a "basically spontaneous and socially activated process."[26] The young people of Gush Emunim (and the religious Zionism embodied in this new fundamentalism is predominantly a movement of young people) confidently step forth into a new life of their own creation. The spirit of Gush Emunim is infused with the miracle of the Six Day War, which some described as a mystical experience.

World-famous Israeli author Amos Oz finds the new religiosity of Gush Emunim a terrifying threat to human freedom in Israel: "A small sect, a cruel and obdurate sect, emerged several years ago from a dark corner of Judaism; and it is threatening to destroy all that is dear and holy to us [Israelis], and to bring down upon us a savage and insane blood-cult. People think, mistakenly, that this sect is struggling for our [Israel's] sovereignty.... The real aim of this cult is ... to force us all to bow to the authority of their brutal false prophets."[27] Oz calls the ideals of Gush Emunim "an ugly and distorted version of Judaism."[28] He describes fundamentalist yeshiva students as "crude, smug and arrogant, power drunk, bursting with messianic rhetoric ... apocalyptic.... signs and oracles, of tidings of 'the end of days.'"[29]

In 1977 Yitzhak Rabin's Labor government ceded the reins to Menachem Begin and Likud. Begin accorded Gush Emunim full legitimacy. They were permitted to settle in Samaria.

A year later things had soured. No official settlement program had been instituted. The American government had exerted pressures. Begin's health had begun to suffer. The government was just too busy with day-to-day governing. Then came the Camp David Accords. The Gush Emunim had placed so much faith in Begin, and what did he do? He agreed to return all of Sinai to Egypt and to initiate the Autonomy Plan for the Palestinians of the West Bank and Gaza.

The philosophy of Gush Emunim allowed for the paradox which arose when secular events appeared to contradict the tenets of ideology. Indeed, Gideon Aran, a student of religious extremism and a lecturer at Hebrew University, asserts that "paradox lies at the very source of the mystic messianism of Gush Emunim."[30] When the facts of secular reality appear as reversals, the opposite is true. Events which would normally prove one's beliefs mistaken serve instead to breathe new vitality into the belief system. Aran says these are people "who refuse to accept the verdict of history proclaiming their belief to be false."[31] The harsher reality flies in their face, the more they are convinced. "Contemptuous of the manifest and the conventional," they relish the contrary as liberating. "The very frustrations brought on by the actual circumstances fill their hearts with certainty of faith."[32] Reversals are interpreted as the "birth pangs of the messiah."[33]

However, paradox and philosophy aside, the Camp David Accords proved too much of a reversal. Late in 1978 Yehuda Etzion began to discuss with others what might be done in the wake of the accords. The result was the formation of an extremist group within Gush Emunim — the Jewish Underground, the Makhteret. A highly regarded expert on Israel's radical right, Ehud Sprinzak lists the Jewish Underground among those movements which he calls "cultural radicals."[34] Robert I. Friedman designates the Makhteret "the most violent anti–Arab terrorist organization since the birth of the Jewish state."[35]

Yehuda Etzion is the figure most responsible for shaping the ideology of the Jewish Underground. Today he has become almost a cult figure in the eyes of a new generation of religious youth. Posters of Etzion adorn settlers' homes in the West Bank and yeshiva dormitories. While he himself did not study at Yeshivat Merkaz ha-Rav, his rabbi at Yeshivat Alon Shvut did. Until the Camp David Accords the 27-year-old Etzion had been a typical product of Gush Emunim. But he needed some theologically satisfactory answer to explain why Begin had capitulated. Then he discovered the forgotten writings of Shabtai Ben-Dov.

Ben-Dov spent his years as an unimportant official in Israel's Ministry of Industry and Commerce. Drawing on the almost forgotten tradition of the ultranationalist poet Uri Zvi Greenberg, he developed a theory of national Redemption. Greenberg's poetry had called for a bloody Joshua-like conquest: "Only that which is conquered in blood, becomes sacred for the nation."[36] Greenberg insisted that traditional Judaism was mistaken in thinking that the Messiah would come without this conquest in blood.

Ben-Dov transformed these 1930s seeds of thought under the hot sunshine of post–1967 enthusiasm. Shabtai Ben-Dov's vision surpassed even that of Yeshivat Merkaz ha-Rav. Where the younger Kook had spoken in generalizations, Ben-Dov talked of the concrete. The key was active Redemption. Why wait for another miracle? The miracle had already happened. The time had come to act. Israel must be transformed into a holy nation of holy people. The biblical kingdom of Israel must be recreated, in possession of all its original territory, the Sanhedrin (the council of 70 wise men) and the house of David reestablished, and a supreme rabbinical court instituted to govern by the Torah. Concrete and total transformation. And at the center of the new theocracy ... a newly constructed Temple, on Temple Mount.

As Etzion read from the master the answer to his question came to him. It wasn't that Begin was a weak man. The setback was a sign from God. God was displeased. The nation of Israel had offended its Lord and the Lord was punishing Israel for its sin. What was that sin? Israel's allowing Muslims to continue to occupy Temple Mount. The Dome of the Rock was an "abomination." Here is how one of the leaders of the Underground put it: "The existence of the abomination on Temple Mount, our holiest place, was the root cause of all the spiritual errors of our generation and the basis of Ishmael's [Islamic] hold in Eretz Yisrael."[37]

Ben-Dov died in 1979. In his last words he requested that the young Etzion destroy the Dome of the Rock. The master had spoken.

Etzion did some hard thinking. He came to see even the younger Kook and Gush Emunim as subservient to the weak-kneed Israeli government. Where both should have been criticizing the government, they were instead supporting it. The rabbis connected with Gush Emunim had failed to read the Torah "correctly."[38]

It made no sense to wait for a secular democracy to act; it would never take action. Even figures like Menachem Begin proved to be soft. Begin and others in government were far too willing to compromise and offer concessions, too eager to have peace at the expense of the accomplishment of revolutionary ideals. Forget world opinion. Forget international relations. Forget practical politics. All that matters is the will of God, the divine commandments. Now was the time to establish the theocracy which Ben-Dov had articulated. The Sanhedrin must replace the Knesset. God's commandments as found in the Torah must become the law of the land. The Third Temple must be constructed. Until these things came to pass it was the duty of every Israeli to disobey the illegal secular government. Etzion called for a response to the holy spirit.

Orthodox Judaism has an expression: "mesirut hanefesh"—complete devotion to a cause. Etzion is completely committed to the ideal of religious revolution in Israel. Sprinzak interviewed Etzion and remarked that he "is the most devoted individual to a cause I have ever met."[39] Here is what Etzion's wife says: "He lives on another plane, having a constant sense of supreme mission.... This is a person who constantly feels he has a role in the course of redemption and who asks himself every day, 'What am I doing for the sake of redemption?'"[40]

Etzion paid no heed to rabbinic constraint. An Israeli Pat Robertson, he received directly from God the "commandment that pounded in the heart of Joshua."[41] Just as Robertson believed his interpretation of the Bible was correct in opposition to that of the church, Etzion believed that he, as opposed to the rabbis, "correctly" interpreted the Torah. Both men want to institute a theocracy, and both men believe they have an active role in bringing about the imminent End to this world.

Etzion was imprisoned in 1984 for acts of terrorism. Here he had time to further formulate his thoughts and to write *Temple Mount*. This influential book broke the taboo over Israel's disgrace regarding Temple Mount. Temple Mount was the centerpiece of Etzion's thinking. Until Temple Mount was cleansed of Muslim defilement and the Third Temple constructed thereon the Messiah would not come and Israel would remain unredeemed. The blissful land of milk and honey could not exist until the Muslims no longer polluted God's holy land: "The expurgation of Temple Mount will prepare the hearts for the understanding and further advancing of our full redemption. The purified Mount shall be — if God wishes — the ground and the anvil for the future process of promoting the next holy elevation."[42]

How, though, did Etzion think the Dome of the Rock could be destroyed without the destruction of Israel by the Arab nations shortly thereafter? Here is his answer. Israel will no longer be merely one secular nation among many. Just as Robertson's raptured Christians will be immune to the horrors of the End Time, Etzion's Israelis will be immune to Arab revenge. Once Temple Mount has been cleansed Israel will be "elevated" to another plane of existence, another dimension of reality, almost like Plato's realm of Ideas — beyond the natural world, untouchable: "But as for ourselves 'our God is not theirs' [the Gentiles]. Not only is our existential experience different from theirs but also from their very definition. For the Gentiles, life is mainly a *life of existence*, while ours is a *life of destiny*, the life of a kingdom of priests and a holy people. We exist in the world in order to actualize destiny."[43]

The constraints of political reality are irrelevant. They have no power over the new kingdom of Israel: "Once adopting the laws of destiny instead of the laws of existence, Israel will be no more an ordinary state.... she will become the kingdom of Israel by its very essence."[44] Anyone familiar with philosophical thought knows that the word "essence" has special meaning, and refers to that which is not part of the everyday world of nature and human actions. Essence is something aloof and other.

With the publication of his *Temple Mount*, Etzion's logic and the originality of his ideas became public, available to influence some young and excitable soul.

As the members of Gush Emunim grew older, more gentrified, and more satisfied with life in general, Etzion realized that they no longer carried the banner of revolution. The state itself Etzion considered illegitimate. It had failed to redeem the land, to assert authority over the Muslims, to rebuild the Temple. God had slowed the process of Redemption because of the secular peace agenda of the Israeli government. Clearly the people were not ready for Redemption. Etzion needed to found a revival movement to replace the tiring Gush Emunim. After seven years in prison Etzion founded Chai Ve-Kayam (Alive and Existing).

The first act of the organization was to draft a new shadow declaration of independence for Israel. The principles of democracy, equality, and human rights gave way to the Bible, Judaic law, and the Kingdom of Israel as it was at the time of the biblical King David. While Chai Ve-Kayam activists have not engaged in violence they have demonstrated their displeasure with the government by their constant attempts to breach the prohibition against praying on Temple Mount. These actions have maintained tension at Temple Mount.

To this day Etzion's thought has not altered. Although "the archterrorist of the Jewish underground"[45] no longer takes an active role in terrorist plots, he prompts others to get involved: "Belief without action is meaningless."[46] He continues to believe that the Temple must be rebuilt: "There are things that people have to do by force. We cannot sit and read books and hope the Temple is rebuilt. We have to rebuild it ourselves."[47]

In a speech to the Israeli parliament in the first year of Israel's existence as a modern state its first prime minister, David Ben Gurion, had said, "When we build the Temple...."[48] Starting with Etzion's lead building the Third Temple on Temple Mount became the focus of life in Israel for the rabidly religious. As Rabbi Shlomo Chaim Hacohen Aviner notes, "The supreme purpose of the ingathering of exiles and the establishment of our state is the building of the temple. The temple is the very top of the pyramid."[49]

A group of hawkish rabbis, Tzfia, has published ideas concerning Temple Mount similar to Etzion's. Unlike Etzion, these rabbis have religious authority. Tzfia claims that all the disasters and suffering of the Jewish people have come as a result of Temple Mount's remaining unredeemed.

Tzfia's loudest advocate for the reclamation of Temple Mount is Rabbi Israel Ariel: "Is control of the Temple Mount no longer a duty and an imperative?"[50] He has set up the Museum of the Temple. Ritual instruments are on display and a guide explains the relevant Torah passages. In 1983 38 yeshiva students met at his home for prayer before proceeding to Temple Mount with plans to dig beneath the Muslim shrines.

Ariel wants the Arabs out of Israel's sacred land. They must be expelled; the threat of war is no deterrent. "Do it."[51] Like religious fanatics east and west, Ariel puts little value on human life when doctrinal ideals are on the line: "Be killed rather than sin."[52] The life of non–Jews counts for nothing. Here is what one rabbi wrote in Tzfia's periodical: "[Some have said that] all human beings are equal, Jews and Gentiles. As we shall now see, this belief stands in total contrast to the Torah of Moses, and is derived from a total ignorance and an assimilation of alien Western values. It would not even merit comment had not so many people been led astray by it."[53] The same rabbi points out that ten Halakhik authorities assert that Gentiles are more beast than human.

Such religious totalitarianism allows no place for concession, no place for toleration, no place for compromise. Morality? Civil rights? Holiness overrides these. God's chosen people are above secular laws and restrictions, those against genocide, for example. Rabbi Israel Hess has published an article in a student paper titled "The Command of Genocide in the Bible." He writes, "The day will still come when we all shall be called to wage this war for the annihilation of Amalek."[54] The Bible commanded that the Amalekites were to be utterly destroyed. They were not to be spared in any way. Man, woman, baby, and beast — all were to be killed. Ethnic cleansing, leading to racial purity. Who are the descendants today of the Amalekites? The Arabs. But what of the words of Isaiah, also in the Bible, that swords should be beaten into ploughshares? Hess would claim these are prophecies for the distant future, for the world to come, after the Messiah has arrived, *after* the warfare and the shedding of blood.

It was a Friday morning, 5:10. Several hundred Muslim worshipers were bowed in Ramadan prayer in the West Bank town of Hebron. Suddenly a man in the uniform of the Israeli Defense Forces broke into the hall and emptied his automatic rifle into the crowd. Before he got to the fifth ammunition clip his gun jammed. The stunned Muslims seized their opportunity. They hurled a fire extinguisher at him, charged, and beat him to death.

Newspaper reports recounted the massacre of February 25, 1994: 29 Muslims killed, over 100 wounded, in just three minutes of mayhem. In the days that followed outraged Palestinians clashed with Israeli soldiers throughout the West Bank, leaving nine Palestinians dead and almost 200 wounded.

Jews were shocked to learn the identity of the killer — Baruch Goldstein, a devout Orthodox Jew, father of four, a respected figure in the community, a doctor who cared for both Israelis and Palestinians (at least one Palestinian said Goldstein had saved his life). Why? And why Goldstein? Israeli Prime Minister Yitzhak Rabin maintained that this was the work of a madman acting alone.

Goldstein had acted purposefully, though. His actions had been carefully planned. He had attended an early Jewish prayer service before perpetrating his heinous deed. Members of the radical fundamentalist Kach movement acknowledged that Goldstein was one of theirs. His act was religiously motivated, a sacred mission. Nobody else had been in on the massacre or knew of it beforehand. It was individually conceived. But members of Kach understood Goldstein's motives. He had acted in the name of God, in accordance with God's will. The course of history needed changing. Israel must be set back on its messianic track. The massacre would send the message to the Rabin government that they must stop the peace process which would sacrifice the sacred land of Israel. Goldstein became revered as a holy man by Kach. His courage and devotion were praised.

Kach (Thus!) was founded by Rabbi Meir Kahane. Goldstein was a personal student of Kahane, and Kahane was his rabbi. Kahane was one of the most rabid figures in the new Israeli messianism. He had seen the time on God's clock, and that time was now. Kahane exhorted Israelis. He incited, he instigated, he agitated, he fomented, he goaded: If only Israel would cleanse the land of all Arabs. If only it would expel the Muslims from Temple Mount. Kach plastered the walls of the Jewish Quarter of the Old City with posters showing a photograph of Temple Mount with the two Muslim mosques gone and a new Temple in their place. Many leaders of the Gush Emunim proudly displayed these same posters on the walls of their homes. If only Israel would annex those territories which rightfully belonged to it without fastidious concern for "the reaction of the Goy," without caring about world opinion — "The State of Israel is not a 'political' creation. *It is a religious one.*"[55] If, and only if, all of these things came to pass, the Messiah would come and bring Redemption to God's chosen people. God had been ready in 1967 but the Jews had stalled. The secular government had not followed through. If this lack of cooperation continued Redemption would come the hard way — through suffering and tribulation.

On July 20, 1984, Kahane was elected to the Knesset by 26,000 voters.[56] The next day he and a group of his supporters led a victory parade to the Western Wall. On their way through the Arab section of the Old City they overturned vegetable stalls, attacked bystanders, and punched the air with clenched fists, yelling to all within earshot that their stay in the Holy Land was nearing its end. During his next four years in office polls showed that Kahane and Kach gained in popularity — up to 7 percent of the population. High school students gave him particular approval — 40 percent agreed with his ideas, and 11 percent said they would vote for him.

American Christian fundamentalists gave Meir Kahane a sympathetic ear. It did not matter that Kahane's Jewish Defense League was listed as a terrorist organization by the FBI. On his trips to the United States where he was on television and introduced at private cocktail parties, Kahane was extremely successful in soliciting funds from Christian fundamentalist and evangelical supporters.

Kahane praised American apocalypticists for their "total and uncon-ditional" support of Israel. He emphasized that Christian fundamentalists and Jewish fundamentalists were heading down the same pathway. East and west united in a common goal. Kahane observed that without God's promise in the Bible the Jews would have no right to a homeland in Pales-tine. Israel can only rightfully exist as a religious entity — a dogma dear to the hearts of Christian dispensationalists, who believe that the Jews are God's chosen people and that the coming of the Messiah depends on a strong Jewish presence in Palestine. Like Kahane, Christian fundamental-ists believe that Israel must expand to its biblical limits, from the Nile to the Euphrates. Back in 1948 Lewis Sperry Chafer had insisted that "Israel must yet possess the entire land as Jehovah has promised."[57]

In 1980 Kahane was jailed without trial for planning to destroy the Dome of the Rock. Ten years later an assassin's bullet ended his life. He was regarded as a dangerous and fanatical extremist by most Israelis, who think terrorism is something only Arabs are morally capable of. Kahane's terrorist proclamations were considered the ravings of a foreign (he was from New York) madman. His acts of terrorism and the plot to destroy the Dome of the Rock shocked the average citizen of Israel.

Yet, as Shlomo Deshen is quick to observe, while most Orthodox Jews stop short of actually joining Kahane's group or extremist movements like the Faithful of the Temple Mount, these extremists "constitute viable alter-natives that people do not reject out of hand." These movements "have an aura of fascination" and make proposals that are seriously "considered and deliberated by young people in particular."[58] Young people, the next gen-eration.

A ceremony was held on the anniversary of the Hebron massacre and Goldstein's death. Goldstein's memory had become the rallying point for the Kahane counterculture, now that Kahane himself was no longer liv-ing. A memorial volume was issued to commemorate Goldstein's bravery. It consisted of essays, testimonies, and letters of support by several con-tributors. Here is what one Kahanist rabbi, a yeshiva instructor, wrote concerning Armageddon: "Revenge against the Gentiles is an inseparable part of the process of redemption. This process will peak in the War of Armageddon, in which all the Gentiles will unite to fight the people of Israel. God initiates this scenario in order to take final revenge against the rest of the nations for all the sorrow and pain they inflicted upon the peo-ple of Israel all through the generations."[59]

The memorial volume is full of phrases like "the killing of a Gentile is not defined as 'murder.'"[60] But the Gentiles were not the real problem, some contributors asserted. "The problem is not the Arabs — the problem is the Jews,"[61] wrote Kahane's son. When Jewish blood was shed it was caused by Jews, by Jews who failed to overthrow the secular state of Israel, by Jews who failed to further the process of Redemption. These failures resulted indirectly in the death of fellow Jews. Hence, Jews who stood in the way of fundamentalist goals could rightfully become targets for fundamentalist assassins.

One who read about this striking theme was 25-year-old Yigal Amir. Amir was a student at the Bar Ilan University's kollel, a religious academy for the study of Halakha (Judaic law). A serious and talented student, he occasionally outperformed his Talmud teachers. For some time he had been active in antipeace protests against the Rabin government.

In the wake of the Goldstein massacre Prime Minister Yitzhak Rabin was warned by his cabinet that Israelis in the Hebron area of the West Bank must be evacuated. This would prevent further provocation and potential conflict, and send a reassuring message to the Palestinians. Perhaps then the peace process could resume after this recent setback.

The plan to begin evacuation furnished a rallying point for religious fundamentalists. Rabbi Shlomo Goren, Israel's former chief rabbi and a highly regarded Halakhik authority, had earlier ruled against any such evacuation. Now the two rabbis who headed Yeshivat Merkaz ha-Rav and another leading rabbi added their voices to that of Goren. They addressed their ruling to Israeli soldiers: evacuation orders were to be considered illegal; soldiers must disobey any such orders. The majority of Israel's Orthodox rabbis approved the ruling. It was a symbolic defeat of Rabin's secular government. The prime minister was forced to back down. The settlers could remain in Hebron.

Rabin did not abandon the peace process, however. His continuation down this path united the Zionist religious groups—almost 400,000 individuals[62]—against him. Protesters constantly gathered in front of his home screaming "traitor," "assassin." One group convened by a former Kachist executed a religious curse on Rabin.

On November 4, 1995 a peace rally of over 100,000 cheered in support of the Rabin government. At its conclusion Rabin received a big hug from Foreign Minister Shimon Peres, chatted with rally organizers, and headed for the VIP parking lot and his armored car. A figure police had assumed was a plainclothes secret agent approached Rabin and fired two bullets into him at point-blank range. An hour and 20 minutes later the prime minister was pronounced dead on the operating table at Ichilov Hospital.

Once again Christian fundamentalists saw signs that the End Time was fast approaching. The same Texas pastor whom Jerry Falwell would a few years later invite to meet Prime Minister Netanyahu, and who collected vast sums to aid Israeli settlement in the West Bank, in 1996 published

Beginning of the End: The Assassination of Yitzhak Rabin and the Coming Antichrist.

Rabin's assassin was young Yigal Amir. It was at Goldstein's funeral that he decided he had to do something just as exemplary as Goldstein's act. He had discussed with rabbis whether Rabin qualified as "rodef" under a Judaic law which permitted a Jew to kill another Jew without a trial. While they failed to give him an unequivocal green light, Amir was convinced that he understood the relevant Halakhik law. But there was a way around lack of rabbinic sanction — the ancient doctrine of zealotry. Amir read again and again the biblical story of Pinchas. Pinchas killed a Jew in God's name and, although denounced by the elders, was forgiven by God, as were the Israelite people — God stopped a plague which had ravaged the nation. In his testimony Amir stressed that God had made it clear to him that he wanted Rabin dead. It was necessary for the survival of Eretz Yisrael.

It was zealotry that led to the destruction of the Second Temple in A.D. 70. Certain that God would not allow his people or his Temple to be destroyed, the zealots of old created civic havoc in order to blackmail God into immediately bringing forth the Messiah. It didn't work. The Romans put down the civil unrest and destroyed the Temple. Ultra-Orthodox Jews believe that the destruction of this Temple and the subsequent scattering of the Jews comprised God's punishment for the hubris of his people. After the destruction the people swore two oaths in return for divine protection: not to return collectively to the Holy Land, and not to attempt to hasten the coming of the Messiah. Only ultra-Orthodox Jews still honor those oaths today.

19

"A Stain on Our Land"

In the Six Day War of 1967 Defense Minister Moshe Dayan ordered General Uzi Narkiss to surround the Old City of Jerusalem, but to stay off Temple Mount. Dayan feared heavy casualties, but more than that. He feared the political consequences of taking Temple Mount, one of Islam's most sacred sites.

The rest of Israel's cabinet overruled Dayan. Not only did Israeli paratroopers land in the area of the Western Wall, the army's rabbinical staff brought the accouterments of worship to the site. The chief rabbi of the army and others of his staff then trooped across the Haram al-Sharif. It was an act of defiance, a sign of victory.

Israel's parliament, the Knesset, allowed Temple Mount to remain under Muslim jurisdiction. Dayan met with the Islamic directors who managed Temple Mount and promised them that they could continue to maintain control. He ordered the Israeli flag, which had been fluttering triumphantly above the Dome of the Rock, to be taken down. Jews would be allowed onto Temple Mount, but could not pray there. Jews were forbidden to worship on Temple Mount, but they could worship freely at the Western Wall. Within days people's homes in front of the Western Wall were bulldozed to clear an open space for Jewish worshipers.

The Chief Rabbinate ordered signs forbidding Jews on Temple Mount to be placed in front of the gates to Temple Mount. It seemed appropriate to give religious rationalization for what seemed an insult to many

Jews: Here, it was believed, had rested the Holy of Holies—the ancient Ark of the Covenant which held the stone tablets on which were inscribed the Ten Commandments given to Moses. Tradition held that any Jew who stepped upon this spot would die instantly.

Gershon Salomon was one Jew among many who saw Dayan's removal of the flag from atop the Dome of the Rock as a betrayal. For Salomon 1967 was the beginning of the fulfillment of God's End Time plans. To counter persons like Dayan he founded the Temple Mount and Land of Israel Faithful Movement to press for liberation of the Mount from "Muslim imperialist occupation." Over the years Salomon's Movement has gained 15,000 adherents worldwide. Periodically members of the organization challenge the Israeli government's stricture against prayer anywhere on Temple Mount except the Wailing Wall.

Shortly after the recapture of Jerusalem historian Israel Eldad was asked whether his people intended to rebuild the Temple. He replied that there had been one generation between David's conquest of Jerusalem and Solomon's construction of the Temple. "So it will be with us."[1]

Sensing this revolutionary thrust of Israeli fundamentalists following the victory in the Six Day War, ultra–Orthodox Jews stressed that rebuilding the Temple must be left to the Messiah. Any effort by human beings to hasten the End Time by taking this task upon themselves was clearly the work of Satan. Israeli Minister for Religious Affairs Zerah Wahrhaftig agreed: Jews should not attempt to reclaim Temple Mount. But this did not slow down those with religious purpose. In addition, after 1967 the religiously zealous were growing as a percentage of the population as a whole. A 1983 newspaper poll revealed that 18.3 percent of Israelis thought it was time that the Temple be rebuilt, while only 3 percent thought rebuilding the Temple should be left until the Messiah came.[2]

That the Mosque of Omar and al-Aqsa Mosque had stood in the capital city of the ancient Israelites for 13 centuries raised questions in the minds of introspective and religiously devout Israelis. Do these mosques symbolize God's punishment of the Jews? If so, why are they being punished?

The two mosques became a bone of contention which polarized the citizens of Israel into two groups—a secular majority and a tiny, but rabidly fundamentalist, religious minority. Fundamentalist Israelis viewed how one thought about the two mosques as a touchstone which determined if one were a truly religious Jew or simply a secular Israeli. "In the beginning when we could practice guerrilla-type tactics to seize land and make our settlements it was exciting.... Now we are getting bored. We are fully armed. And we feel it is a stain on our land to have a mosque sitting in our midst.... One day we will build our Third Temple there. We must do this to show the Arabs, and all the world, that we Jews have sovereignty over all of Jerusalem, over all the Land of Israel."[3] These words of a youthful member of Gush Emunim are repeated by the director of Jerusalem's Temple Institute, Zev Golan: "Every day's delay [in rebuilding the Temple] is a stain on the nation."[4]

After Israel Eldad made his much quoted remark about rebuilding the Temple, a reporter mentioned the obvious problem — that two Muslim mosques occupied the site. Eldad replied, "Who knows? Perhaps there will be an earthquake."[5] Since the onset of religious fervor following the Six Day War there have been several human attempts to help Mother Nature along — more than two dozen separate violent attempts to take Temple Mount. The wish to destroy the symbols of Islamic dominance on Temple Mount attracts religious fanatics of all types — many adventurers, some simply irresponsible hooligans. On August 21, 1969, Michael Dennis Rohan, an Australian Christian — believing he had been chosen by God to erect a Temple to Jesus — set fire to al-Aqsa Mosque. The building was partially gutted. He had been inspired by reading material from the Church of God, a group with traditional ties to the forebears of American Christian fundamentalists. He was declared "insane and psychotic"[6] by the medical director of a nearby mental hospital. The courts ruled that he was suffering from uncontrollable pathological impulses and paranoid schizophrenia and therefore did not merit punishment.

Muslims took a different view. Even though Israeli firefighters put out the fire, many Muslims thought Rohan had been paid up to $100 million — the figures varied — to start the fire. Other Muslims thought Rohan was an Israeli agent. Thousands of outraged Muslims surged through Jerusalem. There was rioting. A few days later a maverick Arab group hijacked a Trans World Airlines plane en route from Rome to Tel Aviv. An Arab foreign ministers' conference in Cairo protested that Israel has "plans against Muslim and Christian shrines" in the Holy Land.[7] Several Islamic nations issued stern warnings to Israel. King Faysal of Saudi Arabia called a pan–Islamic conference at Rabat, Morocco, to capitalize on the anti–Israeli feeling that this act of violence generated. Twenty-five Muslim heads of state attended, most from countries not directly involved in the Israeli-Palestinian conflict. These leaders formed the Organization of the Islamic Conference, a sort of Islamic NATO. Egypt's President Nasser stoked the fires for a "Holy War" to reverse the disaster of 1967. As one editor commented, "That the mosque burning could precipitate a war is obvious; Nasser has used the incident to unify the Arab world against Israel and to create a frenzied response based on an irrational, visceral reaction."[8] The fire at al-Aqsa Mosque had set back a two-year effort to bring Jew and Arab together in Jerusalem. In the words of one observer,

"Whether this fire will touch off the Mideastern powder keg we don't know. But certainly the religious issue is the one thing that can do it."[9] It was months before the situation settled down.

This incident illustrates several significant points: first, the Israeli authorities' attempt to defuse the situation by focusing attention away from the religious motives involved; second, anyone attempting to destroy these shrines must be promptly punished by the Israeli authorities or Muslims could suspect complicity; third, the quick reaction of the Muslim Middle East, even in nations not directly involved.

There have been several other religiously motivated disturbances on Temple Mount. In 1980 Meir Kahane was imprisoned for conspiring to blow up the Dome of the Rock Mosque. In April 1982 Alan Goodman, an Orthodox Jew from the United States and an ardent fan of Kahane, fired on worshipers outside al-Aqsa Mosque with an M-16, killing two and wounding 11 others before police could restrain him. By "liberating the spot holy to the Jews" he had expected to become the "King of the Jews."[10] In the Arab reprisals which followed there were four more deaths and over 100 more people injured.[11] While it was never conclusively proven, it was assumed that he too was acting on his own.[12] His plea of insanity did not succeed; he was a Jew. He was sentenced to life in prison for murder. Meir Kahane paid Goodman's legal costs and made him an honorary member of his Jewish Defense League.

The following winter four Orthodox youths armed with Uzi submachine guns and hand grenades attempted to break into one of the underground passages in East Jerusalem which opens onto Temple Mount. Police caught them before they could plant their explosives in the mosques. Eventually 40 people, including an Orthodox rabbi, would be arrested in connection with this plot.

In January 1984 a night watchman frightened off two intruders placing sacks of explosives against the Dome of the Rock.[13] They belonged to a group of four — the Lifta Gang — who lived in a cave in a deserted village north of Jerusalem. Their world consisted of drugs, wild symbolism, and their own brand of messianism. Their leader, a known criminal, was arrested six years later for conspiring again to blow up the Dome of the Rock, after police discovered a stockpile of weapons including American shoulder-held missiles. Two of the gang were declared mentally unstable and hospitalized.

Yehuda Etzion and the Jewish Underground began to plan an operation to destroy the Dome of the Rock as early as 1978.[14] Several meetings were held and by 1980 a secret meeting was attended by eight men.[15] Etzion presented his Redemption theology. He told the men that the destruction of the Muslim mosques would trigger a national spiritual revolution, that

Israelis would be swept up in a new spirit of religiosity and commitment, and that this bold strike would solve once and for all Israel's problems. Etzion spoke in a tone convincing and prophetic.

A start was made on detailed plans. The first idea was to bomb the Dome from the air. Aerial photographs were procured and an air force pilot was recruited to steal a plane and perform the attack. Eventually this plan was rejected for fear that the Western Wall might be damaged in the process.[16]

Then for two years Etzion and Menachem Livni, an engineer and expert in explosives, studied Temple Mount and the Dome of the Rock in minute detail. Explosives were stolen from a military base in the Golan Heights, and from them 28 precision bombs were made which would destroy the mosques without damaging the Wall and other surroundings. The homemade explosives were tested in the desert. A model of the site was constructed, and practice runs were timed. Men would scale the walls onto the courtyard of the mosque, with 20 people taking part. Guns had silencers. Tear gas would be used to overcome the mosques' guards.

There was some urgency. The final evacuation of Jewish settlements in Sinai was to take place early in 1982. Since Operation Temple Mount was designed to prevent this evacuation no time could be lost.

Then came a hitch. As early as 1980 the question of rabbinical authority had arisen. Most of the group would not go ahead without the blessing of a rabbi, and none of the individuals involved in the planning was a rabbi. Several rabbis were approached in this regard but none would give his blessing. Even the younger Kook, mentor of Gush Emunim, refused. Livni threw up his hands. Sorry. He was out. When the time arrived to act, only the two men who had originated the idea, Etzion and Yeshua Ben Shoshan, were willing to proceed. The operation was shelved.

Two years later many of the group were arrested for other acts of terrorism. At their trial their defense attorney pointed out that Shin Bet (Israel's internal security force) had known the identities of the members of the group and had prior knowledge of their intentions, but failed to make any arrests at that time because "top political and military authorities had urged the underground to take actions that a democratic state cannot."[17] In a speech to young people Yitzhak Shamir pressed for clemency and lauded the members of the underground as "excellent people." Rabbis everywhere were shouting their acclaim. The convicted men were praised as heroes who should get medals. Money began to pour in from Jews in the United States for their legal expenses.

When the judge read the sentences he said the convicted men should be praised "for their pioneering ethos and war records."[18] They were sentenced as leniently as possible under Israeli law. The courtroom erupted into joyfulness and singing. Later, President Chaim Herzog responded to constant petitioning by Knesset members and reduced the sentences, freeing two of the prisoners.

Liberating Temple Mount became a central goal in the political agenda of Gush Emunim. During the mid-1980s dozens of articles calling for Judaizing the site appeared in *Nekuda*, the voice of Gush Emunim.

Temple Mount is the crown jewel in Eretz Yisrael. Efforts to free Temple Mount add momentum to the whole ultranationalist movement. In the short period of time between March 1983 and June 1984 the fraction of Israelis willing to surrender land—captured in 1967 but not yet annexed—in return for a guarantee of peace dropped from 40 percent to 31.4 percent. The more religious the person, the less likely were they to favor surrendering.[19] As Professor Charles S. Liebman notes, "A greater proportion of Israelis who define themselves as 'traditionalists' espouse ultranationalist policies than the proportion of Israelis who define themselves as secularists."[20]

On Jerusalem Day in June 1986 12,000 activists, many from Gush Emunim, marched from Merkaz ha-Rav—the yeshiva made famous by the Kooks—to the Mount of Olives to watch a sound and light show called "The Temple Mount Is the Heart of the People." Pumped up by the presentation, 100 tried to force their way onto Temple Mount but were restrained by police.

In April 1989 during the Muslim observation of Ramadan stones which had been stored on Temple Mount were hurled down onto Jews worshiping at the Western Wall. Authorities believed the attack was organized by members of Hamas—the Islamic fundamentalist group—who had come from the Gaza Strip. The Israeli Ministry of the Interior temporarily restricted entrance to the mount to Muslims from Jerusalem. Roads were blocked into the city and identification papers checked.

On October 8, 1990, Temple Mount was the scene of the most violent incident in Jerusalem since the Six Day War. So threatening to international peace was this event, Israeli authorities temporarily closed Temple Mount, barring Arabs from the two mosques for the first time in 23 years.

It started when Gershom Salomon, the leader of the Temple Mount Faithful, announced his intention to ascend onto the Haram during the Feast of the Tabernacles and lay in place a cornerstone for the new Temple. There were rumors that this cornerstone weighed three tons and had been constructed without metal tools. The Temple Mount Faithful had for years been trespassing on the forbidden ground every major Jewish holiday to pray and to demonstrate a presence. But this was something beyond the ordinary, something that threatened Muslim sovereignty of their holy site. Fearing Muslim reaction, Mayor Teddy Kollek placed ads in all the

Arab newspapers stating that an injunction had been secured from Israel's High Court of Justice against the Temple Mount Faithful, so Muslims need not fear for the safety of their sacred site.

Despite Kollek's actions the Wakf (the Islamic administration of Temple Mount), it appears, did little or nothing to quell Muslim apprehensions. Indeed, the contrary was true. At Friday prayers (October 5) at the mosque a call came over the loudspeaker for volunteers to come and "defend the mosque"[21] on the following Monday.

The day arrived. As they had been doing for years on Jewish holy days, the Temple Mount Faithful made a declaration, but they remained outside the forbidden site, almost a mile away. Over 3,000 Arabs had come to the Haram to prevent the Temple Mount Faithful from achieving their announced goal. Just below was a large crowd of some 14,000 Jews,[22] mixed with tourists, who had come to the Western Wall to pray. When the Arabs heard the words "the Jews are invading" from the mosque's loudspeakers, they began to throw stones, bottles, and bricks at the Israeli police. Many of these missiles fell on Jews worshiping below.

During the riot the local Israeli police station was set on fire. The police fired on the crowd with rubber bullets and tear gas. Repeated cries of "jihad" (Holy War) were heard from the mosque loud speaker, urging the rioters on. Then the Palestinians locked the gates to Temple Mount. Fearing for the lives of the few police trapped inside, those police locked out smashed through the gates. Soon overwhelmed by rioters—some of whom were reported to have wielded chains and axes—the police panicked. They, along with some armed Israeli settlers, began shooting live ammunition into the crowd of "unarmed" Arabs. At the end of the melee 21 Arabs lay dead, another 140 wounded. Nineteen Jews had been injured.

Considerable controversy arose concerning the exact sequence of events and who was to blame.[23] It was claimed that this episode was part of the intifada — a general uprising of Muslims against the Jewish state — and that it had been organized beforehand. As proof it was cited that the rioters had blocked off the access road to Temple Mount with large boulders, and that the rioters came so well prepared. Israeli police Inspector General Ya'acov Terner reported, "We found piles of stones, barrels full of nails, bottles, and bits of iron."[24] Yet Israeli authorities refused to allow a United Nations investigation. Suspecting that Muslim religious leaders had incited the attack, Israeli police arrested the deputy spiritual leader of the Muslims in the Holy Land, Sheik Mohammed Said Jamal.

The Israeli Shin Bet called this act by the Temple Mount Faithful "a provocation." Despite the conclusions of Shin Bet, the prime minister at the time, Yitzhak Shamir, said that the Temple Mount Faithful would be allowed to continue their marches.[25] Indeed, one year later Salomon and his Faithful were back again. Same religious feast, same three-ton corner-stone, same intention. This time Salomon announced that he would be hiring a helicopter to lift the cornerstone onto Temple Mount. Israeli police intervened, but did allow him to parade around the Old City.

Salomon knew that he had plenty of support for his actions. One of his supporters was Monroe Spen, a Florida stockbroker who liked to quip, "I always live by the Golden Rule — whoever has the gold makes the rules."[26] Spen knew how to make money. He had parlayed an inheritance into a fortune, and he liked to spend it on his unabashedly Zionist interests. Among other things he had helped finance Meir Kahane's bid for the Knesset. In 1986 he got the Temple Mount bug. He gathered a handful of like-minded notables at an expensive restaurant, among whom was a former Kach activist who had been imprisoned for attempting to blow up the Dome of the Rock Mosque, a fundraiser for Ateret Cohanim, Meir Kahane, and Stanley Goldfoot with his extensive connections to American Christian apocalypticists. Spen had wanted Yehuda Etzion to make an appearance, but this celebrity had to decline: "Received your dinner invitation, but cannot come as I have been in prison for over two years already for the sin of constant and purposeful loyalty to the Temple Mount."[27]

Representatives from the ultranationalist Tehiya Party were in attendance, but none from the ruling Likud Party. Spen did have a letter of support, however: "Your sentiments regarding the Temple Mount coincide with ours."[28] But the letter went on to say that those in government found it necessary to "proceed with caution and calculation." It was explained that the government could not take a more active stance on the Temple Mount issue until it got a directive from the chief rabbis.

Spen had intended to form an umbrella organization from those present at the meeting, and to set up a means to finance it. He couldn't get a consensus, however, so ended up financing the various Temple Mount organizations separately. But Salomon was special. To Spen he seemed like one of the "prophets of old." Here was a real connection. Spen gave Salomon his full support. He pumped a river of money his way and set up the tax-exempt Friends of the Temple Mount Faithful in Sarasota, Florida.

Again in 1996 the government of Benjamin Netanyahu seemed to play into the hands of Israeli fundamentalists when it authorized the opening of a tunnel beside Temple Mount so tourists could view the Herodian walls from the base. This led to riots resulting in 80 dead.

Netanyahu's government went further in September 1998. The Movement for the Establishment of the Temple had called for a show of strength from the radical religious right. A crowd of 1,500 had gathered in support, and Gershom Salomon of the Temple Mount Faithful had been invited to speak. Salomon sported a cane. He had been injured back in his days as an Israeli military officer, and saw his survival from that mishap as a sign that God had saved him for his role in the rebuilding of the Temple. All ears were attentive as Salomon spoke: "We will liberate the Temple Mount, even if the political leadership doesn't want to.... Instead of the Dome of the Rock and mosques, the flag of Israel and the Temple!... It's the will of Providence that we struggle to remove the abominations from the Mount."[29] Wild cheers, enthusiastic applause. Was the Netanyahu government disturbed by these words and this gathering? On the contrary. Its deputy minister of education sent videotaped greetings from the government. Previous to the event's taking place the chairman of the Knesset Law Committee had mailed out thousands of invitations on parliamentary stationery.

The inflammatory issue of Temple Mount has been purposely underplayed by the secular authorities, and incidents involving the site have attracted surprisingly little media attention outside Israel. Foreign journalists often fail to understand the wider significance of these incidents. Nevertheless, the importance of Temple Mount is not lost on the authorities in Israel. It is today a topic of urgency in the Knesset.

Journalist Susan Sappir observes that "every stone added to it [Temple Mount] and every grain of soil taken away [has] ... historic, political and religious import that threatens to shake the world."[30] Late in 1999 the Muslim authorities in charge of Temple Mount decided that a new exit must be opened to Marwani Mosque for the safety of the large crowds expected to celebrate the last Friday of Ramadan. Marwani Mosque is the underground prayer hall below the surface of Temple Mount which holds about 8,000 worshipers. The caverns beneath the mount had been constructed in the early Muslim period and had been used as stables by the Templar knights during the crusades. In 1996 work began to turn this rough site into a finished mosque to handle overflow crowds. When machinery arrived to start on the new exit antennae began to twitch all over. On December 6 the Temple Mount Faithful filed a petition before Israel's Supreme Court challenging the government to get tough and order the Muslims to halt construction. It was a time for those in the wings to make political hay, while those in positions of power knew their political futures hung by a thread. In the background were attempts to come to a peaceful resolution. The situation called for delicate handling. As Sappir so precisely worded it, "Given the role the holy mount plays in the apocalyptic fantasies of messianic radicals of all stripes.... it is no wonder that the recent dispute over the new opening has been viewed as the potential spark that could ignite the whole Temple Mount powder keg."[31]

The slightest spark could light the fire. David C. Rapoport, a professor of political science at UCLA, has extensively studied the close connection between messianism and terrorism. He says that the expectation of the imminent coming of a messiah pushes believers into "extra-normal behavior."[32] Believers become convinced that traditional conventions of morality and conduct are no longer binding. The situation intensifies if there is some doubt that the imminent expected End, due to some unforeseen circumstances, may not occur. At this point fanatical believers are likely to slip off the edge. They will engage in risky, almost suicidal, acts of terrorism and catastrophic violence because they need to prove to themselves that their expectations remain relevant, or because they want to convince God that they are relevant, or in an effort to blackmail God into hastening redemption.

The same psychology motivates Christian apocalypticists. As Gershom Gorenberg notes, "Each year that passes intensifies the glowing expectations—and the potential for a dangerous letdown."[33]

Hence, ironically, groups like the Jewish Underground can actually become more dangerous, a greater threat to peace, when they meet with outward resistance or internal uncertainty. As Ehud Sprinzak writes—and he puts these words in italics for special emphasis: "The combination of messianic belief in national redemption coupled with a situation of endemic national conflict has within it a built-in propensity for incremental violence — extra-legalism, vigilantism, selective terrorism and finally ... indiscriminate terrorism. A 'majestic' act of 'holy' terrorism may well fit into this scheme."[34]

One doesn't have to be a religious fundamentalist with preconceived notions of violent acts. There is something about Jerusalem, about the environment of Temple Mount itself. Jerusalem psychiatrist Dr. Yair Bar-El has observed a phenomenon he calls the Jerusalem Syndrome. Something happens to certain individuals when they are in the vicinity of Temple Mount. Completely sane before, these persons will suddenly become overwhelmed with religiosity near the sacred site. They may dress completely in white. They may appear near Temple Mount and begin preaching — even if they've never preached a word before. They may identify with Jesus, or with John the Baptist, or with the Virgin Mary. Then the episode passes and they become once again as they were before. When told of how they acted they are embarrassed. A momentary bout of insanity?

What if some crackpot, some religious fanatic, some mad renegade who wants to make a point, and who just coincidentally happens to be a fundamentalist Jew, should cause real damage to Islam's sacred mosques? How would Muslims react? In a part of the world where a child's doll left on the sidewalk is enough to summon the bomb squad, in "a city in which entirely too many people believe that their neighbors are, as a matter of cold theological certainty, bound for hellfire,"[35] the Temple Mount situation is a very touchy and delicate issue. Any messing with the status quo here could precipitate wide and serious consequences. Israel is a nation filled with rival contentious factions that constantly split into smaller groups and change alliances. In a nation where Hasidic Jews throw rocks at other Hasidic Jews, where ultrareligious individuals interrupt operas and destroy government offices, Temple Mount is tempting indeed.

Gershon Salomon and his Temple Mount Faithful know all about this. That is why they persist in marching up the ramp to Temple Mount several times a year only to be told by the guards that they must turn back. Someday something will happen. The situation will be so delicate their march will precipitate an upswelling of emotion and action. Salomon and his Faithful have been joined by others over the years. Meir Kahane regularly participated in these demonstrations. In 1987 Gush Emunim marched with the Faithful, leading to a riot of 2,000 Muslims which lasted three hours. Police had to fire on the crowd and use tear gas. Fifty people were injured.

It is Sukkot — the Feast of Tabernacles — late 1999. Once again Salomon and his Faithful make ready to march up the ramp to Temple Mount. But this time the usual band of two dozen or so is swelled to almost 200. This is good — camera crews from the local media have arrived to witness — although no smile betrays Salomon's pleasure. He carries on as if nothing were different from any of the other hundreds of demonstrations. There is excitement in the air. Thousands are on hand to celebrate Sukkot. There are additional police.

Because the year 2000 is just around the corner apocalypticist Christians have joined the Faithful in their march. Pastor John Small is here with several congregants from his Florida church. Small's T-shirt boasts the words "Space Coast Prophecy Conference." As you draw closer you see that his nametag reads "International Christian Embassy's Feast of Tabernacles" and you recall that the International Christian Embassy is an umbrella organization for Christian groups and individuals who support Eretz Yisrael in all its ramifications — hard-core Zionism. Every year thousands of Christian evangelicals go to Jerusalem to fulfill Zechariah's prophecy in the Bible that in the Last Days all the nations will come to the Holy City to celebrate the Feast of Tabernacles. When asked about his presence Small is quick to respond: "We support building the Temple."[36] A born-again Texan preacher with the improbable name Hayseed Stephens aims to support the building of the Temple by more than just demonstrating. A successful oilman, he hopes to find petroleum near the Dead Sea and with the proceeds fund the construction of the next Temple.

Salomon is ready. He hoists the Faithful's flag, the blue and white of

Israel combined with a yellow map of Eretz Yisrael — a greater Israel comprising all the land between Sinai and Iraq. The crowd moves solemnly but joyfully up the ramp. Ultra-Orthodox adorned with their customary sidecurls accuse them of trying to hurry Redemption. This is wrong; it is blasphemous, they say. The group continues.

At the green gate at the top of the ramp the expected occurs. The police smile and politely indicate that Temple Mount is closed to visitors today (as it always is when the Faithful make their march). Sorry. Salomon and his group do not protest or cause trouble. He turns to his followers and switches on his megaphone. In a quietly confident tone he utters a solemn promise: "Soon we shall see the rebuilding of the Temple ... and the accomplishing of God's End Time plans."[37] The crowd responds enthusiastically. "Amen." "Hallelujah." "Yes."

With that Salomon leads them back down the ramp, through narrow alleys, and out through the Old City gates to a flatbed truck. On the flatbed is a giant stone — the infamous cornerstone of the 1990 escapade. Salomon leans on the stone for the camera crews. Then the demonstrators proceed to Shiloah Spring to rehearse an ancient ceremony — the drawing of water for the Temple.

Recently a group of 50 rabbis has ruled that not only can Jews enter the forbidden area, it is their religious duty to do so. Israeli Nadav Shargai claims that there are over 1,000 active adherents to the most radical Temple Mount movements.[38] Their attitude is worded bluntly: "If destroying the mosque to build a temple creates a big war, then so be it."[39]

20

Holy War

One day a camel visiting the Middle East from western North Africa wanted to swim across the Jordan River and have a look at what was on the opposite side. He had heard that he was at the widest point of the river, but the water was calm and it was a nice day for a swim so he decided to swim across anyway.

Part way across the river he looked to one side and saw a few feet away a scorpion swimming in the same direction. He knew scorpions had a deadly sting, but the scorpion seemed to be absorbed in the pleasure of swimming and paid no attention to the camel — which was fine with the camel. It was a nice relaxing swim. The camel luxuriated in the soft warm water and drank in the blueness of the sky above. But then suddenly a wind came up and the water got choppy. Pleasure quickly turned into hard work as the camel pushed into the wind and waves. The camel looked over and saw the scorpion thrashing about desperately, almost swamped by the rough water. He wasn't going to make it, unless …

"Please help me," the scorpion pleaded. "I'm drowning. Let me get on your back."

The camel was a kind camel; he had always helped those in need. But he wasn't stupid. "I'd like to help you, but I'm afraid you'd sting me. Then we'd *both* die."

"No, no," the scorpion shouted back. "I won't sting you. I'm too smart for that. I know it would only cause my *own* death. Please, you've got to hurry."

The camel realized that what the scorpion said made sense. And, anyway, he didn't want the scorpion's death on his conscience. So he swam over and let the scorpion crawl onto his back for a free ride. The scorpion breathed a sigh of relief. Just in time! Soon he was moving swiftly across the river, secure on the broad back of the camel.

When they were still some distance from the shore the scorpion stung the camel. The camel let out a yelp of pain and, enraged at his betrayal, yelled over his shoulder, "You stupid scorpion. Now I shall die, but you will die with me. Are you crazy? Why?"

The scorpion smiled a crafty smile. "Welcome to the Middle East."

The Middle East is full of scorpions. Human scorpions. Had the camel been resident in the Middle East he would never have trusted the scorpion. For in the Middle East trust is a scarce commodity. Middle Eastern politics is complicated by the "almost universal"[1] phenomenon of the suspicion of conspiracies. Many who are conversant with things Middle Eastern have remarked on this characteristic.[2] Daniel Pipes has written a book on the subject — *The Hidden Hand: Middle East Fears of Conspiracy*. He says it is "one of the region's most distinctive political features"[3] and that unless we take it into account we shall be unable to understand Middle Eastern politics: "Conspiracism provides a key to understanding the political culture of the Middle East. It spawns its own discourse, complete in itself and virtually immune to rational argument.... It helps explain much of what would otherwise seem illogical or implausible, including the region's record of political extremism and volatility, its culture of violence."[4]

Pipes's book is filled with examples of what Westerners would call "paranoid fantasies," but which are everyday fare in Middle Eastern thinking. Here's one example: Saddam Hussein collaborated with Western nations in faking the war known as Desert Storm. Here's another: Ayatollah Khomeini just looked anti–American — he worked hand in glove with the Americans right up until his death. And another: Those six Muslims convicted of bombing the New York World Trade Center in 1993 acted under CIA leadership. Their purpose was to discredit Islam. By another account the bombing was done by Israeli agents, again to make Muslims look bad: "The hands of Zionist agents were behind the bombing."[5]

This lack of trust, and suspicion of deception, frustrates any attempt to arrive at a peace settlement. Former head of the Israeli delegation to the Middle East peace talks Yossi Ben-Aharon says, "It's really difficult to comprehend the Arabs' monumental capacity for deception. It is really something the Western mind cannot absorb and appreciate. It is way beyond anything that Goebbels could have conjured up, because for them, lying is second nature. They believe that deception is part and parcel of the art of war."[6] A Jew invoking the name of Goebbels!

   This lack of trust and suspicion of conspiracy mirrors the overall ethos of the Middle East. For in this part of the world which gave birth to three major religions, what lies immediately before the eyes is considered of less significance than what lies behind the visible surface — the religious dimension. As Ronald Reagan said, "The Middle East is a complicated place — well not really a place, it's more a state of mind."[7]

   The Six Day War of 1967 did much to increase the religious temperature of the region. Not only did it provide a new religious confidence to Israelis, the miraculous Israeli victory in that war was the beginning of a new religious soul-searching among Muslims.

   Military defeat and the symbols of military defeat bear religious connotations in the Middle East. After the Egyptians had been so decisively defeated in the Six Day War they turned toward a more fundamentalist belief in Islam. Here is what was said in the *New York Times*: "Many people feel that the resurgence of Islamic militancy in Egypt dates to that overwhelming defeat ... everyone was questioning themselves after the war ... they kept asking what it was about our society, our culture, our political system that could pave the way for such a defeat."[8] The effects of the 1967 war were felt not just in Egypt, but in all of the Arab states of the Middle East. Bassam Tibi concludes from his extensive research that "the Arab defeat in the Six Day War of 1967 had been one of the major factors underlying the politicization of religion."[9] A former member of the Muslim Brotherhood recalls, "People started to say, why are we defeated? Is it because we are away from Islam?"[10] The events of 1967, he was sure, were the turning point for the Islamic movement, away from Arab nationalism.

   Why would Allah allow the Jews to prevail, allow them to conquer Jerusalem and once again possess it as their own? A young sheik answers: "It is all written in the Koran [Islam's sacred Scripture]. The Koran says that Allah will allow the Jews to return to Palestine. I know this to be Allah's plan from Allah himself: He will bring all the Jews to one place and kill them."[11]

   Robert Harkavy is a Jew. He is also a Ph.D. in international relations (Yale), a professor of political science at a prestigious American university, and has been a visiting research fellow in several countries, including being a Fulbright scholar in Sweden. He states, "At its essence, the Middle East conflict is not fundamentally one of territorial irredentism or self-determination, nor is it simply a zero-sum clash of rival nationalisms over control of Palestine."[12]

   The PLO has operated as if it were. The PLO has traditionally aimed to circumvent the religious dimension: "What we want to create in the historical borders of Palestine is a multi-racial democratic state ... a state without any hegemony in which everyone, Jew, Christian or Muslim, will enjoy full civic rights."[13] "We are not the enemies of Judaism as a religion."[14] Nor are they against Christians. Indeed, Palestinian Arab Christians have had significant influence within the PLO.[15] The PLO wants a Palestinian ministate in the Occupied Territories. Thus it has tacitly recognized the right of Israel to exist as a nation, and has expressed the desire to live in peaceful coexistence with Israel. But the PLO represents moderation. It operates in a secular context.

Harkavy does not deny the secular context. He notes "the deep-seated humiliation" felt by Arabs because they have been defeated in six recent wars with Israel. "This humiliation has caused the Arabs, most importantly in their own eyes, to become virtually a laughing stock of the world."[16] Harkavy asserts that the Arabs have always seen themselves as a proud warrior people, and by contrast have seen the Jews as "an altogether contemptible, despicable bunch of over-intellectualized sissies."[17] That the Arabs were defeated by such sissies, especially when their own warriors held a vast numerical advantage, has resulted in "history's most stunning case of collective national, 'testicular' devastation."[18]

To Western eyes this might appear as two proud peoples reduced to the level of young boys scrapping it out in a sandpit. But no. More is involved. In the Middle East religion is a major part of what it is to be a man. "Testicular devastation" is spiritual and religious devastation. There is always the religious dimension, and it is coming more and more to the fore.

David Th. Schiller did his doctorate on Palestinian paramilitary nationalism. A consultant for the Rand Corporation and other research institutes and government agencies, he is an editor of the periodical *Terrorism, Violence, and Insurgency*. Schiller stresses the importance of the Six Day War of 1967 in spawning a spiritual renewal among Middle Eastern peoples. Paramilitary groups called the fedayeen ("those willing to sacrifice themselves")[19] took over the PLO. Since that time insurgent Palestinian factions have sneered at Arafat and the PLO as "moderates," at times killing their fellow Palestinians in cold blood. They oppose the PLO's rapprochement with the enemy. Any sign of peace fosters a new round of violence.

There is another, new force in the battle for Palestinian nationality. The Temple Mount escapades by fundamentalist Jews helped to give birth to a rising star of the Islamic fundamentalist movement — the Islamic Resistance Movement, known by its acronym "Hamas." Extremism begets extremism. Thanks to the Temple Mount exploits, Hamas began to rival the PLO in popular Palestinian allegiance.

Hamas operates in a religious context. It refuses, on theological grounds, to acknowledge the existence of Israel — Israel is illegitimate. Hamas, therefore, opposes any peace process, and wants Palestine to be Islamic. Islamic, not Arabic: "Giving up part of Palestine is like giving up part of religion."[20]

Hamas grew out of the Muslim Brotherhood which blamed the military disasters of 1967 and 1973 on the failure of modern Westernized Arab states to embrace Islam and gain full control and possession of Temple Mount. A Westernized democratic state of Palestine, such as the PLO envisions, is anathema to Hamas. Like other Islamic fundamentalist movements, Hamas challenges the existence of secular nation-states as an "import from the West,"[21] Israel being the best example of such a nation-state. As an alternative to the secular nation-state they favor an Islamic state. As Bassam Tibi notes, "At issue is an alleged divine order to replace the existing secular nation-state."[22] Tibi sees the new militant Islamic movement as "a threat to most of the existing secular nation-states," not just Israel, and part of a wider trend pitting "politicized religion against the existing secular order."[23]

Conflict formerly confined to the cooler arena of secular politics escalates into a more heated, dangerous, and volatile religious conflict. Conflict becomes holy war. Hamas's slogan reads, "Jihad [holy war] is its path, and death for the sake of Allah is the loftiest of its wishes."[24]

As editor Joyce M. Davis notes: "Hamas's *jihad* against Israel was the foundation of its popularity with the Palestinian people and especially with youths searching for a way out of the daily misery of occupation.... More and more, Palestinians were ready to accept the hard and angry message of Hamas: that the only hope lay in *jihad* and that negotiating peace with Israel was treason."[25]

Time, Hamas believes, is on its side. As Khalil Shikaki, professor of political science and director of the Center for Palestine Research and Studies warns, "Arafat will not live forever, and Hamas will not stay on the sidelines forever."[26]

However, some see signs that Hamas is on the decline. Even if that were true other Islamic fundamentalists will rise in its place. Splinter fedayeen groups continually appear to fill the gap. They "have experienced now more than two decades of set-backs and defeats, with no tangible results for years of trouble and bloodshed."[27] Their unrest "will spill over into the international arena with more senseless terrorist acts."[28] These acts will be perpetrated by terrorists like Osama Bin Laden, whom Yossef Bodansky describes as a "super-terrorist."[29]

The holy war of the Middle East is not always carried on in Western fashion — nation against nation. Instead, it is often waged in the form of terrorism. Some of that is provocative terrorism. The purpose of provocative terrorism is to keep the kettle boiling, to draw the opposing side into retributive action. Christian apocalypticists are indirectly engaging in this type of terrorism at Temple Mount. They want to draw Muslims into a holy war with Israel that will eventuate in Armageddon.

They may succeed. Temple Mount is of prime importance to Islam. If Palestine is to become part of Islam — much like fundamentalist Jews see Eretz Yisrael, as holy land — then possession of Temple Mount as a central sacred site is necessary. Just as the building of the Third Temple would signal that Israel had moved from being a secular state to a being a religious entity, complete possession of Temple Mount by Islamic peoples would indicate that Westernized Arab nationality had been abandoned for religious polity. As Ghosheh says, "Al-Aqsa Mosque is not only for the Palestinians. It is for all the Muslims all over the world."[30] And Hamas is supported by Muslims all over. Ghosheh cites support from Muslims in Jordan, the Gulf, Saudi Arabia, Yemen, Pakistan, and Turkey.

The Mosque of Omar and al-Aqsa Mosque are important in themselves, but they are also important as symbols. Symbols are important in Jerusalem, in the Middle East. "In the Middle East ... the symbolic is what is most real," observes Gershom Gorenberg, an expert on matters relating to Temple Mount.[31] Because the two mosques were constructed shortly after the Muslim conquest of Jerusalem 1,300 years ago they have become symbols of military victory and acknowledged defeat. For religious Israelis the two mosques on Temple Mount have for too long been resented memorials to the fact that God apparently at one time favored the forces of Islam over those of Judaism. Somewhere deep in the blood of religious Israelis the mosques seem to say, You have been conquered.

Then came the Six Day War, however. Everything changed. For religious Israelis it became clear that God was once again on Israel's side. All that remains is for Israel to repossess Temple Mount and wipe the stain from their holy place. Until that time the two mosques remain an insult to fundamentalist Jews. They mock, they jeer, they challenge. Victory at Temple Mount, sole possession of the holy site, will insure — both sides believe — that God/Allah is fully behind their endeavors, and that, therefore, total and final victory is guaranteed.

Final victory. A dream that seems never to be fulfilled. Conflict has been, and remains, part of the culture of the Middle East. Those who study the region remark that it is "sadly unique in its potential for violent and often irrational conflict."[32] Irrational, religious conflict — holy war. Holy war, for this is the Holy Land. All war is holy war in the Middle East. To fail to understand this is to fail to understand much of the ethos of the Middle East. One should pick up the Bible and scan chapters 13 through 23 of the book of Isaiah. The Old Testament, the literature of the ancient

Israelites, is salted with what we today would call hate literature. Their God was the god of war. He would bring victory over the enemies of the Israelites. Here is best expressed the nexus of religion and murderous hate so endemic to the region. Holy war. Ironically, both sides of today's conflict are blessed by the same God, hence both sides are confident of eventual victory. Maybe not victory today, maybe not tomorrow, but eventual victory. Future victory. Final victory. Because of this religious confidence on both sides, neither side is going to surrender. Neither side is going to give up, to sue for peace.

Robert Harkavy knows this. Harkavy's shoot-from-the-hip bluntness is refreshing for one steeped in academic life. He places his cards "face-up on the table," and warns that his "values and predictions will ... appear raw and unvarnished, somewhat lacking in ... nuance."[33] Harkavy is not optimistic about peace in the Middle East: "A 'permanent' peace in the Middle East, or even a semipermanent one involving a lengthy peaceful truce following a 'comprehensive peace agreement,' is highly unlikely, in the near or distant future."[34]

Past experience suggests this is an accurate assessment. There have been more than 50 thwarted peace proposals since the First World War.[35] Harkavy is not optimistic about peace even in an imaginary best-case scenario — an Arab-Israeli peace agreement signed by all the local nations and the superpowers, in which Israel would return all land beyond the boundaries of the pre–1948 United Nations partition proposal, in which a fully independent Palestinian state under the Palestine Liberation Organization would be created, and in which Jerusalem would be internationalized. Even this would grant no more than a temporary interlude of peace. As Ehud Sprinzak notes, "Even under ... optimal conditions, Jewish and Muslim extremists can be expected to make every effort to sabotage the emerging understanding."[36]

Ibrahim Ghosheh is a small intense man and a leading light in Hamas. He stresses that while Hamas is an Islamic movement "we are not against the religion of the Jews or, of course, the Christians."[37] He points out that for centuries Jew, Muslim, and Christian had lived together in Palestine. Hamas is against the Jews not because of their faith and beliefs — the three religions worship the same God — but because they came from outside, took Palestine by force, and kicked the Muslims out. Not that the Jews are to be blamed for this, he notes. It is the fault of Western Zionists, particularly in the United States. The conflict is "between Islam and Zionism."[38] Moreover, the conflict will be long, but Islam will win. Look at the Crusades, he says. Two hundred years "and they were turned back."

Ghosheh and Hamas are most vociferous in their opposition to American interference in Middle Eastern affairs. Hamas does not oppose Americans because they are Americans. It opposes Americans because it sees Americans as representing Christian Zionism. Hamas clearly opposes the actions of Christian Zionists and apocalypticists like Jerry Falwell, Pat Robertson, and their cohorts.

Gershom Gorenberg agrees that the actions of Christian apocalypticists are stoking a dangerous religious fire. Just the opposite is needed: "Israeli officials should take every chance to meet evangelical and fundamentalist leaders, and urge them to lower rhetoric about Armageddon or a rebuilt Temple. We should seek the best relations we can get in the real world — rather than remaining unwitting actors in the apocalypse."[39]

The gunpowder is in place. It needs only a lighted match. Ehud Sprinzak writes, "In the next decade [the first decade of the 21st century], whether or not they succeed politically, Muslim and Jewish religious radicals are likely to hold the center stage of their respective societies and attract the attention of the community of nations."[40] With increased polarization the Middle East is rapidly approaching the stage where, as Robert I. Friedman so aptly phrases it, "Belfast will seem like Disneyland."[41]

"We Will Go Crazy"

In October 1986 the London-based *Sunday Times* broke a stunning story. A young Israeli technician had provided the newspaper with top secret information concerning Israel's production of materials for use in nuclear weapons.[1] Mordechai Vanunu had worked at the Dimona plant in the Negev desert south of the populous part of Israel for nine years. He supplied 57 photographs and handwritten notes, and had undergone intense interrogation by nuclear physicists to certify that his information was correct.

From Vanunu's revelations experts calculated that Israel had enough material to manufacture 150 nuclear weapons,[2] 35 of which could be thermonuclear[3]—many more than had been suspected and many more than would be required for a policy of deterrence.[4] The numbers have gone up in recent years—as high as 300 nuclear weapons of several varieties, some large yield and thermonuclear.[5]

Israel's official response to the Vanunu incident was a time-weary line. Its prime minister at the time, Shimon Peres, repeated the standard formula: "Israel would not become the first country to introduce nuclear weapons into the Middle East."[6] This is the standard mantra to this day.[7] Some have suggested that this statement could be correct, if "only in a Talmudic sense"[8]—they couldn't be "first" because American vessels carrying nuclear weapons had been in the eastern Mediterranean for decades.

Israel had long been suspected of a nuclear weapons program and as the years passed the evidence grew. During the October War of 1973 the Soviet Union dispatched nuclear warheads from its naval base in Odessa to Alexandria where they were to be fitted onto Russian Scud missiles based in Egypt. United States intelligence observed the Soviet ships as they passed through the Bosphorus. On October 25 U.S. forces were put on global military alert—a stage IV nuclear alert (where stage V is nuclear weapons launch). It was a warning to the Soviets to back off. They did, but nuclear war and nuclear disaster had been a whisker away.

It was believed that the Soviets responded with nuclear weapons because they knew Israel had nuclear weapons. Perhaps, as some Israelis have speculated, the Soviets gleaned this information through their Cosmos spy satellite. Some Western intelligence experts believed the Israelis conducted an underground test in the Negev in 1963 which the Soviets detected.

At three o'clock in the morning of September 22, 1979, an American satellite passing over the Prince Edward Islands more than a thousand miles off the southern coast of Africa records the two almost simultaneous flashes that indicate a nuclear explosion. Meanwhile a radio-telescope at the United States observatory in Arecibo, Puerto Rico, detects a ripple speeding through the ionosphere — also the sign of a nuclear blast. A third piece of evidence: the U.S. Naval Research Laboratory registers two pings echoing off the Antarctic ice shelf.

A nuclear test? Nothing was ever conclusively proved. But suspicions have remained that Israel tested a bomb with the help of the South African government. There was some indirect evidence at the time, and then five months later the scoop by CBS News. Dan Raviv, an Israeli-American junior correspondent in Tel Aviv, flew to Rome to avoid Israeli military censorship and make his announcement. But Raviv had relied on only two sources and could produce no hard evidence that Israel and South Africa were involved.[9]

Until Vanunu's exposure Dimona had remained a well-kept secret. The Dimona complex is buried six levels below the desert and had escaped the notice of even the most sophisticated spy satellites. So touchy was Israel's security concerning this project, its ground-to-air missile batteries had standing orders to shoot down any aircraft approaching the plant. *Any* aircraft. In 1967 an Israeli Air Force jet accidentally flew too close. It was blasted out of the sky. Six years later a Libyan airliner was approaching the airspace over Dimona. It had apparently become lost through navigational error. Israeli fighters tried to get it to turn back. When their efforts failed they shot the airliner down.

The American Central Intelligence Agency had suspected Dimona back in 1968. American scientists returning from Israel informed the CIA that the Israelis appeared to be working with bomb-grade uranium. The CIA checked air and soil samples from the area around Dimona with sophisticated instruments. The scientists were right. There was enough enriched uranium to make several bombs. A CIA report covering these findings was finally revealed in 1976.

Also, in 1976 Homer A. Jack wrote about Israel's "reported stockpile of a dozen atomic bombs."[10] During the same year *Time* magazine began its cover story with the words, "For years there has been widespread speculation about Israel's nuclear potential — speculation that has now been confirmed."[11] The article mentioned a CIA estimate of ten to 20 nuclear weapons "available for use."

From an undivulged source *Time* had learned something even more disconcerting. At the beginning of the October War of 1973 Israel's forces were being pressed back on every front. When it appeared that her troops could not hold out much longer Israel's Defense Minister, Moshe Dayan, approached Prime Minister Golda Meir: "This is the end of the Third Temple." Golda Meir did not hesitate. She gave the order to activate the "Doomsday weapons." Nuclear warheads were dispatched to the waiting air force units. But before they could be used news came that the battle was turning. The Israeli forces were routing the enemy. The nuclear bombs — 13 of 20-kiloton capacity, each equivalent to those released over Hiroshima and Nagasaki — were then stored in an underground arsenal, ready to be dropped from aircraft or missiles whenever they might be needed. They remain there to this day, the *Time* article noted ominously.

In an interview with *The New York Times* in June 1981 Israel's former defense minister Moshe Dayan continued to deny that his country had nuclear arms: "We don't have any atomic bomb now. But we ... can do that in a short time. We ... do have the capacity to produce nuclear weapons."[12]

There is, of course, the fine point of definition. According to the Nuclear Non-Proliferation Treaty, a nuclear weapon exists only when its major components are screwed together. It is standard practice for nuclear-weapons powers to store the components separately. This makes the weapons more difficult to steal. Israel could be a mere screw turn away from being armed for nuclear combat and still claim it has no such weapons. It could "have" them at 78 hours' notice.[13] The question remains: If Israel does not have nuclear weapons, why refuse international inspections?[14]

Today we know that Israel had operational nuclear weapons capability back in 1967 on the eve of the Six Day War.[15] It was the sixth nation in the world to do so. Yet to this day "Israel's nuclear status has remained an enigma, referred to both as 'the world's worst kept secret' and 'the bomb that never is.'"[16] However, as long as Israel does not conduct a full-yield test it is given the benefit of the doubt.

Israel has always been extremely careful neither to confirm, nor deny that it has nuclear weapons[17] — a policy that Avner Cohen terms "nuclear opacity."[18] Nuclear opacity allows Israel to maintain a position of psychological strength. What little stability exists in the Middle East, people like Cohen contend, is the result of Israel having the bomb and remaining opaque about that fact. If Israel openly declared itself nuclear the Arab nations would have to go nuclear, changing the whole military-political environment in the Middle East. Then Israel would have to be on hairtrigger alert — she is only ten minutes from an Arab missile launch. There would be no time for wait and see, no time to assess the situation. Use them or lose them. Israel would have to launch on warning, with all the potential for miscalculation and accident. Use-them-or-lose-them logic might some day even lead to one side's launching a first strike.[19]

Another reason for neither confirming nor denying its possession of nuclear weapons is the $4 to $5 billion of aid which the United States government provides annually to its tiny Middle Eastern ally. Since the United States government cannot by law give economic aid to Israel if it is certain that Israel has nuclear weapons, it would be foolish for Israel to come clean. Both parties tacitly recognize that the letter of the law is important here, not the spirit. Ronald Reagan turned a deaf ear to Vanunu's revelations. Today if Israel openly admitted having nuclear weapons she would risk condemnation and international sanctions, and be under pressure to forfeit her weapons.

King Saud is alleged to have said that it is worth six million people dead to get rid of Israel.[20] Which is why Israel considers it necessary to have nuclear weapons. Many in the Israeli government are convinced that "the whole world is against us."[21] This is a fear voiced over and over through Israel's brief existence as a nation.[22] Israel fears for her survival. A nation of four million surrounded by 150 million Arabs, it has the highest ratio of soldiers to civilians in the world. It has more tanks than France and Germany, and the world's third-largest air force. Overall, Israel is judged the fourth-greatest military power in the world.[23] It has the latest state-of-the-art equipment — supplied by the United States, or from its own drawing boards— and military personnel who have been highly trained in its use. Israel has some of the best military intelligence and communications in the world, and a nuclear-capable missile that can reach all parts of the Arab world.

Yet Israel fears. The Arab world in total has many more tanks, soldiers, and aircraft. The right alliance of Arab nations could defeat Israel in a conventional war, hence the perceived need for nuclear weapons. In the final analysis nuclear weapons represent "the ultimate Zionist project ... to ensure the physical existence of the State of Israel, the product of the Zionist movement."[24] Avner Cohen writes, "The Jews of Israel will never be like the Jews in the Holocaust. Israel will be able to visit a terrible retribution on those who would attempt its destruction."[25]

The United States yearns to calm Israel's fear that the rest of the world might abandon it to its enemies. However, Israel cannot be calmed. In her memoirs, written shortly after the shock of the October War of 1973, former prime minister Golda Meir promised that Israel would never again be caught in a position of dependency, begging for arms. Israel could not by itself manufacture enough conventional weapons, nor could it be sure of winning a war of attrition. Israel was alone among the nations. The unspoken implication was that Israel needed nuclear weapons.

Israel has used this recognized paranoia and the belief that it possesses nuclear weapons to gain advantages. By threatening to go nuclear, Israel can blackmail the United States—give us more conventional weapons, or else. Such nuclear blackmail worked during the October War and has functioned as a powerful tool in Israel's foreign policy.

Much of the force behind Israel's nuclear blackmail results from the "Samson complex." In the biblical story Samson was being tormented by the Philistines. He lusted for vengeance: "O God, that I may be avenged upon the Philistines" (Judges 16:28). "Let me die with the Philistines," he shouted, and then pulled the building down upon the Philistines, and upon himself. Given this biblical precedent, Westerners find it difficult to forget the words of Israeli Defense Minister Pinhas Lavon: "We will go crazy."[26] Samson lives. He is Israel's secret weapon, its final strategy.

Israel holds a lighted match over a hill of gunpowder — an unspoken threat to the international community. Israel milks every drop out of the threat that, if pressed, it may be a "wild country." In 1981 Begin's defense minister warned, "[The Islamic nations] must not force us into a corner where we might — albeit reluctantly — have no recourse but nuclear weapons."[27] In his book, *In the Land of Israel*, Amos Oz has recorded the words of an Israeli settler: "Let them know in Washington, in Moscow, in Damascus, and in China that if they shoot one of our ambassadors, or even a consul, or even the attaché in charge of stamp collecting, we're capable of starting, suddenly, just for the hell of it, before breakfast, World War Three. ...the important thing is that they walk on tiptoe around Israel, so as not to provoke the wounded animal."[28]

22

Nuclear Orgasm

It was 1945. The first atomic bomb had just been detonated. The cheering and celebratory dancing was soon replaced with an eerie silence. No longer the usual croaking frogs. Desert life had been killed or scared off for miles around. The silence was punctuated by the whinnying of frightened horses in nearby army stables. After the scientists' initial elation and euphoria came fatigue. Then fear and worry. The question mark in smoke, formed from the nuclear funnel by the variation of air currents with height, gave tangible expression to questions arising in the minds of those who had witnessed this dawn of a new era in human history. It was a moment in time which could never be reversed and from which humankind would never be able to retreat. What was done could not be undone. The genie had been let loose from its bottle and the bottle was in pieces. There would, and could, be no turning back.

In recent years meteorologists and climatologists have learned just how vulnerable are the earth's atmosphere and climate to what appear to be relatively minor events. The ash from a single volcano has a surprisingly far-reaching and long-lasting chain of effects. Increased use of certain chemicals and some engine exhausts have already diluted the ozone layer to the point where skin cancers are on the rise. Finally, although it isn't knowledge that came quickly, scientists have learned the dangers of nuclear radiation.

Since 1940 the United States has spent $400 billion on nuclear warheads and $5 trillion on the delivery vehicles for these warheads.[1] The military has developed scenarios for the execution of "successful" nuclear war, but these involve best-case assumptions and conveniently ignore innumerable "ifs." The postulated survivors inherit a remarkably intact world. Little or no notice is taken that local and international communications would be virtually wiped out — loss of computer data bases, power utilities, transportation, services. Who would assist the injured and the sick?

Those who study the prospect of nuclear war from a more objective nonmilitary perspective see no hope for optimism. Water supplies would be polluted. Hospitals would be destroyed. Disease would run amok. Widespread panic and chaos would render civilization a mere ideal. Environmental radiation — food, water, air — would make existence outside some science-fiction shelter impossible. The delicate equilibrium, the miraculous balance that allows life to exist would be at risk. Millions of tons of dust catapulted into the higher regions of the atmosphere would darken the skies and cool the earth's surface in a nuclear winter which would interrupt food supplies and alter weather patterns for the unforeseeable future. Lethal levels of ultraviolet radiation would filter through an attenuated ozone layer. The sun would become our enemy. The ecosphere would revert to conditions the earth knew billions of years ago — conditions in which the existence of life as we know it is impossible.

Yet even with this knowledge, Israel deployed nuclear weapons during the 1973 October War[2] and the Soviet Union sent nuclear weapons to Egypt and probably Syria. Both superpowers put their nuclear forces on alert. World War III was only a sneeze away.

Surely today we can leave those fears behind. Are not the days of superpower confronting superpower past? The Soviet Union no longer exists. Russia is on peaceful terms with the West, the cold war history. With Russia in financial meltdown, there remains only one superpower.

Nevertheless, trouble can quickly arise anywhere in the world. Peace is never a sure thing. In 1998 Ashton Carter, John Deutch, and Philip Zelikow in a *Foreign Affairs* article wrote: "The danger of weapons of mass destruction being used against America and its allies is greater now than at any time since the Cuban missile crisis of 1962."[3]

The Islamic Middle East is today rapidly arming with nuclear weapons. Iraq is assumed to be moving toward nuclear capability, with possible help from Russia, Pakistan, and China.[4] Professor Geoffrey Kemp, a security specialist, is director of regional strategic programs in the Nixon Center for Peace and Freedom. He and Robert E. Harkavy have written *Strategic Geography and the Changing Middle East*, in which they state that the Middle East "is the region where there is most expectation that weapons of mass destruction [including nuclear weapons] will be used in war (chemical weapons have already been used extensively)."[5] Kemp says there is some concern that the Palestinians might turn to "nuclear blackmail."[6]

The instruments of destruction are available. Russia has inherited the major portion of the former Soviet Union's nuclear arsenal. While Russia once presented a military threat to peace, now it presents another threat. The West has virtually given up attempting to help Russia reform. "Tactical disengagement" is the new watchword. As a result Russia is reduced to an almost barter economy. Elaborate international networks of organized crime, arms dealers, drug traffickers, and money launderers provide the infrastructure to facilitate Russia's barter system. As Bruce Blair and Clifford Gaddy warn in their 1999 article in *Brookings Review*, "surrender to economic pressures ... could open the floodgates to the illicit transfer of nuclear materials, weapons, and delivery technologies to America's adversaries."[7] North Korea and China already sell their nuclear wares to the highest bidder.

A lot of money is tied up in Russia's nuclear stockpile and in desperate financial need the Russians might some day decide to cash it in. The Ministry of Atomic Energy has already informed managers of Russia's nuclear facilities that they must meet their own operating costs by marketing goods and services. In one year exports of nuclear technology increased by 20 percent. Then in June 1997 Minister of Atomic Energy Viktor Mikhailov announced a plan to double exports of nuclear materials and technology by the year 2000.

A greater danger, at least for the present, is that some of the Russian nuclear arsenal could be stolen or "diverted" by individuals. Carter and colleagues fear the Russian storehouse of nuclear weapons and material "may be descending into turmoil,"[8] making it likely that some of that arsenal could "go missing." As far back as 1994 an official of the Russian Ministry of Atomic Energy remarked, "The question is not whether large quantities of highly enriched nuclear material will be stolen, but when."[9]

Material can be "diverted" without arousing outside suspicions. Accounting is lax. During the Soviet period nuclear facilities produced excess material to ensure they could meet production quotas in case of a future shortfall. As much as ten percent of production may have gone unaccounted for in this way.[10] These secret caches are tempting targets in Russia's present economic climate.

Staffing the stores of nuclear material is a problem. Draft evasion has meant fewer staff, and this has led to extended shifts of duty. To get new recruits standards of admission have been lowered. To save money troops are replaced by old women on guard duty. Those who do baby-sit Russia's nuclear arsenal are demoralized and alienated from the state. Too long have they suffered a lack of esteem, food shortages, and pay arrears. They are underpaid, overworked, hungry, and unhappy. Moonlighting, suicide, and crime prevail.

Nuclear weapons material is often stored in gym-type lockers secured with only the equivalent of bicycle locks. In 1996 the American Central Intelligence Agency reported that some nuclear weapons had broken locking devices. The locking devices had not been repaired for lack of spare parts. The Russian Ministry of Internal Affairs says that 80 percent of the storage facilities have no monitors to detect the passage of nuclear materials through the gates.[11] But why use the gates when the fences have gaping holes? It is not surprising that eight thefts of nuclear materials have been confirmed.[12] Which raises the obvious question: How many thefts have *not* been confirmed?

Once the material is out of the facility it is moved out of Russia at weak border points. When the Soviet Union broke up, 15 new countries resulted. New borders, new border guards and customs police, and embryonic or nonexistent nuclear export control systems.[13] Where border guards do exist they are poorly paid and corruption is rampant. Large segments of these new borders are completely unguarded. Borders of the Baltic states and new nations to the south are notoriously porous, and this is where a substantial portion of the former Soviet Union's nuclear infrastructure is located.

It all seems so easy. One member of Greenpeace says he came close to buying a nuclear warhead from a Russian soldier at a storage site. The soldier claimed to have found a way to gain access to the warheads during the transition between shifts. Apparently security was oriented against military attack but not against small-scale theft.

The real danger is not the everyday workers at the facilities or amateur thieves, but the professionals. Corrupt senior officials and intelligence agents know the system. Working with organized crime they can easily export the goods. According to one senior United States intelligence official this threat "is no longer hypothetical."[14] Members of organized crime have run for Parliament so they can be granted parliamentary immunity. Organized crime has infiltrated law enforcement agencies, commercial banking, and political and military leadership. Russian financial news agencies report that it controls more than 40,000 businesses, including 550 banks.[15] Testimony before the United States House Committee on International Relations revealed that organized crime controls 40 percent of Russian business, 60 percent of the remaining state-owned enterprises, and more than half of Russia's 1,740 banks.[16]

These criminals do not always fit the customary mold. Many of Russia's unemployed nuclear engineers are fleeing the motherland for wherever they can sell their talents. Some, though, have stayed and joined the ranks of organized crime. Teaming up with former senior KGB agents, they have access to sophisticated techniques.

In 1997 the chief of the organized-crime control section of the Lithuanian police received an anonymous tip that someone was storing smuggled goods in a bank in Vilnius. As a pretext for searching the bank, police staged a bomb threat. They discovered 27 crates filled with metallic cylinders. The cylinders, it turned out, were made of beryllium — an extremely light metal used in the production of nuclear weapons. Lengthy investigation showed that the beryllium originated at the Institute of Physics and Power Engineering near Moscow. Senior government officials had signed off on the illegal shipment. It had been purchased by a company with links to organized crime. Some experts suspect that a large Austrian company that trades in metals and is alleged to have been founded with KGB funds was also involved. The United States National Security Agency had found the same company implicated in nuclear smuggling in 1993 and 1994.[17] The destinations were Iran and North Korea.

In May 1997 the former head of Russia's Security Council General Alexander Lebed told a visiting American congressional delegation that 84 of 132 "nuclear suitcase bombs"— developed for the KGB during the 1970s, and until recently a part of the former Soviet arsenal—could not be accounted for. In 1998 Lebed testified before the United States House of Representatives that 43 of these weapons had gone missing. Lebed stated that a single individual could carry and detonate one of these devices (they weighed 30 kilograms), and that the force of the explosion could kill 100,000 people (they had a yield of two kilotons). The perfect terrorist device.

Sometime later Israeli-born leader of the United States House Task Force on Terrorism and Unconventional Warfare Yossef Bodansky was virtually certain he knew what had happened to some of the missing bombs: During the confusion following the collapse of the former Soviet system Muslim superterrorist Osama Bin Laden had obtained them from the Chechnyan mafia in exchange for money and two tons of heroin. Bodansky's suspicions were confirmed. Russian intelligence has acknowledged that Bin Laden has a few bombs. The intelligence services of moderate Arab regimes put the number in excess of 20.

Nuclear physicist Frank Barnaby notes that any Arab nation or group — like the PLO — could make an atomic bomb.[18] There is no need for access to classified literature, because the technology is readily available, and the cost is a fraction of a million dollars. Materials are obtainable on the black market. Recently those who design nuclear weapons were commissioned to find out whether terrorists, with or without state sponsorship, could make their own nuclear device. With some qualifications the answer was yes.[19] But terrorists like Bin Laden or rogue nations clearly do not need to build their own weapons. They can steal them, or better, purchase them "off the shelf." Russian nuclear weapons laboratory Arzamas-16 has had foreign requests for nuclear warheads. One letter, allegedly faxed by Islamic Jihad, offered to buy one warhead. The director of Arzamas-16 says that on another occasion, in 1993, Iraqi agents offered $2 billion for a warhead.[20]

Terrorists can be employed by rogue states—such as Saddam Hussein's Iraq—which transgress international norms and violate human rights with impunity. Student of terrorism Ovid Demaris cautions that "nuclear terrorism is the wave of the future."[21] In *Vision and Violence* Arthur P. Mendel speaks of Armageddon. He finds the Middle East "a likely flash point for sparking a first and last global nuclear exchange."[22] One way or another the Middle East is armed and ready.

Armageddon

The Middle East is armed and ready. The Middle East spends a higher portion — about one quarter — of its GNP on the military than any other region in the world. There are 15 soldiers for every thousand population — again the highest level; the next region on the list has only four per thousand.[1] Populations are exploding in Arab nations. That means a high portion of young people — median age of 14 and 15 in some cases[2] — emotional, feisty, energetic, active. Ready for a fight.

Could there be a nuclear war in the Middle East? Certainly it would be a mistake to try to understand the Middle East with Western concepts. As Weissman and Krosney note, "The ins and outs, the shifting alliances, the religious fervor, and the basic instability in the region all make a cruel joke of any rational calculation, or of the kind of game theory that Western strategists use[d] to analyze the nuclear conflict between the United States and the Soviet Union."[3]

Western secular logic of war and peace assumes rational behavior — the premium placed on self-preservation, for example. However, this logic has no place in the religious realm, and the Middle East is becoming more and more the captive of the fundamentalists of the three religions. Gush Emunim, Hamas, and other extremist religious groups are gaining a grasp on the reins of Middle East politics. In recent years the religious fanaticism of the minority is more and more becoming the ethos of the majority. Meir Kahane was regarded as a racist madman by most Israelis while he was alive, but today his idea that Israel has a right to exist as a nation only in the religious context is making sense to a growing portion of the nation's citizenry.

The apocalyptic drama is played on another stage, remote from secular thought and actions, an otherworldly metahistorical stage. Fundamentalists dream of the final metahistorical cataclysm of the apocalypse. Their hearts beat to the rhythm of holy war. Holy war (it is strange that no one speaks of holy peace!) fought by true believers is something that defies reason. Both sides believe that one and the same deity will bless them with victory. Both Jews and Muslims believe God/Allah is on their side. They cannot lose, hence both sides will fight to the end and accept no compromise. "En brerah" ("no alternative") is the rallying cry. As one fundamentalist says, "Fundamentalists don't place a high value on compromise and negotiation."[4] They will go to any lengths to pursue their dreams. Ayatollah Yusuf Sani'i, a senior member of Iran's ruling council, gives voice to the concept of religious sacrifice: "All religious persons and Islamic leaders must encourage and teach the value of the deed of suicide. We ask God to illuminate all Muslims and to seat all the fallen in the front row, particularly the most courageous martyrs who were killed in suicide actions."[5] Holy war. Holy war operates in the domain of the irrational. It is madness, and madness has no rules. Such madness is fitting context for nuclear war. For nuclear war is, after all, madness.

At the threshold of a new century the Middle East has become the world's most politically sensitive region. Because of its oil and central location the Middle East has always been a political hot spot. But with the rise of Jewish fundamentalism and the doctrine of Eretz Yisrael, opposed by a growing militant Islamic fundamentalism, the political temperature has risen in recent years. If one adds American Christian apocalypticists eager to bring on the End (*The Nation* editor Christopher Hitchens calls them "dogmatic Christians ... who hope that Israeli fanatics will bring about Armageddon"[6]) by financing and backing rabid Jewish fundamentalists in Israel, then the tension level rises to an unsupportable level.

Fundamentalists are only a fanatic minority within their respective religious traditions. The vast majority of Christians, Muslims, and Jews are not fundamentalists. The majority of believers in the three faiths have no desire for holy war, or war of any kind. While it may be true, as Ferdynand Zweig points out, that "the three great religions were born of violence and grew on violence,"[7] there is much in all three religious traditions that aims at peace, and charity to one's fellow human beings. The vast majority of Christians, Muslims, and Jews wish to worship their God in peace. They most emphatically do not want the world to end. But they are passive, whereas their fundamentalist brothers are fanatically active.

The upsurge in fundamentalism in these three world religions is something new, a new force thrown into ever delicate Middle East politics. Jewish fundamentalists claim to be returning to the "true" Judaism, and Christian fundamentalists claim to be returning to the "true" Christianity, but all three fundamentalisms are recent developments, differing from the traditions of their respective faiths. Christianity: Even Hal Lindsey admits that his message has a history of scarcely more than a century. Donald E. Wagner of Evangelicals for Middle East Understanding states emphatically that "Christian Zionism should be considered a Western heresy detrimental to peace and understanding in the Middle East."[8] Judaism: Jewish fundamentalism dates from 1967. Islam: Professor of International Relations at the University of Göttingen, Germany, Bosch Fellow at Harvard, and an expert in things Middle Eastern Bassam Tibi calls the idea of Islamic fundamentalism "a recent creation."[9] He insists that "Islam and fundamentalism are different issues. It is a great mistake to refer to them in an identical manner!"[10]

Israeli Prime Minister Netanyahu knew the difference when he said: "I do not view Islam as the enemy of the West or the enemy of Israel. Islam is one of the world's great religions. We have no quarrel with Islam, we have no enmity with Islam. We have a problem with a militant few who want to twist Islam into a perverted ideology of violence and aggression."[11] In this connection editor Joyce M. Davis writes, "It is puzzling but true that the religion whose name is built on the root word *salaam*, or 'peace,' also has been used as a justification for murder and terror."[12]

Fundamentalists of all three religions have chosen violence and discord and holy war — justified by the demonization of one's enemies. As one Christian minister contemplating the increasing violence of the New Christian Right commented, when you demonize your opponents "you are just a hair away from killing the person or people associated with that view, because to kill something evil becomes something good.... you could be killed 'for Christ's sake'."[13]

There have been some viable attempts at a peaceful resolution in the Middle East in recent years, yet most experts on the region do not predict a lasting peace. Bassam Tibi believes religious fundamentalism provides the "major threat" to peace and security in the Middle East, and a challenge to the existence of Western nation-states such as Israel: "The threat to the peace arrangement comes basically from fundamentalist or religio-ethnic groups, be they those of Islamic Hamas or of the Jewish settlers."[14]

Tibi doesn't see war in the Middle East arising from a political conflict between nation-states. Instead, a "global shift" is taking place to "a new kind of war."[15] The Arab-Israeli conflict henceforth will feature "paramilitary groups," "non-state armies," and "postmodern terrorists."[16] A war between nation-states may result, but it would start not in the confrontation between the governments of two nations, but in the actions of some religiously fanatic group or individual.

Here is how it could happen. After many aborted attempts, the Israeli government and the Palestinian leaders recognize each other's positions and agree to a peace concord which allows the creation of a Palestinian state in the Occupied Territories. International hopes run high. Finally, the foundation for a lasting peace in the Middle East. Gush Emunim and other fundamentalist groups are stunned. This is a catastrophic defeat for their ideology. Religious fundamentalists, such as Gush Emunim, Tibi points out, seek "an alternative order" based upon ideology.[17] How can the Messiah come if some of holy Eretz Yisrael is surrendered — and by Jews, voluntarily? As one of the founders of Gush Emunim puts it: "The fulfillment of the Redemption ... [is] more important than any hypothetical peace."[18]

Those who study religious extremism have learned that messianic fundamentalists become most dangerous and most likely to engage in risky acts of fanaticism when events appear to deny the imminent fulfillment of their cherished religious ends. Any whiff of peace spurs the actions of religious fanatics like Gush Emunim. They begin to panic. Observes journalist Jeffrey Goldberg, "Middle-Eastern extremists ... traditionally make their moves when political compromise is in the air."[19] Religious fundamentalists of the three faiths — Judaism, Islam, and Christianity — "share a fear of the peace process."[20]

Gush Emunim and other Jewish fundamentalists then decide that the peace process must be abrogated. They know the best way to do it, too. Temple Mount. To strike here would be to smite Islam at its very soul. Former Israeli security boss Carmi Gillon points out that "Jewish extremists would be energized to act anytime the peace process moved forward.... Extremists who want to stop the peace process ... know that the best way to end anything is to attack the mosques."[21] Robert I. Friedman studied Gush Emunim and the settler movement in Israel for a decade and a half. In the concluding chapter of his monumental study he writes, "The ultimate settler provocation would be blowing up the Dome of the Rock Mosque. In view of the intensity of feeling prevalent on the extreme religious and secular right, the threat of a peace settlement that could destroy their hopes of establishing 'Greater Israel' makes it altogether possible that settlers might attempt to blow up the famous mosque." He then quotes Ehud Sprinzak. "When you try to think of one single act that could torpedo a peace process — and one that would blow apart the Arab world — it's the bombing of the mosque."[22] As Hebrew University's Avishai Margalit observed a decade ago, "If the peace talks progress, I have no doubt that a new [settler] underground will emerge. And the way to destroy a peace agreement is very clear: blow up the Dome of the Rock Mosque. Then the whole world will be against us."[23]

Asked what would happen if the Jews destroyed the mosques on Temple Mount, Sheik Ahmed Yassin, the quadriplegic leader of the Hamas suicide bombers, replies, "This would be the end of Israel."[24] Plain and simple, no qualification. Temple Mount is the focal point of "the colliding eschatologies of monotheism."[25] All three monotheistic religions — Judaism, Islam, and Christianity — see their respective messiahs reigning from Temple Mount in the End Time. Only in the case of the Islamic Mahdi can the present mosques remain on the site. Before the Christian and Jewish messiahs arrive the mosques must be destroyed. However, any attempt to do so will lead to certain holy war. Author Menachem Klein writes, "There is tension surrounding the Temple Mount. Any change in favor of the Jews will bring about a big explosion. All the Palestinians, and all the Arab world, are closely following the preparations of Jewish radical groups to reclaim the Temple Mount. They are mobilizing to protect the Mount. They are calling the masses to prayers, raising their voices to defend al-Aqsa."[26] As an official at al-Aqsa Mosque asserts, Muslims "will defend the Islamic holy places to the last drop of their blood."[27] Muslims, too, believe in Armageddon.

What might happen, then, if the mosques on Temple Mount are destroyed? Islamic states may sponsor terrorists to seek revenge. Big-time terrorism. Who can predict what religiously inspired terrorists might do? One expert observes, "Terrorist groups on the verge of defeat or acting on apocalyptic visions may not hesitate to apply all destructive means at their disposal."[28] Jessica Stern, in her book *The Ultimate Terrorists*, agrees: "Religious groups are more likely than others to turn to WMD [weapons of mass destruction]."[29] Among terrorists, she cites "religious fanatics" as those "most likely to attempt to use WMD."[30] If some "premillennial tension" is added, one has the recipe for disaster: "Millenarian organizations operating during periods when apocalyptic fears are common are more likely to become violent."[31] Stern finds religious and apocalyptic terrorists not only more violent than secular groups, but on the increase. "Religious zealots" are least likely to be deterred by fears of government crackdown. "Worldly consequences are not a central concern for religious terrorists, since they believe their actions are dictated by a divine authority."[32]

Divine sanction is exactly what emboldens Jewish apocalypticists. Ismar Schorsch, chancellor of the Jewish Theological Seminary: "If you believe that God isn't going to abandon you, then you're not intimidated by a billion Muslims."[33] But what if the destruction of Temple Mount caused Israel the loss of international support, leaving her alone to face her enemies in the Middle East? Fine, says Gush Emunim. God would see this as an act of faith and respond by coming to the aid of his chosen people. When the Jewish Underground planned an attack on the Dome of the Rock in the 1980s they were not unaware of the risks. They willingly and purposefully courted disaster. They wanted to provoke a Muslim holy war, and they hoped it would result in the "war of Gog and Magog"—Armageddon. Then the Messiah would come. Scholars at the Harvard Center for International Affairs conducted a simulation game to analyze what would have happened had the Jewish Underground Temple Mount conspirators succeeded. Some were convinced that the result would have been World War III.[34]

Threatened by terrorist action and anti–Israeli rhetoric, Israel feels its existence threatened, and with good reason. During a recent military parade in Teheran, the capital of Iran, a new missile was proudly flaunted. Written on the banners which draped this missile were the words "Israel should be wiped from the map."[35] Religious apocalyptic thinking—a mode of thought that comes to the fore whenever the boundaries of secular existence seem about to disintegrate—quickly comes to predominate as Israel becomes convinced it is not going to survive as a nation. The suicidal madness of the Samson complex coalesces with the religious madness of the Temple Mount activists. In the former all hope is abandoned; in the latter, hope is multiplied beyond hope. At such a moment of collective psychological distress, Israel might be ready to take the rest of the world with it in a nuclear bonfire. Israel is not beyond making of itself a whole burnt offering. The memory of the Holocaust is never too far away in the minds of Israelis. Ferdynand Zweig remarks, "Most Israelis are convinced that, if by any chance a second Holocaust should afflict Israel, this would be the forerunner of a third and total Holocaust involving the whole human race."[36] In their study of nuclear weapons in the Middle East, Steve Weissman and Herbert Krosney write, "If the Israelis ever felt their survival at stake, they could well threaten to unleash their ultimate weapon of destruction [nuclear weapons]."[37]

Nuclear weapons? Since chemical weapons have already been used in the Middle East, conflict might begin with them. The next step might be nuclear. As Kemp and Harkavy remark, "The use of chemical weapons may have implications for the lowering of the nuclear threshold, raising the probability that conventional wars might quickly get out of hand, moving up the ladder of escalation through the use of chemical weapons and then a reactive use of nuclear arms."[38] But things could unravel much more quickly. Escalation could be virtually instant, given the "primordial hatreds," the short distances, and the hair-trigger environment of the

Middle East.[39] Indeed, if Israel felt truly threatened it might launch a first strike. It did so in the Six Day War when Egypt threatened Israel's existence. It could do so again.

This scenario for the beginning of a Middle East Armageddon is no mere remote possibility. Again, to quote Friedman, "Israeli experts fear that Jewish extremists are planning an incident that could spark an international conflagration. Attempts to establish a Jewish foothold on the Temple Mount could trigger a bloodbath of unimaginable horror. Because the Temple Mount is a focus of Muslim passions, it is an easy political instrument with which to rally the Islamic world to the defense of the faith against the infidels. A successful attack by these zealots for Zion on Muslim holy places could result in a kind of Armageddon — one in which the use of nuclear weapons is not unimaginable."[40]

Two domes, resplendent in the oriental sunshine. One silver, one gold. Al-Aqsa Mosque. The Mosque of Omar. One hundred thousand square meters of real estate. The epicenter of Middle East tensions. Since the Israeli conquest of Jerusalem in 1967, the focal point of rabid religious emotions.

The Dome of the Rock is reputed to be the site where Cain killed Abel — the first act of violence between humans. The last act of human violence — Armageddon ... will it start at the Dome of the Rock?

Notes

1— Time Bomb

1. Gorenberg, "Tribulations" (1999) 20.
2. Sontag, "Apocalyptic" (1999) 1.
3. Beyer, "Target" (1999) 39.
4. *Ibid.*
5. Sontag, "Apocalyptic" (1999) 11.
6. *Ibid.*
7. Ackerman, "Millennial" (1999) 32.
8. Sontag, "Apocalyptic" (1999) 11.
9. Boston, *Dangerous* (1996) 141.
10. "Israel Deports" (1999) 50.
11. "Israel Deports" (1999) 51.
12. Sontag, "Apocalyptic" (1999) 11.
13. Leland, "Millennium" (1999) 70.
14. Kirn, "The End" (1999) 39.
15. Fields-Meyer & Pick, "In Heaven's" (1998) 139.
16. Woodward, "The Way" (1999) 68.
17. Kirn, "The End" (1999) 39.
18. *Ibid.*
19. Fields-Meyer & Pick, "In Heaven's" (1998) 140.
20. *Ibid.*
21. "Democracy and the Religious Right" (1997) 55.
22. *End of the World* (1997) 214.
23. Sheler, "Christmas" (1994) 64.
24. Leland, "Millennium" (1999) 70.
25. Sheler, "Dark" (1997) 63.
26. Wojcik, *End* (1997) 212.
27. Stern, *The Ultimate* (1999) 72–73.
28. Lacayo, "End" (1999) 38.
29. Lacayo, "End" (1999) 37.
30. Lacayo, "End" (1999) 36.
31. Sheler, "Dark Prophecies" (1997) 70.
32. Lacayo, "End" (1999) 42.
33. Boston, *Dangerous* (1996) 203–205.
34. Leland, "Millennium" (1999) 70.
35. Govier, "Religious" (1999) 24.
36. Teresi, "Zero" (1997) 88.
37. Govier, "Religious" (1999) 24.
38. Sennott, "Millennium" (2000) 54.
39. Beyer, "Target" (1999) 39.
40. Goldberg, "Israel's Y2K" (1999) 42.
41. Gorenberg, "Waiting" (1998) 12.
42. Goldberg, "Israel's Y2K" (1999) 40.
43. Friedland & Hecht, "Sacred" (1991) 21.
44. Friedland and Hecht, "Sacred Place" (1991) 38.
45. Words of Homer A. Jack, "Security Council's" (1976) 382.
46. Lane, "Time Bomb" (1990) 38.
47. *Ascendance* (1991) 288.
48. Goldberg, "Israel's Y2K" (1999) 40.
49. "Tensions Mount" (2000) 42.

50. Beyer, "Target" (1999) 39.
51. Ackerman, "Millennial" (1999) 33.
52. Gorenberg, "Tribulations" (1999) 21.
53. Beyer, "Target" (1999) 39.
54. *Salvation* (1988) 363.
55. (1992) 1.
56. "Postmodern Terrorism" (1996) 32–33.
57. Tharp, "Scary" (1999) 58.
58. Wojcik, *End* (1997) 214.
59. "The Beginning" (2000) 26

2 — Countdown

1. Rhodes, *Making* (1986) 673.
2. Stoff et al., *Manhattan* (1991) 192.
3. Stoff et al., *Manhattan* (1991) 190.
4. Rhodes, *Making* (1986) 673.
5. Rhodes, *Making* (1986) 677.
6. Stoff et al., *Manhattan* (1991) 226.
7. Rhodes, *Making* (1986) 734.
8. *Ibid.*
9. Stoff et al., *Manhattan* (1991) 226.
10. Rhodes, *Making* (1986) 715.
11. *Ibid.*
12. *Ibid.*
13. *Ibid.*
14. *Ibid.*
15. Rhodes, *Making* (1986) 777.
16. Hansen, *Nuclear* (1988) 58.
17. Hansen, *Nuclear* (1988) 105.
18. Barnaby, "Nuclear War?" (1985) 35.
19. Knelman, *America* (1987) 45.
20. Bradley, *No Place* (1983) 184–85.
21. Bradley, *No Place* (1983) 186.
22. Rhodes, *Making* (1986) 784.
23. Barnaby, "Nuclear War?" (1985) 35.
24. Schell, *Fate* (1982) 3.
25. *Ibid.*
26. Hansen, *Nuclear* (1988) 105–6.
27. Knelman, *America* (1987) 115.
28. Knelman, *America* (1987) 285.
29. Greene et al., *Nuclear Winter* (1985) 12.
30. Boyer, *Bomb's Early* (1985) 14.
31. Boyer, *When Time* (1992) 116.
32. Wojcik, *End* (1997) 1.
33. Boyer, *When Time* (1992) 329.
34. Negri, "Scholars" (1984) 27.
35. Boyer, *When Time* (1992) 330.
36. Boyer, *When Time* (1992) 328–29.
37. "Millennial Task Force" (1999) 43

3 — Religious Hardliners

1. Jensen, "Trouble" (1990) 33.
2. *Ibid.*
3. *Ibid.*
4. Woodward, "The Way" (1999) 68.
5. The editor of a Baptist newspaper defines a fundamentalist as someone who is willing to "do battle royal" to defend the fundamentals of his or her faith (Strozier, *Apocalypse* [1994] 190).
6. Martin, *With God* (1996) 7.
7. Elwell, "Dispensationalisms" (1994) 28.
8. Strozier, *Apocalypse* (1994) 120–21.
9. Gardella, "Ego" (1995) 201.
10. Gardella, "Ego" (1995) 200.
11. Stozier, *Apocalypse* (1994) 4,5,120.
12. Sandeen, *Roots* (1970) 223.
13. Scofield, *Study Bible* (1984) x.
14. *Ibid.*
15. Crutchfield, *Origins* (1992) preface.
16. Sandeen, *Roots* (1970) 222.
17. Crutchfield, "C. I. Scofield" (1989) 376.
18. Halsell, *Prophecy* (1986) 15.
19. Richards, *Promise* (1991) 40.
20. Richards, *Promise* (1991) 40, 44.
21. Sheler, "Stains" (1994) 97.
22. Toulouse, "W. A. Criswell" (1989) 96.
23. Halsell, *Prophecy* (1986) 14.
24. Halsell, "Why" (1986) 7

4 — End Time Scenario

1. Lindsey, *1980s* (1980) 4.
2. Negri, "Who Biblical" (1984) 27.
3. Weber, *Living* (1983) 211.
4. Lindsey, *Road* (1989) dust jacket.
5. Gardella, "Ego" (1995) 197, mentions Lindsey's professor, J. Dwight Pentecost, and cites his book, *Things to Come* (1958, 1980).
6. Marmon, *People* (July 4, 1977) 70–72.
7. Lindsey, *Late* (1970) 131–32.
8. Lindsey, *Late* (1970) introduction.
9. Lindsey, *Late* (1970) 168.
10. *Late Great Planet* (1970) 137; Peter Gardella, "Ego" (1995) 197, says apocalypticists find scriptural support for the Rapture in Revelation, 1 Thessalonians 4:17, 1 Corinthians 15, Matthew 24:40, Luke 17:34–35, and in the stories of Enoch's and Elijah's being taken up without dying. Nonapocalypticists strongly

contest these interpretations of Scripture.

11. Strozier, *Apocalypse* (1994) 120.
12. Sheler, "Dark" (1997) 69.
13. Boyer, *When Time* (1992) 329.
14. Sheler, "Christmas" (1994) 64.
15. Lindsey, *Late* (1970) 131–32

5 — The Dawning of the Last Days

1. Lindsey, *1980s* (1980) 41.
2. "Jews in Old Jerusalem!" (1967) 973.
3. Armstrong, *Holy War* (1988) 200.
4. Lindsey, *Late* (1970) 56.
5. "Next Year" (1967) 997.
6. Bell, "Unfolding" (1967) 1045.
7. Bell, "Unfolding" (1967) 1044. A quotation often cited — see Weber, *Living* (1983) 211, and Wagner, "Evangelicals" (1998) 1021.
8. "War Sweeps," (1967) 957.
9. Boyer, *When Time* (1992) 188.
10. Baker, "Jerusalem: A Third Temple?" (1967) 1050.
11. "Jews in Old Jerusalem!" (1967) 973

6 — Christian Zionists

1. Boyer, *When Time* (1992) 189.
2. Sandeen, *Roots* (1970) 10.
3. Strozier, *Apocalypse* (1994) 199.
4. Boyer, *When Time* (1992) 186.
5. Wilson, *Armageddon* (1977) 25.
6. Wagner, "Evangelicals" (1998) 1021.
7. Armstrong, *Holy War* (1988) 59.
8. Boyer, *When Time* (1992) 187.
9. *Ibid.*
10. Boyer, *When Time* (1992) 189.
11. *Ibid.*
12. *Ibid.*
13. Wright, "Forcing" (1998) 48.
14. Wilson, *Armageddon* (1977) 61.
15. Wilson, *Armageddon* (1977) 62.
16. Strozier, *Apocalypse* (1994) 206. A few words about the term "anti-Semitic." It has been used by Jews to describe Arabs (see, for example, Friedman, *Zealots* [1992] 22). It has

even been used by Jews to describe other Jews — usually right-wing Jews who wish to smear their liberal brothers. Arabs, as well as Jews, are Semites. "Anti-Semite" should properly be used in reference to persons who hate *all* Semitic peoples. "Anti-Jew" should be used only for those who specifically hate Jews. Nevertheless, to conform with common usage we shall use the term "anti-Semitic" to refer to hatred of Jews.
17. Boyer, *When Time* (1992) 209.
18. *Ibid.*
19. *Ibid.*
20. Weber, "How Evangelicals" (1998) 43. Premillennialism is the theological position that Christ will come back and establish the millennium — the thousand years of Christ's reign on earth. It is a part of dispensationalist thought.
21. *Ibid.*
22. Boyer, *Time* (1992) 209.
23. Weber, "How Evangelicals" (1998) 43.
24. *Ibid.*
25. Weber, "How Evangelicals" (1998) 44.
26. Boyer, *When Time* (1992) 216.
27. Wright, "Forcing" (1998) 50–51.
28. Willoughby, *Does America* (1981) 146.
29. "Next Year in the New Jerusalem?" (1967) 997.
30. Willoughby, *Does America* (1981) 146.
31. Wright, "Forcing" (1998) 48.
32. Halsell, *Prophecy* (1986) 140.
33. Halsell, *Prophecy* (1986) 141.
34. Jonathan Kuttab, quoted in Halsell, "Palestinian Christian" (1986) 49.
35. Armstrong, *Holy War* (1988) 370

7 — Jerry and the Jews

1. Wagner, "Evangelicals" (1998) 1022.
2. Simon, *Jerry* (1984) 88.
3. Boyer, *When Time* (1992) 189.
4. Gorenberg, "Tribulations" (1999) 18.
5. Weber, "How Evangelicals" (1998) 49.
6. Halsell, "Why" (1986) 4.
7. Halsell, *Prophecy* (1986) 75.
8. Wagner, "Evangelicals" (1998) 1023.
9. Wagner, "Evangelicals" (1998) 1020.

10. Simon, *Jerry* (1984) 5–6.
11. Halsell, *Prophecy* (1986) 74.
12. Halsell, *Prophecy* (1986) 118.
13. Halsell, *Prophecy* (1986) 161.
14. Simon, *Jerry* (1984) 66.
15. Halsell, *Prophecy* (1986) 121.
16. Simon, *Jerry* (1984) x.
17. Simon, *Jerry* (1984) ix.
18. Simon, *Jerry* (1984) xi.
19. Simon, *Jerry* (1984) 13.
20. Capps, *New Religious* (1990) 38

8 — Militant Apocalypticism

1. Lindner, *Yearbook* (1999) 350.
2. Dollar, *A History* (1973) 105.
3. *Ibid.*
4. Falwell, quoted in D'Souza, *Falwell* (1984) 42.
5. Falwell, quoted in D'Souza, *Falwell* (1984) 190.
6. *Ibid.*
7. Falwell, *Strength* (1987) 130.
8. Falwell, *Strength* (1987) 191.
9. Falwell, "I'd Do" (1999) 50.
10. Capps, *New Religious* (1990) 32, and other sources.
11. Capps, *New Religious Right* (1990) 31.
12. Falwell, "I'd Do It All Again" (1999) 50.
13. Capps, *New Religious* (1990) 31.
14. Falwell, quoted in D'Souza, *Falwell* (1984) 84.
15. *Ibid.*
16. *College Blue Book* (1999) 850.
17. *Ibid.*
18. Capps, *New Religious* (1990) 25.
19. Quoted in Capps, *New Religious* (1990) 25.
20. Quoted in Capps, *New Religious* (1990) 30.
21. Quoted in D'Souza, *Falwell* (1984) 85.
22. Taylor, *International Handbook* (1996) 1761.
23. *College Blue Book* (1999) 850.
24. Quoted in Capps, *New Religious* (1990) 44.
25. Quoted in "Biblical" (1987) 246.
26. Quoted in Capps, *New Religious* (1990) 45.
27. Quoted in Halsell, *Prophecy* (1986) 39.
28. Quoted in Boyer, *When Time* (1992) 137.
29. Leland, "Millennium" (1999) 70.
30. Falwell, "Agenda" (1987) 114–15.
31. Reichley, *Religion* (1985) 326.
32. Brown, "Religious Right" (1987) 259.
33. Falwell, quoted in Goodman and Price, *Jerry Falwell* (1981) 125

9 — In from the Political Cold

1. Ostling, "Those Mainline" (1989) 54–56. Gardella, "Ego" (1995) 197, disagrees about who is mainstream: "In fact, fundamentalists, evangelicals, and interpreters of apocalyptic have always been part of American politics; arguably, they have been the mainstream of American politics."
2. Nash, *Evangelicals in America* (1987) 21.
3. Wills, *Under* (1990) 19.
4. Gallup and Castelli, *People's* (1989) 66.
5. Gallup and Castelli, *People's* (1989) 93.
6. Falwell, "Agenda" (1987) 119.
7. Falwell, "Agenda" (1987) 120.
8. *Ibid.*
9. Falwell, "Agenda" (1987) 121.
10. Falwell, "Agenda" (1987) 122–23.
11. Negri, "Why Biblical" (1984) 27.
12. Nash, *Evangelicals* (1987) 35.
13. Jorstad, *Holding* (1990) 95.
14. *Ibid.*
15. Jorstad, *Holding* (1990) 103–4.
16. Barna, *Vital Signs* (1984) 76.
17. Barna, *Vital Signs* (1984) 75.
18. *Ibid.*
19. Barna, *Vital Signs* (1984) 150.
20. Jorstad, *Holding* (1990) 9.
21. Barna, *Vital Signs* (1984) 34.
22. *Ibid.*
23. *Ibid.*
24. *Ibid.*
25. Barna, *Vital Signs* (1984) 37.
26. Robertson, *New World* (1992) 152.
27. Goodman and Price, *Jerry Falwell* (1981) 42.
28. Giorgianna, *Moral Majority* (1989) 143.
29. Liebman, "Mobilizing" (1983) 58.
30. Guth, "New Christian Right" (1983) 32.

31. Goodman and Price, *Jerry Falwell* (1981) 42.
32. *Ibid.*
33. McDonald, "Fire" (1988) 22–23.
34. D'Souza, *Falwell* (1984) 129.
35. *Ibid.*
36. *Ibid.*
37. Jorstad, *New Christian Right* (1987) 231.
38. *Ibid.*
39. D'Souza, *Falwell* (1984) 10.
40. *Ibid.*
41. Diamond, *Spiritual* (1989) 63.
42. Ajemian, "Jerry" (1985) 44–54. This figure is perhaps an exaggeration. Other estimates give two million for Moral Majority in combination with other new right-wing groups (Guth, "New Christian Right" [1983] 37).
43. Jorstad, *New Christian* (1987) 231.
44. Guth, "New Christian Right" (1983) 36.
45. Barna, *Vital Signs* (1984) 93–94.
46. D'Souza, *Falwell* (1984) 18.
47. Walker, "Falwell Claims" (1989) 58–59.
48. Falwell, "I'd Do" (1999) 51.
49. Martin, "Christian Right" (1999) 67–68.
50. Martin, "Christian Right" (1999) 71.
51. Gardella, "Ego" (1995) 200. Surely, most Americans would argue, an excessive exaggeration

10 — God's Instrument

1. Morris, *Dutch* (1999) 586.
2. Ducat, *Taken In* (1988) 95.
3. Cannon, *Reagan* (1982) 21.
4. Thomas and Meacham, "Book on Reagan" (1999) 23.
5. *Ibid.*
6. *Ibid.*
7. Thomas and Meacham, "Book on Reagan" (1999) 25.
8. *Ibid.*
9. Thomas and Meacham, "Book on Reagan" (1999) 24.
10. Morris, *Dutch* (1999) 644.
11. Morris, *Dutch* (1999) 668.
12. Slosser, *Reagan Inside Out* (1984) 118.
13. Brown, "Religious Right" (1987) 259.
14. Goodman and Price, *Jerry Falwell* (1981) 44.
15. Falwell, "Agenda" (1987) 111.
16. Falwell, "I'd Do" (1999) 51.
17. Straub, *Salvation* (1988) 305.
18. Halsell, *Prophecy* (1986) 48.
19. Jones and Sheppard, "Ronald Reagan's 'Theology'" (1986) 35.
20. Jones and Sheppard, "Ronald Reagan's 'Theology'" (1986) 32.
21. Reagan, *American* (1990) 217.
22. Reagan, *American* (1990) 219.
23. Reagan, *American* (1990) 246.
24. Reagan, *American* (1990) 247.
25. Boyarsky, *Ronald Reagan* (1981) 192.
26. Reagan, *American* (1990) 635.
27. Reagan, *American* (1990) 665.
28. Cannon, *President Reagan* (1991) 287.
29. Cannon, *President Reagan* (1991) 212.
30. Reagan, *American* (1990) 21.
31. Cannon, *President Reagan* (1991) 212.
32. Dallek, *Ronald Reagan* (1984) 9.
33. Slosser, *Reagan Inside Out* (1984) 14.
34. Slosser, *Reagan Inside Out* (1984) 14–15.
35. Slosser, *Reagan Inside Out* (1984) 15.
36. Slosser, *Reagan Inside Out* (1984) 19.
37. Woodward, "Arguing Armageddon" (1984) 91.
38. Reagan, *American* (1990) 228.
39. Reagan, *American* (1990) 226.
40. Reagan, *American* (1990) 316–17.
41. Slosser, *Reagan Inside Out* (1984) 40.
42. Reagan, *American* (1990) 262.
43. Slosser, *Reagan Inside Out* (1984) 82.
44. Reagan, *American* (1990) 263.
45. Slosser, *Reagan Inside Out* (1984) 22.
46. Morris, *Dutch* (1999) xii

11 — Hooked on Armageddon

1. Reagan, *American* (1990) 413.
2. Weissman and Krosney, *Islamic Bomb* (1981) 317.
3. Barrett, *Gambling* (1983) 274–275.
4. Morris, *Dutch* (1999) 462.
5. Barrett, *Gambling* (1983) 272.
6. Barrett, *Gambling* (1983) 265.
7. Morris, *Dutch* (1999) 339.
8. Reagan, *American* (1990) 554.
9. Dallek, *Ronald Reagan* (1984) 59.

10. Van der Linden, *Real Reagan* (1981) 243.
11. Reagan, *American* (1990) 220.
12. Reagan, *My* (1981) 297.
13. Van der Linden, *Real Reagan* (1981) 243.
14. Reagan, *American* (1990) 566.
15. Weissman and Krosney, *Islamic Bomb* (1981) 315.
16. *Ibid.*
17. Green and MacColl, *There He* (1983) 33.
18. Cannon, *President Reagan* (1991) 536.
19. Morris, *Dutch* (1999) 330.
20. Halsell, *Prophecy* (1986) 43.
21. Halsell, *Prophecy* (1986) 43. This was a more cautious prediction than the youthful Graham's 1950 prognostication: "Two years and it's all going to be over" (Sheler, "Christmas" [1994] 67).
22. Boyer, *When Time* (1992) 143.
23. Woodward, "Doom" (1977) 51.
24. Cannon, *President Reagan* (1991) 289.
25. Morris, *Dutch* (1999) 632.
26. Cannon, *President Reagan* (1991) 39.
27. Cannon, *President Reagan* (1991) 214.
28. *Ibid.*
29. Slosser, *Reagan Inside Out* (1984) 37.
30. Reagan, *American* (1990) 21.
31. Halsell, *Prophecy* (1986) 41.
32. Slosser, *Reagan Inside Out* (1984) 118.
33. Jones and Sheppard, "Ronald Reagan's 'Theology'" (1986) 30.
34. Halsell, *Prophecy* (1986) 43.
35. *Ibid.*
36. Woodward, "Arguing" (Nov.5, 1984) 91.
37. Halsell, *Prophecy* (1986) 47.
38. Cannon, *President Reagan* (1991) 289n.
39. Morris, *Dutch* (1999) 587.
40. Halsell, *Prophecy* (1986) 44–45; Boyer, *When Time* (1992) 142; Mendel, *Vision and Violence* (1992) 275–276.
41. Barrett, *Gambling* (1983) 6. Morris, *Dutch* (1999) 548, also calls Reagan "an ideologue."
42. Morris, *Dutch* (1999) 415.
43. Morris, *Dutch* (1999) 569.
44. Morris, *Dutch* (1999) 203.
45. Morris, *Dutch* (1999) 202–203.
46. Reagan, *American* (1990) 31.
47. *Ibid.*
48. Thomas and Meacham, "Book on Reagan" (1999) 23.
49. "The Book on Reagan" (1999) 25. Thomas and Meacham are speaking of "Morris's Reagan," with reference to Edmund Morris's biography *Dutch: A Memoir of Ronald Reagan*, but the content of their remark rings true.
50. Morris, *Dutch* (1999) 121.
51. Morris, *Dutch* (1999) 414.
52. Morris, *Dutch* (1999) 442.
53. Morris, *Dutch* (1999) 579.
54. Morris, *Dutch* (1999) 443.
55. Kenneth and Valerie Lynn, quoted in Morris, *Dutch* (1999) 629.
56. Knelman, *America* (1987) 23.
57. Knelman, *America* (1987) 178.
58. Cannon, *President Reagan* (1991) 34.
59. Morris, *Dutch* (1999) 202.
60. Boyarsky, *Ronald Reagan* (1981) 15
61. Cannon, *President Reagan* (1991) 293–94.
62. Scheer, *With Enough* (1982) 100.
63. Cannon, *President Reagan* (1991) 296.
64. Thomas and Meacham, "Book on Reagan" (1999) 25.
65. Knelman, *America* (1987) 250.
66. Morris, *Dutch* (1999) 661.
67. Morris, *Dutch* (1999) 661.
68. Mojtabai, *Blessèd* (1986) 152.
69. Knelman, *America* (1987) 267.
70. *Ibid.*
71. Bobi Hromas, quoted in Knelman, *America* (1987) 267.
72. Conway and Siegelman, *Holy Terror* (1984) 363.
73. Conway and Siegelman, *Holy Terror* (1984) 363.
74. Watt, quoted in Cannon, *Reagan* (1982) 361.
75. Cannon, *Reagan* (1982) 368.
76. Bobi Hromas, quoted in Knelman, *America* (1987) 267.
77. Boyer, *When Time* (1992) 145.
78. Lindsey, *1980s* (1980) 157.
79. Wagner, "Evangelicals and Israel" (1998) 1021.
80. Lindsey, *1980s* (1980) 3.
81. Lindsey, *1980s* (1980) 5.
82. Lindsey, *1980s* (1980) 6.
83. *Ibid.*
84. Halsell, *Prophecy* (1986) 47.
85. Lindsey, *1980s* (1980) 5-6.

86. Lindsey, *1980s* (1980) 6.
87. *Ibid.*
88. Halsell, *Prophecy* (1986) 47. Also see Knelman, *America* (1987) 228–29.
89. Baranowski, "Jerry Falwell" (1989) 139.
90. Knelman, *America* (1987) 230.
91. Halsell, *Prophecy* (1986) 190-91.
92. Haddad and Wagner, *All in the Name* (1986) 106.
93. Wagner, "Evangelicals and Israel" (1998) 1023.
94. Cannon, *President Reagan* (1991) 289n.
95. Friedman, *Zealots for Zion* (1992) 151.
96. Boyer, *When Time* (1992) 142.
97. Jones and Sheppard, "Ronald Reagan's 'Theology'" (1986) 33.
98. Reagan, *American* (1990) 410.
99. Reagan, *American* (1990) 418.
100. Wagner, "Evangelicals and Israel" (1998) 1023.
101. D'Souza, *Falwell* (1984) 129.
102. *Ibid.*
103. Jones and Sheppard, "Ronald Reagan's 'Theology'" (1986) 31.
104. Reagan, *My* (1981) 302.
105. Halsell, *Prophecy* (1986) 45.
106. *Ibid.*
107. *Ibid.*
108. Slosser, *Reagan Inside Out* (1984) 196.
109. *Ibid.*
110. *Ibid.*
111. Scheer, *With Enough* (1982) 42.
112. Dugger, *On Reagan* (1983) 430.
113. Reagan, *American* (1990) 550.
114. Reagan, *American* (1990) 229.
115. Slosser, *Reagan Inside Out* (1984) 194.
116. Slosser, *Reagan Inside Out* (1984) 195.
117. *Ibid.*
118. Reagan, *American* (1990) 552.
119. Cannon, *President Reagan* (1991) 314.
120. Goodman and Price, *Jerry Falwell* (1981) 44.
121. Slosser, *Reagan Inside Out* (1984) 70.
122. Scheer, *With Enough* (1982) 34–35.
123. Scheer, *With Enough* (1982) 41.
124. Thomas and Meacham, "Book on Reagan" (1999) 24.
125. Knelman, *America* (1987) 55.
126. Dugger, *On Reagan* (1983) 395.
127. Scheer, *With Enough* (1982) 99.
128. Dugger, *On Reagan* (1983) 425.
129. Figures and quote from Morris, *Dutch* (1999) 450.

130. Friedman, *Zealots for Zion* (1992) 151.
131. Reagan, *American* (1990) 238.
132. Reagan, *American* (1990) 316.
133. Reagan, *American* (1990) 552.
134. Reagan, *American* (1990) 555.
135. *Ibid.*
136. *Ibid.*
137. *Ibid.*
138. Boyer, *When Time* (1992) 137.
139. Boyer, *When Time* (1992) 143.
140. Boyer, *When Time* (1992) 142.
141. Woodward, "Arguing Armageddon" (1984) 91.
142. Jones and Sheppard, "Ronald Reagan's 'Theology'" (1986) 29.
143. Jones and Sheppard, "Ronald Reagan's 'Theology'" (1986) 35.
144. Wojcik, *End of the World* (1997) 30.
145. Reagan, *My* (1981) 298.
146. Reagan, *My* (1981) 299.
147. Morris, *Dutch* (1999) 643.
148. Reagan, *American (1990) 257.*
149. Scheer, *With Enough* (1982) 100.
150. Cannon, *President Reagan* (1991) 212.
151. Green and MacColl, *There He* (1983) 15.
152. Reagan, *American* (1990) 257.
153. Morris, *Dutch* (1999) 548.
154. Wills, *Under God* (1990) 150

12 — "The Time Has Come"

1. Hadden and Shupe, *Televangelism* (1988) 179–80.
2. Strozier, *Apocalypse* (1994) 293.
3. Boston, *Most* (1996) 52.
4. Boston, *Most* (1996) 32.
5. Junod, "365 Days" (1999) 96.
6. *Ibid.*
7. Junod, "365 Days" (1999) 98.
8. Hitchens, "Minority" (1995) 375.
9. Mendel, *Vision and Violence* (1992) 309.
10. Quoted in Harrell, *Pat* (1987) 221.
11. Robertson quoted in Straub, *Salvation* (1988) 14.
12. Stafford, "Robertson" (1996) 26.
13. Boston, *Most Dangerous* (1996) 183.
14. Boston, *Most Dangerous* (1996) 186.
15. Hosenball, "Rendering" (1999) 47.
16. Martin, "Christian Right" (1999) 71.
17. Capps, *New Religious* (1990) 164.

18. Boston, *Most Dangerous* (1996) 29.
19. Martin, "Christian Right" (1999) 71.
20. Straub, *Salvation* (1988) 62.
21. Taylor, "Pat Robertson's" (1994) 79.
22. Boston, *Most Dangerous* (1996) 183.
23. Boston, *Most Dangerous* (1996) 42.
24. Friedman, *Zealots* (1992) 144.
25. Boston, *Most Dangerous* (1996) 149.
26. Boston, *Most Dangerous* (1996) 154.
27. *Ibid.*
28. Junod, "365 Days" (1999) 98.
29. Robertson, quoted in Straub, *Salvation* (1988) 339.
30. "Pat Robertson, Novelist" (1997) 25.
31. Haddad and Wagner, *All in the Name* (1986) 122.
32. "Republicans Court Religious Right" (1992) 770.
33. Robertson, *New World* (1992) 133.
34. Robertson, *New World* (1992) 148.
35. Robertson, *New World* (1992) 150.
36. Robertson, *New World* (1992) 168.
37. Robertson, *New World* (1992) 211.
38. Robertson, *New World* (1992) 11.
39. Robertson, *New World* (1992) 64. The Council on Foreign Relations is at the hub. It "reaches out to many power centers" (140). Robertson lists "just a few," a list requiring half a page (140–141).
40. Robertson, *New World* (1992) 12.
41. Robertson, *New World* (1992) 104–105.
42. Robertson, *New World* (1992) 12.
43. Robertson, *New World* (1992) 53–54.
44. Robertson, *New World* (1992) 246.
45. Robertson, *New World* (1992) 256
46. Robertson, *New World* (1992) 246.
47. Robertson, *New World* (1992) 185.
48. Straub, *Salvation* (1988) 334.
49. Boston, *Most Dangerous* (1996) 145.
50. Boston, *Most Dangerous* (1996) 142.
51. Straub, *Salvation* (1988) 339.
52. Straub's words, in *Salvation* (1988) 342.
53. Straub, *Salvation* (1988) 341.
54. Straub, *Salvation* (1988) 333.
55. *Ibid.*
56. Straub, *Salvation* (1988) 341.
57. Straub, *Salvation* (1988) 334

13 — The Chosen One

1. Taylor, "Pat Robertson's" (1994) 79.

2. Donovan, *Pat Robertson* (1988) 6.
3. Donovan, *Pat Robertson* (1988) 11.
4. *Ibid.*
5. Taylor, "Pat Robertson's" (1994) 78.
6. From *Shout It from the Housetops*, as quoted in Capps, *New Religious* (1990) 162.
7. Harrell, *Pat* (1987) 41.
8. Harrell, *Pat* (1987) 83. It was Bredesen who converted Slosser to a charismatic.
9. Harrell, *Pat* (1987) 83.
10. Harrell, *Pat* (1987) 234–35.
11. Harrell, *Pat* (1987) 58.
12. Straub, *Salvation* (1988) 18.
13. Straub, *Salvation* (1988) 343.
14. Straub, *Salvation* (1988) 21.
15. Straub, *Salvation* (1988) 20.
16. Straub, *Salvation* (1988) 359.
17. Straub, *Salvation* (1988) 343.
18. Straub, *Salvation* (1988) 367.
19. Straub, *Salvation* (1988) 363.
20. Harrell, *Pat* (1987) 148.
21. Alter, "Pat" (1988) 18–19.
22. Harrell, *Pat* (1987) 190.
23. Harrell, *Pat* (1987) 190.
24. Boston, *Most Dangerous* (1996) 56.
25. Alter, "Pat" (1988) 18–19.
26. *Ibid.*
27. Boston, *Most Dangerous* (1996) 41.
28. Taylor, "Pat Robertson's" (1994) 81.
29. Boston, *Most Dangerous* (1996) 41.
30. Alter, "Pat" (1988) 18–19.
31. *Ibid.*
32. Straub, *Salvation* (1988) 195.
33. Straub, *Salvation* (1988) 376.
34. Boston, *Most Dangerous* (1996) 36.
35. Harrell, *Pat* (1987) 231.
36. Boston, *Most Dangerous* (1996) 37.
37. Boston, *Most Dangerous* (1996) 146

14 — Virus

1. "Religious Right" (1992) 770.
2. Conason, "Political" (1993) 35.
3. As quoted in Barrett, "Religious Right" (1993) 34.
4. Conason "Political" (1993) 36.
5. Boston, *Most Dangerous* (1996) 59.
6. Boston, *Most Dangerous* (1996) 21.
7. Christian Coalition promotional literature; Boston, *Most Dangerous* (1996) 87.

8. Martin, *With God* (1996) 265.
9. *Ibid.*
10. Taylor, "Pat Robertson's" (1994) 82.
11. Conason, "The Religious" (1992) 541, 553–559.
12. Taylor, "Pat Robertson's" (1994) 80.
13. Boston, *Most Dangerous* (1996) 91. Those words have haunted Reed ever since. Critics keeping throwing them back in his face. Reed left the executive of Christian Coalition in 1997 to become a political consultant. Robertson has resumed control of its daily operations.
14. "Religious Right" (1992) 770.
15. *Ibid.*
16. Reed, "We Can't" (1999) 47.
17. Robertson, quoted in Conason, "The Religious" (1992) 541, 553–559.
18. "Pep Talk" (1997) 865.
19. Strozier, *Apocalypse* (1994) 293, reports that in many local races only 10 percent of registered voters vote.
20. Boston, *Most Dangerous* (1996) 108.
21. Martin, *With God* (1996) 262.
22. Conason, "The Religious" (1992) 541, 553–559.
23. Strozier, *Apocalypse* (1994) 293.
24. Green et al., "1998 Election" (1998) 1239.
25. Isikoff, "Taxing" (1999) 39.
26. Kennedy, "Christian" (1999) 9.
27. Martin, "Christian Right" (1999) 70.
28. Kennedy, "Christian" (1999) 9.
29. Boston, *Most Dangerous* (1996) 110.
30. Green et al., "1998 Election" (1998) 1238.
31. Greeley and Hout, "Measuring" (1999) 810.
32. Boston, *Most Dangerous* (1996) 237.
33. "Pat Robertson Deconstructed" (1995) 10.
34. Boston, *Most Dangerous* (1996) 60, 87.
35. Martin's words, "Christian Right" (1999) 77.
36. Green et al., "1998 Election" (1998) 1239.
37. *Ibid.*
38. Reed, "We Can't" (1999) 46.
39. Martin, "Christian Right" (1999) 68.
40. Carnes, "Republicans" (1998) 20.
41. *Ibid.*
42. Martin, "Christian Right" (1999) 79.
43. Leo, "Looking" (1998) 16.
44. Boston, *Most Dangerous* (1996) 16.
45. Boston, *Most Dangerous* (1996) 87.
46. Boston, *Most Dangerous* (1996) 239.
47. Ibid.
48. Boston, *Most Dangerous* (1996) 164.
49. Boston, *Most Dangerous* (1996) 181.
50. Boston, *Most Dangerous* (1996) 137.
51. Sloan, "Robertson" (1997) 60.
52. *Graduate Programs* (1999) 1189.
53. Martin, *With God* (1996) 325

15 — The War of Good Versus Evil

1. Harrell, *Pat* (1987) 108.
2. Taylor, "Pat Robertson's" (1994) 80.
3. *Ibid.*
4. Robertson, quoted in Harrell, *Pat* (1987) 121.
5. Boston, *Most Dangerous* (1996) 55.
6. Simon, "Miracle" (1996) 11.
7. Harrell, *Pat* (1987) 118.
8. *Ibid.*
9. Harrell, *Pat* (1987) 119.
10. Robertson, quoted in Harrell, *Pat* (1987) 117.
11. Woodward, "This Way" (July 5, 1982) 79.
12. Simon, "Miracle" (1996) 11.
13. *Ibid.*
14. Donovan, *Pat* (1988) 78.
15. Taylor, "Pat Robertson's" (1994) 81.
16. Quoted in Frost, "Gospel" (Feb.22, 1988) 21–22.
17. As quoted in Straub, *Salvation* (1988) 378.
18. Simon, "Miracle" (1996) 11.
19. Boston, *Most Dangerous* (1996) 144.
20. Donovan, *Pat* (1988) 112.
21. Wilhelm, "Getting Ready" (1999) 175.
22. Boston, *Most Dangerous* (1996) 139.
23. Harrell, *Pat* (1987) 210.
24. Harrell's words, *Pat* (1987) 213.
25. Robertson, quoted in Harrell, *Pat* (1987) 213.
26. Boston, *Most Dangerous* (1996) 125.
27. Boston, *Most Dangerous* (1996) 122.
28. Robertson, quoted in Harrell, *Pat* (1987) 194.
29. Harrell, *Pat* (1987) 193.

30. Straub, *Salvation* (1988) 287.
31. Robertson, *New World* (1992) 313–314.
32. Robertson, *New World* (1992) 224.
33. Robertson, *New World* (1992) 226.
34. The words of Richard Falk, as quoted by Robertson in *New World* (1992) 225.
35. Robertson, *New World* (1992) xiii.
36. Straub, *Salvation* (1988) 329.
37. Harrell, *Pat* (1987) 150.
38. Weber, "How Evangelicals" (1998) 47.
39. Wieseltier, "Gog" (1995) 46.
40. Boston's words, *Most Dangerous* (1996) 126. Nowhere in *The New World Order* does Robertson make a directly anti–Semitic statement, but there is plenty of innuendo. Those who make a habit of searching for hints of anti–Semitism would find *The New World Order* profitable. Robertson constantly speaks of the Rothschilds, even when there seems no point in doing so (e.g., p.9). He mentions that Jews were admitted to the Freemasons and if the Rothschilds were among these Jews "we may have discovered the link between the occult and the world of high finance" (266–267). Also Robertson claims that "communism was the brainchild of German-Jewish intellectuals" (24). Communism is an assumed evil force, and the whole book makes the claim that a supposed international banking establishment is behind a demonic conspiracy to take over the world. Reading between the lines it is not difficult to imagine that the last line of the syllogism has the Jews conspiring to take over the world. But this goes unstated. Robertson allows his readers to make the logical connections.
41. Kennedy, "Christian" (1999) 9.
42. While not denying that Robertson is anti–Semitic, Michael Kinsley, an editor with *The New Republic*, writes, The "debate [whether Robertson is anti–Semitic] ... has overshadowed the issue of whether he is a complete nut case." ["Pat Robertson Deconstructed" (1995) 10.]
43. "Is Pat Robertson an Anti–Semite?" (1996) 13.
44. Podhoretz, "In the Matter" (1995) 30.
45. Hitchens "Minority" (1995) 479.
46. Harrell, *Pat* (1987) 76.
47. Wilson, *Armageddon* (1977) 213.
48. *Ibid.*
49. Diamond, *Spiritual Warfare* (1989) 18.
50. Wagner, *Anxious* (1995) 221.
51. Wagner, *Anxious* (1995) 220.
52. Wagner, *Anxious* (1995) 182.
53. Wagner, *Anxious* (1995) 52.
54. Straub, *Salvation* (1988) 356.
55. Harrell, *Pat* (1987) 146.
56. Harrell, *Pat* (1987) 148.
57. Boston, *Most Dangerous* (1996) 196.
58. Taylor, "Pat Robertson's" (1994) 79.
59. "Is Pat Robertson an Anti–Semite?" (1996) 10.
60. Podhoretz, "In the Matter" (1995) 29.
61. "365 Days" (1999) 98.
62. "Ego" (1995) 201.
63. "Ego" (1995) 200.
64. *Vision and Violence* (1992) 309

16 — The Jerusalem Connection

1. Wagner, "Evangelicals" (1998) 1023. Information on and quotations from this ad come from Wagner's article. I was unable to locate the ad in this issue of *New York Times*.
2. Wagner, "Evangelicals" (1998) 1025.
3. Weber, "How Evangelicals" (1998) 39.
4. Halsell, "Why Christian Zionists" (1986) 4.
5. Haddad and Wagner, *All in the Name* (1986) 97.
6. Gorenberg, "Waiting" (1998) 13.
7. Haddad and Wagner, *All in the Name* (1986) 107.
8. Haddad and Wagner, *All in the Name* (1986) 106.
9. See, for example, Haddad, "Cult of Israel" (1986) 12.
10. Halsell, "Why Christian Zionists" (1986) 8.

11. Wagner "Evangelicals" (1998) 1022.
12. *Ibid.*
13. *Ibid.*
14. Lindsey, *1980s* (1980) 158.
15. Weber, "How Evangelicals" (1998) 39.
16. Jordan, "Intifada" (1990) 13. Jordan laments this money going to Israel when only a fraction of it would, she thinks, solve many health and social problems at home in the United States.
17. Bierman, "Defying" (1990) 45.
18. Friedman, *Zealots* (1992) xxv.
19. Friedman, *Zealots* (1992) 79.
20. Wall, "Missing" (1999) 699.
21. Haddad and Wagner, *All in the Name* (1986) 119, in which is reproduced an article from the *Jerusalem Post* by Louis Rapoport titled "Slouching towards Armageddon: Links with Evangelicals."
22. Wagner, "Evangelicals" (1998) 1021.
23. Friedman, *Zealots for Zion* (1992) 236, says Congress is "terrified of AIPAC"—without question the most powerful lobby in America." Friedman tells how one senator who challenged AIPAC lost his seat in the next election. That such a powerful body should solicit the support of Christian apocalypticists points to the latter's strength and significance.
24. Wagner, "Evangelicals" (1998) 1023.
25. Weber, "How Evangelicals" (1998) 39.
26. Wagner, "Evangelicals" (1998) 1025.
27. Wojcik, *End* (1997) 159.
28. Wagner, "Evangelicals" (1998) 1025.
29. *Ibid.*
30. Weber, "How Evangelicals" (1998) 47.
31. Weber, "How Evangelicals" (1998) 49.
32. Haddad and Wagner, *All in the Name* (1986) 120, in which is reproduced an article from the *Jerusalem Post* by Louis Rapoport titled "Slouching towards Armageddon: Links with Evangelicals."
33. Wagner, *Anxious* (1995) 101.
34. Wagner, *Anxious* (1995) 99.
35. Wagner, *Anxious* (1995) 107.
36. *Ibid.*

37. Wagner, *Anxious* (1995) 100.
38. Wagner, *Anxious* (1995) 104.
39. Friedman, *Zealots* (1992) 143.
40. *Ibid.*
41. Wagner, "Evangelicals" (1998) 1026.
42. Halsell, *Prophecy* (1986) 178.
43. Wright, "Forcing" (1998) 48.
44. Goldberg, "Israel's Y2K" (1999) 43.
45. *Ibid.*
46. Gorenberg, "Tribulations" (1999) 21.
47. Halsell, *Prophecy* (1986) 171.
48. Halsell, *Prophecy* (1986) 173.
49. Knelman, *America* (1987) 267.
50. Haddad and Wagner, *All in the Name* (1986) 113, in which is reproduced an article from the *Jerusalem Post* by Louis Rapoport titled "Slouching towards Armageddon: Links with Evangelicals."
51. Halsell, *Prophecy* (1986) 96.
52. Haddad and Wagner, *All in the Name* (1986) 116, in which is reproduced an article from the *Jerusalem Post* by Louis Rapoport titled "Slouching towards Armageddon: Links with Evangelicals."
53. Friedman, *Zealots* (1992) 151.
54. Mendel, *Vision and Violence* (1992) 288.
55. Halsell, *Prophecy* (1986) 100.
56. Friedman, *Zealots* (1992) 147.
57. Wagner, "Anxious" (1986) 25.
58. See Haddad and Wagner, *All in the Name* (1986) 113–114, in which is reproduced an article from the *Jerusalem Post* by Louis Rapoport titled "Slouching towards Armageddon: Links with Evangelicals."
59. Halsell, *Prophecy* (1986) 97.
60. Wagner, "Anxious" (1986) 26.
61. Friedman, *Zealots* (1992) 151-152.
62. Goldberg, "Israel's Y2K" (1999) 52.
63. Haddad and Wagner, *All in the Name* (1986) 1

17 — The Red Heifer

1. Ostling, "Time" (1989) 71.
2. Shargai, "Baby Priests" (1998) 46.
3. Hamilton, "The Strange Case" (1997) 16.
4. *Ibid.*

5. *Ibid.*
6. Perhaps he had seen photographs in which Moses is depicted with horns. The idea that Moses had horns arose from confusion concerning a word in the Hebrew Exodus 34:35. The Hebrew Old Testament originally did not have vowels. The verb "shone" in the sentence "the skin of Moses' face shone" comes from a Hebrew word that could mean "shone" or "horn," depending on which vowels are supposed to be meant.
7. Wright, "Forcing" (1998) 50

18 — Mesirut Hanefesh

1. Wright, "Forcing" (1998) 48.
2. Sharot, "Sociological Analyses" (1995) 21.
3. Deshen, "Religion" (1995) 115.
4. Deshen, "Religion" (1995) 110.
5. Sprinzak *Brother* (1999) 300–301.
6. Sharot, "Sociological Analyses" (1995) 21.
7. Sharot, "Sociological Analyses" (1995) 22.
8. Friedman, *Zealots* (1992) 180. The quoted words are Friedman's.
9. Peres, "Religious Adherence" (1995) 95, 97.
10. Sprinzak, "From Messianic" (1988) 202.
11. Sprinzak, *Ascendance* (1991) 45.
12. Liebman, "Religious" (1987) 132–133.
13. Haddad and Wagner, *All in the Name* (1986) 119, in which is reproduced a *Jerusalem Post* article by Louis Rapoport.
14. Friedman, *Zealots* (1992) 14.
15. Aran, "Jewish Zionist" (1991) 271.
16. Aran, "Mystic-Messianic" (1995) 200.
17. Aran, "Mystic-Messianic" (1995) 199.
18. Aran, "Mystic-Messianic" (1995) 201.
19. Aran, "Mystic-Messianic" (1995) 199.
20. Tal, "Foundations" (1986) 59.
21. Kook, quoted in Sprinzak, *Ascendance* (1991) 46.
22. Friedman, *Zealots* (1992) 245.
23. Friedman, "Jewish" (1992) 159.
24. Friedman, "Jewish" (1992) 171.
25. Friedman, "Jewish" (1992) 159.
26. Friedman, "Jewish" (1992) 172.
27. Liebman, "Jewish Fundamentalism" (1993) 79.
28. *Ibid.*
29. Armstrong, *Holy War* (1988) 211.
30. Aran, "Mystic-Messianic" (1995) 206.
31. *Ibid.*
32. Aran's wording, "Mystic-Messianic" (1995) 207.
33. Quoted in Sharot, "Sociological Analyses" (1995) 25.
34. Sprinzak, *Ascendance* (1991) 251–52.
35. Friedman, *Zealots* (1992) 23.
36. Sprinzak, *Ascendance* (1991) 357 n.5
37. Sprinzak, "From Messianic" (1988) 208.
38. Sprinzak, "From Messianic" (1988) 205.
39. Sprinzak, *Ascendance* (1991) 358.
40. Sprinzak, *Ascendance* (1991) 254.
41. Lustick, *For the Lord* (1988) 98.
42. Etzion, quoted in Sprinzak, "From Messianic" (1988) 206.
43. Etzion, quoted in Sprinzak, "From Messianic" (1988) 207.
44. *Ibid.*
45. Goldberg, "Israel's Y2K" (1999) 38.
46. Goldberg, "Israel's Y2K" (1999) 40.
47. *Ibid.*
48. Sprinzak, *Brother Against Brother* (1999) 32.
49. Halsell, *Prophecy* (1986) 103.
50. Liebman, "Religious" (1987) 133.
51. Sprinzak, *Ascendance* (1991) 271.
52. *Ibid.*
53. Sprinzak, *Ascendance* (1991) 272.
54. Tal, "The Foundations" (1986) 64.
55. Kahane, quoted in Smith, "They Must Go" (1986) 56.
56. Sprinzak, *Brother Against Brother* (1999) 145.
57. Boyer, *When Time* (1992) 194.
58. Deshen, "Religion" (1995) 109.
59. Sprinzak, *Brother Against Brother* (1999) 261.
60. Sprinzak, *Brother Against Brother* (1999) 262.
61. Sprinzak, *Brother Against Brother* (1999) 264.
62. Sprinzak, *Brother Against Brother* (1999) 252

19 — "A Stain on Our Land"

1. "Should the Temple Be Rebuilt?" (June 30, 1967) 48.
2. Ostling, "Time" (1989) 69.
3. Halsell, *Prophecy* (1986) 106–7.
4. Ostling, "Time" (1989) 71.
5. "Should the Temple Be Rebuilt?" (June 30, 1967) 48.
6. "Eschatalogical Stirrings" (Feb. 27, 1970) 35.
7. "An Emotional Arab World Aroused" (1969) 153.
8. "Arson in Jerusalem" (1969) 33.
9. "Fire at a Mosque" (1969) 6.
10. Friedland and Hecht, "The Bodies" (1998) 123.
11. Silver, "West" (1982) 40.
12. Smith, "Attack" (1982) 49.
13. Deming, "Who Owns" (1984) 62.
14. Sprinzak, "From Messianic" (1988) 208–209.
15. Sprinzak, "From Messianic" (1988) 199–200.
16. Deming, "Who Owns" (1984) 62.
17. Halsell, *Prophecy* (1986) 109.
18. *Ibid.*
19. Liebman, "Religious" (1987) 128.
20. Liebman, "Religious" (1987) 130.
21. Submission by Bridges for Peace, a Christian nonprofit organization based in Jerusalem in "Letters from Readers: The Temple Mount" (1991) 9.
22. Nemeth, "Blood" (1990) 30.
23. See the claims of biased reporting in "Letters from Readers: The Temple Mount," in the April 1991 edition of *Commentary.* Friedman, *Zealots* (1992) 128–135, discusses the controversy surrounding conflicting reports of the incident.
24. Submission by Bridges for Peace, a Christian nonprofit organization based in Jerusalem, in "Letters from Readers: The Temple Mount" (1991) 9.
25. Masland, "Bloody Monday" (1990) 36–40.
26. Friedman, *Zealots* (1992) 145.
27. Friedman, *Zealots* (1992) 146.
28. Friedman, *Zealots* (1992) 145.
29. Gorenberg, "Tribulations" (1999) 20.
30. Sappir, "Tensions" (2000) 42.
31. *Ibid.*
32. Sprinzak, "From Messianic" (1988) 208.
33. Gorenberg, "The Beginning" (2000) 26.
34. Sprinzak, "From Messianic" (1988) 214.
35. Goldberg's description, in "Israel's Y2K" (1999) 41.
36. Gorenberg, "Faithful" (1999) 120.
37. *Ibid.*
38. Wright, "Forcing the End" (1998) 46.
39. Halsell, *Prophecy* (1986) 106

20 — Holy War

1. Pipes, Pipes, *The Hidden Hand* (1996) 2.
2. Bronner, "Psycho-Semitic" (1993), for example.
3. Pipes, *The Hidden Hand* (1996) 2.
4. Pipes, *The Hidden Hand* (1996) 1–2.
5. Pipes, *The Hidden Hand* (1996) 116.
6. Friedman, *Zealots* (1992) 233–234.
7. Morris, *Dutch* (1999) 505.
8. Harkavy, "Imperative" (1986) 98.
9. Tibi, *Conflict and War* (1998) 225.
10. Ibrahim Ghosheh, quoted in Davis, *Between Jihad* (1999) 199.
11. Goldberg, "Israel's Y2K" (1999) 42.
12. Harkavy "Imperative" (1986) 98.
13. Armstrong, *Holy War* (1988) 90.
14. Armstrong, *Holy War* (1988) 90-91.
15. Wagner, *Anxious* (1995) 164.
16. Harkavy "Imperative" (1986) 98.
17. Harkavy "Imperative" (1986) 99.
18. *Ibid.*
19. Schiller, "A Battlegroup" (1988) 91.
20. Friedland and Hecht, "The Bodies" (1998) 131.
21. Tibi, *Conflict and War* (1998) 219.
22. Tibi, *Conflict and War* (1998) 224.
23. Tibi, *Conflict and War* (1998) 225.
24. Friedland and Hecht, "The Bodies" (1998) 131.
25. David, *Between Jihad* (1999) 197–198.
26. Shikaki, "Peace Now" (1998) 30.
27. Schiller, "The Bodies" (1988) 105.
28. Schiller, "The Bodies" (1988) 106.
29. Bodansky, an American Jew born in Israel, has written a biography on

Bin Laden. Journalist Yael Haran notes that Bodansky is affiliated with right-wing Jewish groups critical of the peace process in the Middle East. He says Bodansky's book on Bin Laden "reads like the 'Protocols of the Elders of Islam'"—in clear reference to the similarly titled rabidly anti–Jewish literature ("The Counterterrorist" [1999] 50).

30. Davis, *Between Jihad* (1999) 205.
31. Goldberg, "Israel's Y2K" (1999) 40.
32. Weissman and Krosney, *The Islamic Bomb* (1981) 22.
33. Harkavy, "Imperative" (1986) 97.
34. *Ibid.*
35. Wagner, *Anxious* (1995) 131–132.
36. Sprinzak, *Brother Against Brother* (1999) 305.
37. Davis, *Between Jihad* (1999) 205.
38. Davis, *Between Jihad* (1999) 208.
39. Gorenberg, "The Beginning" (2000) 26.
40. Sprinzak, *Brother Against Brother* (1999) 8.
41. Friedman, *Zealots* (1992) xxxvii

21 — "We Will Go Crazy"

1. Barnaby, *Invisible Bomb* (1989) vii.
2. Barnaby, *Invisible Bomb* (1989) xiv.
3. Barnaby, *Invisible Bomb* (1989) 25.
4. Barnaby, *Invisible Bomb* (1989) xiv.
5. Kemp and Harkavy, *Strategic* (1997) 381–383.
6. Barnaby, *Invisible Bomb* (1989) ix.
7. Cohen, *Israel and the Bomb* (1998) 343.
8. Weissman and Krosney, *The Islamic Bomb* (1981) 128.
9. Buheiry, "Implications" (1986), outlines the historical symbiosis between the two nations, noting that they have "basic impulses which have served to reinforce their community of interests in the political, military, economic and colonial spheres" (76). Buheiry makes special mention of their close cooperation in the nuclear field, with South Africa being a leading producer of uranium.
10. Jack, "Security Council's" 383.
11. Anonymous, "How Israel Got the Bomb" 21.
12. Pry, *Israel's Nuclear Arsenal* (1984) 42.
13. Pry, *Israel's Nuclear Arsenal* (1984) 110.
14. Jordan, "Intifada" (1990) 13.
15. Cohen, *Israel and the Bomb* (1998) 1.
16. Cohen, *Israel and the Bomb* (1998) 339.
17. Cohen, *Israel and the Bomb* (1998) 343.
18. His book *Israel and the Bomb* (1998) deals primarily with this policy and how and why it developed. His desire to write a comprehensive history of Israel's nuclear project was foiled—the archives of the Israel Atomic Energy Commission remain sealed (2).
19. Schoenfeld, "Thinking" (1998) 38.
20. Yuval Ne'eman quoted in Weissman and Krosney, *The Islamic Bomb* (1981) 306. With sentiments like that in the air Ne'eman asks, "Do you really believe that a balance of fear would preserve peace in the Middle East?"
21. Chomsky, *Fateful Triangle* (1983) 468.
22. See, for example, Zweig, *Israel: The Sword* (1969) 206.
23. Chomsky, *Fateful Triangle* (1983) 441.
24. Cohen, *Israel and the Bomb* (1998) 340.
25. Cohen, *Israel and the Bomb* (1998) 342.
26. Chomsky, *Fateful Triangle* (1983) 467.
27. Weissman and Krosney, *The Islamic Bomb* (1981) 305.
28. Oz, *In the Land* (1983) 89–90

22 — Nuclear Orgasm

1. Blair and Gaddy, "Russia's Aging" (1999) 13.
2. Barnaby, *Invisible Bomb* (1989) xii, 24.
3. Carter, Deutch, and Zelikow, "Catastrophic" (1998) 81.
4. Kemp and Harkavy, *Strategic Geography* (1997) 381.
5. (1997) xiii.
6. Friedlander, "Armageddon Factor" (1986) 156.
7. Weissman and Krosney, "The Islamic Bomb" (1999) 13.
8. Carter, Deutch, and Zelikow "Catastrophic" (1998) 81.
9. Stern, *The Ultimate Terrorists* (1999) 87.

10. Stern, *The Ultimate Terrorists* (1999) 96–97.
11. Stern, *The Ultimate Terrorists* (1999) 95.
12. Stern, *The Ultimate Terrorists* (1999) 9.
13. Kemp and Harkavy, *Changing Middle East* (1997) 293.
14. Stern, *The Ultimate Terrorists* (1999) 89.
15. Stern, *The Ultimate Terrorists* (1999) 104.
16. Stern, *The Ultimate Terrorists* (1999) 193, n.52.
17. Kemp and Harkavy, *Strategic* (1997) 294.
18. Barnaby, "Nuclear Arsenal" (1987) 97–106.
19. Stern, *The Ultimate Terrorists* (1999) 58.
20. Stern, *The Ultimate Terrorists* (1999) 183, n.34.
21. Friedlander, "Armageddon Factor" (1986) 156.
22. Mendel, *Vision and Violence* (1992) 309

23 — Armageddon

1. Wagner, *Anxious* (1995) 188.
2. Wagner, *Anxious* (1995) 197.
3. Weissman and Krosney, *The Islamic Bomb* (1981) 29–30.
4. Ed Dobson, quoted in Martin, *With God on Our Side* (1996) 236.
5. Schoenfeld, "Thinking" (1998) 37.
6. Hitchens, "Minority Report" (1995) 479.
7. Zweig, *Israel: The Sword* (1969) 213.
8. Wagner, *Anxious* (1995) 201.
9. Tibi, *Conflict and War* (1998) 227.
10. Tibi, *Conflict and War* (1998) 231.
11. Davis, *Between Jihad* (1999) xi.
12. Davis, *Between Jihad* (1999) xii.
13. Reverend James Lewis; Martin, *With God on Our Side* (1996) 131.
14. Tibi, *Conflict and War* (1998) 220, 218.
15. Tibi, *Conflict and War* (1998) 214.
16. Tibi, *Conflict and War* (1998) 215.
17. Tibi, *Conflict and War* (1998) 217.
18. Armstrong, *Holy War* (1988) 213.
19. Goldberg, "Israel's Y2K" (1999) 76.
20. Goldberg, "Israel's Y2K" (1999) 41.
21. Goldberg, "Israel's Y2K" (1999) 42.
22. Friedman, *Zealots* (1992) 247–248.
23. Friedman, *Zealots* (1992) 41.
24. Goldberg, "Israel's Y2K" (1999) 40.
25. Jeffrey Goldberg's apt phrase, in "Israel's Y2K" (1999) 40.
26. Sappir, "Tensions Mount" (2000) 43.
27. Ostling, "Time" (1989) 69.
28. Laqueur, "Postmodern Terrorism" (1996) 36.
29. Stern, *The Ultimate Terrorists* (1999) 7.
30. Stern, *The Ultimate Terrorists* (1999) 70.
31. Stern, *The Ultimate Terrorists* (1999) 71, 72.
32. Stern, *The Ultimate Terrorists* (1999) 8, 79–80.
33. Goldberg, "Israel's Y2K" (1999) 77.
34. Aran, "Jewish Zionist" (1991) 267.
35. Schoenfeld, "Thinking" (1998) 38.
36. Zweig, *Israel: The Sword* (1969) 217.
37. Weissman and Krosney, *The Islamic Bomb* (1981) 29.
38. Kemp and Harkavy, *Strategic Geography* (1997) 269.
39. Kemp and Harkavy, *Strategic Geography* (1997) 387.
40. Friedman, *Zealots* (1992) 152

Bibliography

Ackerman, Elise. "Millennial Madness, Jerusalem Jitters: Israel Deports One Cult, Worries about Others," *U.S. News & World Report*, Jan. 18, 1999, 32–33.

Ajemian, Robert. "Jerry Falwell's Crusade," *Time*, Sept. 2, 1985, 44–54.

Alter, Jonathan. "Pat Robertson: The Telepolitician," *Newsweek*, Feb. 22, 1988, 18–19.

"'The American Whey' Promo Raises Eyebrows," *The Christian Century*, Oct. 13, 1993, 972.

Andersen, Kurt. "For God and Country," *Time*, Sept. 10, 1984, 12–14.

Aran, Gideon. "Jewish Zionist Fundamentalism: The Bloc of the Faithful in Israel (Gush Emunim)," in *Fundamentalisms Observed*, vol. 1, edited by Martin E. Marty and R. Scott Appleby. Chicago: University of Chicago Press, 1991. pp. 265–344.

_____. "The Mystic-Messianic Interpretation of Modern Israeli History: The Six-day War in the Religious Culture of Gush Emunim," in *Israeli Judaism: The Sociology of Religion in Israel*, edited by Shlomo Deshen, Charles S. Liebman and Moshe Shokeid. New Brunswick, New Jersey: Transaction, 1995. pp. 197–209.

Armstrong, Karen. *Holy War*. London: Macmillan, 1988.

"Arson in Jerusalem," *Christianity Today*, Sept. 12, 1969, 33.

Aviad, Janet. "The Contemporary Israeli Pursuit of the Millennium," *Religion* 14 (1984) 199–222.

Averill, Lloyd J. *Religious Right, Religious Wrong: A Critique of the Fundamentalist Phenomenon*. New York: Pilgrim, 1989.

Baker, Dwight L. "Jerusalem: A Third Temple?" *Christianity Today*, July 21, 1967, 1050.

Baranowski, Shelley. "Jerry Falwell," in *Twentieth-Century Shapers of American Popular Religion*, edited by Charles H. Lippy. Westport: Greenwood Press, 1989. pp. 133–141.

Bar-Illan, David. "'60 Minutes' & the Temple Mount," *Commentary*, Feb. 1991, 17–24.

Barna, George, and William Paul McKay. *Vital Signs: Emerging Social Trends and the Future of American Christianity*. Westchester, Illinois: Crossway Books, 1984.

Barnaby, Frank. *The Invisible Bomb: The Nuclear Arms Race in the Middle East*. London: I. B. Tauris, 1989.

_____. "The Nuclear Arsenal in the Middle East," *Journal of Palestine Studies*, vol. 17, no. 1 (1987), 97–106.

_____. "Will There Be a Nuclear War?" in *Dropping the Bomb: The Church and the Bomb Debate*, edited by John Gladwin. London: Hodder and Stoughton, 1985. pp. 35–49.

Barr, James. *Fundamentalism*. Philadelphia: Westminster, 1978.

Barrett, Laurence I. "The `Religious Right' and the Pagan Press," *Columbia Journalism Review*, July/August 1993, 33–34.

_____. *Gambling with History: Ronald Reagan in the White House*. New York: Doubleday, 1983.

Bell, L. Nelson. "Unfolding Destiny," *Christianity Today*, July 21, 1967, 1044–1045.

Benjamin, Milton R., and Richard M. Smith. "A War That Broke the Myths," *Newsweek*, Oct. 22, 1973, 60–86.

Berger, Peter L. "Democracy and the Religious Right," *Commentary*, January 1997, 53–56.

Beyer, Lisa. "Target: Jerusalem," *Time*, Jan. 18, 1999, 39.

Bierman, John. "Defying Both Friends and Foes," *Maclean's*, Oct. 29, 1990, 45.

_____. "Inviting Skepticism," *Maclean's*, Nov. 5, 1990, 34.

Blair, Bruce, and Clifford Gaddy. "Russia's Aging War Machine: Economic Weakness and the Nuclear Threat," *Brookings Review*, Summer 1999, 10–13.

Bock, Darrell L. "Why I Am a Dispensationalist with a Small 'd.'" *Journal of the Evangelical Theological Society* 41 (1998) 383–396.

Boston, Robert. *The Most Dangerous Man in America? Pat Robertson and the Rise of the Christian Coalition*. Amherst, New York: Prometheus Books, 1996.

Bouchier, David. "No More Mr. Good Guy," *The Humanist*, July/Aug. 1990, 21–22.

Boyarski, Bill. *Ronald Reagan: His Life and Rise to the Presidency*. New York: Random, 1981.

Boyer, Paul. "A Brief History of the End of Time," *The New Republic*, May 17, 1993, 30–33.

_____. *By the Bomb's Early Light: American Thought and Culture at the Dawn of the Atomic Age*. New York: Pantheon, 1985.

_____. *When Time Shall Be No More: Prophecy Belief in Modern American Culture*. Cambridge: Harvard University Press, 1992.

Bradley, David. *No Place To Hide, 1946/1984*. Hanover, New Hampshire: University Press of New England, 1983.

Bronner, Ethan. "Psycho-Semitic," *The New Republic*, May 24, 1993, 17.

Brown, Robert McAfee. "The Religious Right and Political/Economic Conservativism," in *Border Religions of Faith: An Anthology of Religion and Social Change*, edited by Kenneth Aman. Maryknoll, N.Y.: Orbis, 1987. pp. 258–63.

Brummet, Barry. *Contemporary Apocalyptic Rhetoric*. New York: Praeger, 1991.

Budiansky, Stephen. "Prayers for the Dying, Politics for the Living," *U.S. News & World Report*, Oct. 22, 1990, 14–15.

Buheiry, Marwan. "Implications of the Israel-South Africa Alliance," in *All in the Name of the Bible: Selected Essays on Israel and American Christian Fundamentalism*, edited by Hassan Haddad and Donald Wagner. 2nd ed. Brattleboro, Vermont: Amana Books, 1986. pp. 71–77.

Cannon, Lou. *President Reagan: The Role of a Lifetime*. New York: Simon & Schuster, 1991.

_____. *Reagan*. New York: G. P. Putnam's Sons, 1982.

Capps, Walter H. *The New Religious Right: Piety, Patriotism, and Politics*. Columbia: University of South Carolina Press, 1990.

Carnes, Tony. "Republican Candidates Court Conservatives Early, Often," *Christianity Today*, April 5, 1999, 16–17.

_____. "Republicans, Religious Right Stunned by Voter Rebuke," *Christianity Today*, Dec. 7, 1998, 20.

Carter, Ashton, John Deutch, and Philip Zelikow. "Catastrophic Terrorism: Tackling the New Danger," *Foreign Affairs*, November/December 1998, 80–94.

Case, Shirley Jackson. *The Millennial Hope: A Phase of War-time Thinking*. Chicago: University of Chicago Press, 1918.

Chattaway, Peter T. "Christian Filmmakers Jump on End-times Bandwagon," *Christianity Today*, Oct. 25, 1999, 26–27.

Chidester, David. *Patterns of Power: Religion and Politics in American Culture*. Englewood Cliffs: Prentice Hall, 1988.

Chomsky, Noam. *The Fateful Triangle: The United States, Israel and the Palestinians*. Boston: South End Press, 1983.

Claybaugh, Gary K. *Thunder on the Right: The Protestant Fundamentalists*. Chicago: Nelson-Hall, 1974.

Cohen, Avner. *Israel and the Bomb*. New York: Columbia University Press, 1998.

Cohen, Gary. "On God's Green Earth," *U.S. News & World Report*, Aug. 24, 1995, 32–33.

Cohen, Geula. *Women of Violence: Memoirs of a Young Terrorist, 1943–1948*. New York: Holt, Rinehart and Winston, 1966.

The College Blue Book: Narrative Descriptions. 27th ed. New York: Macmillan, 1999.

Conason, Joe. "A Political Story — Chapter and Verse," *Columbia Journalism Review*, July/August 1993, 35–36.

_____. "The Religious Right's Quiet Revival," *The Nation*, April 27, 1992, 1553–1559.

Conway, Flo, and Jim Siegelman. *Holy Terror: The Fundamentalist War on America's Freedoms in Religion, Politics and Our Private Lives*. New York: Dell, 1984.

Cox, Harvey. "The Warring Visions of the Religious Right," *The Atlantic Monthly*, November 1995, 59–69.

Crutchfield, Larry V. "C. I. Scofield," in *Twentieth-Century Shapers of American Popular Religion*, edited by Charles H. Lippy. Westport: Greenwood Press, 1989. pp. 371–381.

_____. *The Origins of Dispensationalism: The Darby Factor*. Lanham, Maryland: University Press of America, 1992.

Dabney, Dick. "God's Own Network: The TV Kingdom of Pat Robertson," *Harper's*, Aug. 1980, 33–52.

Dallek, Robert. *Ronald Reagan: The Politics of Symbolism*. Cambridge: Harvard University Press, 1984.

Davenport, Elaine, Paul Eddy, and Peter Gillman. *The Plumbat Affair*. London: André Deutsch, 1978.

Davis, Joyce M. *Between Jihad and Salaam: Profiles in Islam*. 2nd ed. New York: St. Martin's Griffin, 1999.

Deming, Angus. "Who Owns the Temple Mount?" *Newsweek*, Nov. 5, 1984, 62.

Denton, Robert E., Jr. *The Primetime Presidency of Ronald Reagan: The Era of the Television Presidency*. New York: Praeger, 1988.

Deshen, Shlomo. "Religion in the Israeli Discourse on the Arab-Jewish Conflict," in *Israeli Judaism: The Sociology of Religion in Israel*, edited by Shlomo Deshen, Charles

S. Liebman and Moshe Shokeid. New Brunswick, New Jersey: Transaction, 1995. pp. 107–123.

_____, Charles S. Liebman, and Moshe Shokeid (editors). *Israeli Judaism: The Sociology of Religion in Israel.* New Brunswick, New Jersey: Transaction, 1995.

Diamond, Sara. *Spiritual Warfare: The Politics of the Christian Right.* Boston: South End Press, 1989.

Doan, Ruth Alden. *The Miller Heresy, Millennialism, and American Culture.* Philadelphia: Temple University Press, 1987.

Doerr, Edd. "Falwell's Farewell," *The Humanist,* Jan./Feb. 1988, 40–41.

Dollar, George W. *A History of Fundamentalism in America.* Greenville, South Carolina: Bob Jones University Press, 1973.

"Dome of the Rocks," *The New Republic,* Oct. 29, 1990, 7–8.

Donovan, John B. *Pat Robertson: The Authorized Biography.* New York: Macmillan, 1988.

Dror, Yehezkel. *Crazy States: A Counterconventional Strategic Problem.* Lexington, Mass.: D. C. Heath, 1971.

D'Souza, Dinesh. *Falwell: Before the Millennium, A Critical Biography.* Chicago: Regnery Gateway, 1984.

Ducat, Stephen. *Taken In: American Gullibility and the Reagan Mythos.* Tacoma: Life Sciences, 1988.

Dugger, Ronnie. *On Reagan: The Man & His Presidency.* New York: McGraw-Hill, 1983.

Efird, James M. *End-Times: Rapture, Antichrist, Millennium.* Nashville: Abingdon, 1986.

Ehteshami, Anoushiravan. *Nuclearization of the Middle East.* London: Brassey's, 1989.

Elwell, Walter A. "Dispensationalisms of the Third Kind," *Christianity Today,* Sept. 12, 1994, 28.

"An Emotional Arab World Aroused," *America,* Sept. 13, 1969, 153.

English, E. Schuyler. *A Companion to the New Scofield Reference Bible.* New York: Oxford University Press, 1972.

"Eschatological Stirrings: Madman at the Mosque?" *Christianity Today,* Feb. 27, 1970, 35.

"Evangelicals Differ on Middle East Policy," *The Christian Century,* Feb. 25, 1998, 197–198.

"The Expanding CBN Empire," *The Christian Century,* July 27–Aug. 3, 1994, 712–713.

Falwell, Jerry. "An Agenda for the 1980s," in *Piety and Politics: Evangelicals and Fundamentalists Confront the World,* edited by Richard John Neuhaus and Michael Cromartie. Washington: Ethics and Public Policy Center, 1987. pp. 111–23.

_____. "A Biblical Plan of Action," in *Border Regions of Faith: An Anthology of Religion and Social Change,* edited by Kenneth Aman. Maryknoll, New York: Orbis, 1987. pp. 244–50.

_____. "I'd Do It All Again," *Christianity Today,* Sept. 6, 1999, 50–51.

_____. *Strength for the Journey: An Autobiography.* New York: Simon and Schuster, 1987.

Festinger, Leon, Henry W. Riecken, and Stanley Schachter. "When Prophecy Fails," in *Extending Psychological Frontiers: Selected Works of Leon Festinger.* New York: Russell Sage Foundation, 1989. pp. 258–269.

Fields-Meyer, Thomas, and Grant Pick. "In Heaven's Name," *People Weekly,* Dec. 14, 1998, 139–140.

Finch, Phillip. *God, Guts, and Guns.* New York: Seaview/Putnam, 1983.

Fineman, Howard. "God and the Grass Roots," *Newsweek,* Nov. 8, 1993, 42–45.

"Fire at a Mosque Sparks New Crisis," *U.S. News & World Report*, Sept. 1, 1969, 6.

Friedland, Roger, and Richard D. Hecht. "The Bodies of Nations: A Comparative Study of Religious Violence in Jerusalem and Ayodhya," *History of Religions* 38 (1998) 101–149.

_____. "The Politics of Sacred Place: Jerusalem's Temple Mount / al-haram al-sharif," in *Sacred Places and Profane Spaces: Essays in the Geographics of Judaism, Christianity, and Islam*, edited by Jamie Scott and Paul Simpson. Westport, Connecticut: Greenwood, 1991. pp. 21–61.

Friedlander, Robert A. "The Armageddon Factor: Terrorism and Israel's Nuclear Option," in *Security or Armageddon: Israel's Nuclear Strategy*, edited by Louis René Beres. Lexington, Mass.: D.C. Heath, 1986. pp. 151–58, 216–19.

Friedman, Menachem. "Jewish Zealots: Conservative Versus Innovative," in *Fundamentalism in Comparative Perspective*, edited by Lawrence Kaplan. Amherst: University of Massachusetts Press, 1992. pp. 159–76.

_____. "Life Tradition and Book Tradition in the Development of Ultraorthodox Judaism," in *Israeli Judaism: The Sociology of Religion in Israel*, edited by Shlomo Deshen, Charles S. Liebman and Moshe Shokeid. New Brunswick, New Jersey: Transaction, 1995. pp. 127–147.

Friedman, Robert I. *The False Prophet: Rabbi Meir Kahane from FBI Informant to Knesset Member*. Brooklyn: Lawrence Hill, 1990.

_____. *Zealots for Zion: Inside Israel's West Bank Settlement Movement*. New York: Random, 1992.

Friedrich, Otto. "City of Protest and Prayer," *Time*, April 12, 1982, 26–35.

Frost, David. [interview with Pat Robertson] "The Gospel According to Robertson," *U.S. News & World Report*, Feb. 22, 1988, 21–22.

Fuller, Daniel P. *Gospel and Law: Contrast or Continuum?: The Hermeneutics of Dispensationalism and Covenant Theology*. Grand Rapids: Eerdmans, 1980.

Gallup, George, Jr., and Jim Castelli. *The People's Religion: American Faith in the 90's*. New York: Macmillan, 1989.

Gardella, Peter. "Ego and Apocalypse in America," *Religious Studies Review*, vol. 21 (1995), 196–201.

Garrison, David. "Tim and Beverly LaHaye," in *Twentieth-Century Shapers of American Popular Religion*, edited by Charles H. Lippy. Westport: Greenwood Press, 1989. pp. 233–240.

Giorgianna, Sharon Linzey. *The Moral Majority and Fundamentalism: Plausibility and Dissonance*. Lewiston, New York: Edwin Mellen, 1989.

Goffney, Mark. *Dimona: The Third Temple?: The Story Behind the Vanunu Revelation*. Brattleboro, Vermont: Amana Books, 1989.

Goldberg, Jeffrey. "Israel's Y2K Problem," *The New York Times Magazine*, Oct. 3, 1999, 38–43, 52, 65, 76–77.

Goldman, Peter, and Tom Mathews. *The Quest for the Presidency 1988*. New York: Simon & Schuster, 1989.

Goodman, William R., Jr., and James J. H. Price. *Jerry Falwell: An Unauthorized Profile*. Lynchburg: Paris & Associates, 1981.

Gorenberg, Gershom. "The Beginning Is Nigh," *The Jerusalem Report*, Jan. 3, 2000, 26.

_____. "More Faithful Than Ever," *The Jerusalem Report*, Oct. 25, 1999, 12.

_____. "Tribulations: Jerusalem's Y2K Problem," *The New Republic*, June 14, 1999, 18–21.

_____. "Waiting for the End in the Holy Land," *World Press Review*, July 1998, 12–13.

Gould, Stephen Jay. "Dousing Diminutive Dennis's Debate," *Natural History*, April 1994, 4–12.

Govier, Gordon. "Preparing for Pilgrims: Religious Rivalry Complicates Millennial Planning," *Christianity Today*, June 14, 1999, 24.

Graduate Programs in the Humanities, Arts & Social Sciences, Book 2. 33rd ed. Princeton: Peterson's, 1999.

Graham, Stephen R. "Hal Lindsey," in *Twentieth-Century Shapers of American Popular Religion*, edited by Charles H. Lippy. Westport: Greenwood Press, 1989. pp. 247–255.

Greeley, Andrew, and Michael Hout. "Measuring the Strength of the Religious Right," *The Christian Century*, Aug.25–Sept. 1, 1999, 810–815.

Green, John C., James L. Guth, Lyman A. Kellstedt, and Corwin E. Smidt. "A Defeat, Not a Debacle: The Religious Right and the 1998 Election," *The Christian Century*, Dec. 23–30, 1998, 1238–1240.

Green, Mark, and Gail MacColl. *Ronald Reagan's Reign of Error*. expanded and updated edition. New York: Pantheon, 1987.

_____. *There He Goes Again: Ronald Reagan's Reign of Error*. New York: Pantheon, 1983.

Greene, Owen, Ian Percival, and Irene Ridge. *Nuclear Winter: The Evidence and the Risks*. Cambridge: Polity, 1985.

Gritsch, Eric W. *Born Againism: Perspectives on a Movement*. Philadelphia: Fortress, 1982.

Guth, James L. "The New Christian Right," in *The New Christian Right: Mobilization and Legitimation*, edited by Robert C. Liebman and Robert Wuthnow. New York: Aldine, 1983. pp. 31–45.

Guth, James L., John C. Green, Lyman A. Kellstedt, and Corwin E. Smidt. "God's Own Party: Evangelicals and Republicans in the '92 Election," *The Christian Century*, Feb. 17, 1993, 172–76.

Hackett, George. "Where Have You Been, Mr. Robertson?" *Newsweek*, Aug. 8, 1988, 29.

Haddad, Hassan. "The Cult of Israel and Palestinian Human Rights," in *All in the Name of the Bible: Selected Essays on Israel and American Christian Fundamentalism*, edited by Hassan Haddad and Donald Wagner. 2nd ed. Brattleboro, Vermont: Amana Books, 1986. pp. 9–15.

Hadden, Jeffrey K., and Anson Shupe. *Televangelism: Power and Politics on God's Frontier*. New York: Henry Holt, 1988.

Hall, Chris. "What Hal Lindsey Taught Me about the Second Coming," *Christianity Today*, Oct. 25, 1999, 83–85.

Halsell, Grace. "A Palestinian Christian Response: An Interview with Jonathan Kuttab," in *All in the Name of the Bible: Selected Essays on Israel and American Christian Fundamentalism*, edited by Hassan Haddad and Donald Wagner. 2nd ed. Brattleboro, Vermont: Amana Books, 1986. pp. 48–49.

_____. *Prophecy and Politics: Militant Evangelists on the Road to Nuclear War*. Westport, Connecticut: Lawrence Hill, 1986.

_____. "Why Christian Zionists Support Israel," in *All in the Name of the Bible: Selected Essays on Israel and American Christian Fundamentalism*, edited by Hassan Haddad and Donald Wagner. 2nd ed. Brattleboro, Vermont: Amana Books, 1986. pp. 4–8.

Hamilton, Kendall. "The Strange Case of Israel's Red Heifer," *Newsweek*, May 19, 1997, 16.

Hansen, Chuck. *U.S. Nuclear Weapons: The Secret History*. Arlington, Texas: Aerofax, 1988.

Haran, Yael. "Bin Laden Has Several Nuclear Suitcases," *The Jerusalem Report*, Oct. 25, 1999, 8.

_____. "The Counterterrorist," *The Jerusalem Report*, Dec. 20, 1999, 50–51.

Harkavy, Robert. "The Imperative to Survive," in *Security or Armageddon: Israel's Nuclear Strategy*, edited by Louis René Beres. Lexington, Mass.: D.C. Heath, 1986. pp. 97–118, 208–10.

Harrell, David. "The Roots of the Moral Majority: Fundamentalism Revisited," in *Border Regions of Faith: An Anthology of Religion and Social Change*, edited by Kenneth Aman. Maryknoll, New York: Orbis, 1987. pp. 227–43.

Harrell, David Edwin, Jr. *Pat Robertson: A Personal, Religious, and Political Portrait.* San Francisco: Harper & Row, 1987.

Harris, Michael P. "Paradise under Siege," *Time*, Aug. 28, 1989, 52.

Heilman, Samuel C., and Menachem Friedman. "Religious Fundamentalism and Religious Jews: The Case of the Haredim," in *Fundamentalisms Observed*, vol.1, edited by Martin E. Marty and R. Scott Appleby. Chicago: University of Chicago Press, 1991. pp. 197–264.

Hirschfield, Robert. "The Temple Mount and the New Apocalypse," *The Christian Century*, vol. 102, no. 28 (Sept. 25, 1985), 820–1.

Hitchens, Christopher. "Minority Report," *The Nation*, April 10, 1995, 479.

_____. "Minority Report," *The Nation*, Oct. 9, 1995, 375.

"Hooliganism in the Holy City," *Time*, June 27, 1983, 62.

Hosenball, Mark. "Rendering unto Laura," *Newsweek*, Feb. 8, 1999, 47.

"How Israel Got the Bomb," *Time*, April 12, 1976, 21–22.

Hull, Jon D. "Anatomy of a Tragedy," *Time*, Oct. 22, 1990, 22–23.

Hunter, James Davison. "Before the Shooting Begins," *Columbia Journalism Review*, July/August 1993, 29–32.

Ide, Arthur Frederick. *Evangelical Terrorism: Censorship, Falwell, Robertson & the Seamy Side of Christian Fundamentalism.* Irving: Scholars Books, 1986.

Idinopulos, Thomas. "Theopolitics at Jerusalem's Dome of the Rock," *The Christian Century*, vol. 100, no. 33 (Nov.9, 1983), 1018–21.

"If You Don't Swing, You Can't Zing," *U.S. News & World Report*, June 26, 1989, 12.

"Is Pat Robertson an Anti-Semite?," *Commentary*, January 1996, 3–13.

Isikoff, Michael. "Taxing Times for Robertson," *Newsweek*, June 21, 1999, 39.

Isikoff, Michael, and Mark Hosenball. "With God There's No Cap," *Newsweek*, Oct. 3, 1994, 42–44.

"Israel Deports Cult Members," *The Christian Century*, Jan. 20, 1999, 50–51.

Jabber, Fuad. *Israel and Nuclear Weapons: Present Option and Future Strategies.* London: Chatto & Windus, 1971.

Jack, Homer A. "The Security Council's Temple Mount Debate," *The Christian Century*, April 21, 1976, 380–383.

Jacoby, Tamar. "Is It Time to Take Pat Seriously?" *Newsweek*, Jan. 4, 1988, 21–22.

Jensen, Holger. "Trouble in Paradise," *Maclean's*, May 7, 1990, 33–35.

"Jerusalem Deaths," *The Christian Century*, Oct. 24, 1990, 961–962.

Jewett, Robert. *The Captain America Complex: The Dilemma of Zealous Nationalism.* Philadelphia: Westminster, 1973.

"Jews in Old Jerusalem!: A Historic Re-entry," *Christianity Today*, June 23, 1967, 973–974.

Jones, Larry, and Gerald T. Sheppard. "Ronald Reagan's 'Theology' of Armageddon," in *All in the Name of the Bible: Selected Essays on Israel and American Christian Fundamentalism*, edited by Hassan Haddad and Donald Wagner. 2nd ed. Brattleboro, Vermont: Amana Books, 1986. pp. 29–36.

Jordan, June. "Intifada, U.S.A.," *The Progressive*, December 1990, 13.

Jorstad, Erling. *Holding Fast / Pressing On: Religion in America in the 1980s.* Westport, Connecticut: Greenwood, 1990.

_____. *The New Christian Right, 1981–1988: Prospects for the Post-Reagan Decade.* Lewiston, New York: Edwin Mellen, 1987.

_____. *The Politics of Doomsday: Fundamentalists of the Far Right.* New York: Abingdon, 1970.

_____. *Popular Religion in America: The Evangelical Voice.* Westport, Connecticut: Greenwood, 1993.

Junod, Tom. "365 Days to the Apocalypse and We Still Don't Know Where to Hide the Jews," *Esquire,* January 1999, 94–99.

Kahane, Meir. *Uncomfortable Questions for Comfortable Jews.* Secaucus, New Jersey: Lyle Stuart, 1987.

Kedem, Peri. "Dimensions of Jewish Religiosity," in *Israeli Judaism: The Sociology of Religion in Israel,* edited by Shlomo Deshen, Charles S. Liebman and Moshe Shokeid. New Brunswick, New Jersey: Transaction, 1995. pp. 33–59.

Kelly, Dean M. *Why Conservative Churches Are Growing: A Study in Sociology of Religion.* New York: Harper & Row, 1977.

Kemp, Geoffrey, and Robert E. Harkavy. *Strategic Geography and the Changing Middle East.* Washington: Brookings Institution Press, 1997.

Kennedy, John W. "Christian Coalition Loses Exempt Status," *Christianity Today,* July 12, 1999, 9.

_____. "Wild Card Election," *Christianity Today,* Oct. 26, 1998, 80–84.

Kermode, Frank. *The Sense of an Ending: Studies in the Theory of Fiction.* New York: Oxford University Press, 1967.

Keylock, Leslie R. "Evangelical Protestants Take Over Center Field," *Publishers Weekly,* Mar. 9, 1984, 32–33.

Kinsley, Michael. "Long Sentence: Pat Robertson Deconstructed," *The New Republic,* May 8, 1995, 10–11.

Kirn, Walter. "The End Is Here, Pt. 6," *Time,* Sept. 13, 1999, 39.

Kirsch, Jonathan. "Hal Lindsey," *Publishers Weekly,* vol. 211, no. 11 (1977), 30–32.

Klebnikov, Peter. "Time of Troubles," *Newsweek,* April 7, 1997, 48–48b.

Knelman, F. H. *America, God and the Bomb: The Legacy of Ronald Reagan.* Vancouver: New Star, 1987.

Kraus, C. Norman. *Dispensationalism in America: Its Rise and Development.* Richmond: John Knox, 1958.

Kraybill, J. Nelson. "Apocalypse Now," *Christianity Today,* Oct. 25, 1999, 31–40.

Küng, Hans, and Jürgen Moltmann (editors). *Fundamentalism As an Ecumenical Challenge.* London: SCM, 1992.

Lacayo, Richard. "The End of the World as We Know It?" *Time,* Jan. 18, 1999, 34–42.

Lane, Charles. "A Time Bomb at the City's Heart," *Newsweek,* Oct. 22, 1990, 38.

Laqueur, Walter. "Postmodern Terrorism," *Foreign Affairs,* September/October 1996, 24–36.

Ledeen, Barbara, and Michael Ledeen. "The Temple Mount Plot: What Do Christian and Jewish Fundamentalists Have in Common?" *The New Republic,* June 18, 1984, 20–23.

Leland, John. "Millennium Madness," *Newsweek,* Nov.1, 1999, 70–71.

Leo, John. "Looking for a Scapegoat," *U.S. News & World Report,* Nov. 23, 1998, 16.

"Letters from Readers: The Temple Mount," *Commentary,* April 1991, 2–12.

Liebman, Charles S. "Jewish Fundamentalism and the Israeli Polity," in *Fundamentalisms and the State,* vol.3, edited by Martin E. Marty and R. Scott Appleby. Chicago: University of Chicago Press, 1993. pp. 68–87.

_____. "The Religious Component in Israeli Ultra-Nationalism," *The Jerusalem Quarterly*, vol. 41 (1987) 127–144.

Liebman, Robert C. "Mobilizing the Moral Majority," in *The New Christian Right: Mobilization and Legitimation*, edited by Robert C. Liebman and Robert Wuthnow. New York: Aldine, 1983. pp. 49–73.

Lief, Louise. "Bloodshed in a Holy Place: The Battle on the Temple Mount," *U.S. News & World Report*, Oct. 22, 1990, 45.

Lifton, Robert Jay. *Death in Life: Survivors of Hiroshima*. New York: Random, 1967.

Lindner, Eileen W. *Yearbook of American and Canadian Churches, 1999*. Nashville: Abingdon, 1999.

Lindsey, Hal. *The Late Great Planet Earth*. Grand Rapids: Zondervan, 1970.

_____. *The 1980's: Countdown to Armageddon*. New York: Bantam, 1980.

_____. *The Road to Holocaust*. New York: Bantam, 1989.

Linenthal, Edward Tabor. "Pat Robertson," in *Twentieth-Century Shapers of American Popular Religion*, edited by Charles H. Lippy. Westport: Greenwood Press, 1989. pp. 349–356.

Lord, Lewis. "UPI, Born Again," *U.S. News & World Report*, May 25, 1992, 25.

Lustick, Ian S. *For the Land and the Lord: Jewish Fundamentalism in Israel*. New York: Council on Foreign Relations, 1988.

_____. "Reinventing Jerusalem," *Foreign Policy*, vol.93 (winter 1993–1994), 41–59.

Maloney, Lawrence D., and Kathleen Phillips. "At Eastertide, a Resurgence of Religion," *U.S. News & World Report*, April 30, 1984, 82–83.

Marmon, Lucretia. [article on Hal Lindsey] *People*, July 4, 1977, 70–72.

Marsden, George M. *Understanding Fundamentalism and Evangelicalism*. Grand Rapids: Eerdmans, 1991.

Martin, David. "Mystery of Israel's Bomb," *Newsweek*, Jan. 9, 1978, 26–27.

Martin, William. "The Christian Right and American Foreign Policy," *Foreign Policy*, Spring 1999, 66–80.

_____. *With God on Our Side: The Rise of the Religious Right in America*. New York: Broadway Books, 1996.

Marty, Martin E. "Reckoning with the Millennium," *The Christian Century*, Feb. 4–11, 1998, 159.

_____. "Religious Books," *The Critic*, vol. 31, no. 4 (1973), 85.

Masland, Tom. "Bloody Monday on the Temple Mount," *Newsweek*, Oct. 22, 1990, 36–37.

_____. "The High Price of Hatred: Kahane's Murder Unleashes a Wave of Retribution," *Newsweek*, Nov. 19, 1990, 48.

_____. "Israel: The Word Is Defiance," *Newsweek*, Oct. 29, 1990, 53.

Maudlin, Michael G. "The Bible Study at the End of the World," *Christianity Today*, Sept. 1, 1997, 22–26.

Maxwell, Joe. "Liberty U. Weathers Debt Crisis; Falwell's 'Worst Year,'" *Christianity Today*, Feb. 10, 1992, 46–49.

McDonald, Marci. "Fire on the Religious Right," *Maclean's*, Jan. 18, 1988, 22–23.

McLoughlin, William G., Jr. *Billy Sunday Was His Real Name*. Chicago: University of Chicago Press, 1955.

McManus, Jason, and Ron Kriss. "How Israel Won the War," *Time*, June 16, 1967, 26–36.

Melton, J. Gordon. *Religious Leaders of America*. Detroit: Gale Research, 1991.

Mendel, Arthur P. *Vision and Violence*. Ann Arbor: University of Michigan Press, 1992.

Mergui, Raphael, and Philippe Simonnot. *Israel's Ayatollahs: Meir Kahane and the Far Right in Israel*. London: Saqi Books, 1987.

"Middle East," *Time*, June 23, 1967, 25–29.

"The Mideast Erupts," *Newsweek*, Oct. 15, 1973, 38–41.

Miller, Richard L. *Under the Cloud: The Decades of Nuclear Testing*. New York: Free Press, 1986.

"Millennial Task Force," *The Christian Century*, Jan. 20, 1999, 43.

"Missing Millennialists Turn Up in Israel," *The Christian Century*, Dec. 16, 1998, 1208.

Mojtabai, A. G. *Blessed Assurance: At Home with the Bomb in Amarillo, Texas*. Boston: Houghton Mifflin, 1986.

Morris, Edmund. *Dutch: A Memoir of Ronald Reagan*. New York: Random, 1999.

Nash, Ronald H. *Evangelicals in America: Who They Are, What They Believe*. Nashville: Abingdon, 1987.

Negri, Maxine. "Why Biblical Criticism by Scholars Is Imperative," *The Humanist*, vol. 44, no.3 (1984), 27–28.

Nemeth, Mary. "Blood on Sacred Soil," *Maclean's*, Oct. 22, 1990, 30–31.

"Next Year in the New Jerusalem?," *Christianity Today*, July 7, 1967, 997.

"No Tax-Exemption for Christian Coalition," *The Christian Century*, June 30–July 7, 1999, 671–672.

O'Keefe, Mark. "Faculty Complaint Clouds Regent Law Accreditation," *Christianity Today*, Jan. 10, 1994, 40.

_____. "'Religious Bigotry' Alleged," *Christianity Today*, Dec. 13, 1993, 66–67.

O'Leary, Stephen D. *Arguing the Apocalypse: A Theory of Millennial Rhetoric*. New York: Oxford University Press, 1994.

Olsen, Ted. "Robertson Gets Roasted," *Christianity Today*, Aug. 12, 1996, 31.

Ostling, Richard N. "Power, Glory — and Politics: Right-wing Preachers Dominate the Dial," *Time*, Feb. 17, 1986, 54–65.

_____. "Those Mainline Blues," *Time*, May 22, 1989, 54–56.

_____. "Time for a New Temple?" *Time*, Oct. 16, 1989, 69–71.

Oz, Amos. *In the Land of Israel*. New York: Harcourt Brace Jovanovich. 1983.

"Pat Robertson, Novelist," *Christianity Today*, Sept. 1, 1997, 25.

Peres, Yochanan. "Religious Adherence and Political Attitudes," in *Israeli Judaism: The Sociology of Religion in Israel*, edited by Shlomo Deshen, Charles S. Liebman and Moshe Shokeid. New Brunswick, New Jersey: Transaction, 1995. pp. 87–106.

Pipes, Daniel. *The Hidden Hand: Middle East Fears of Conspiracy*. New York: St. Martin's, 1996.

Podhoretz, Norman. "In the Matter of Pat Robertson," *Commentary*, August 1995, 27–32.

Pry, Peter. *Israel's Nuclear Arsenal*. Boulder: Westview, 1984.

Radner, Ephraim. "New World Order, Old World Anti-Semitism," *The Christian Century*, Sept. 13–20, 1995, 844–849.

Rapoport, David C. "Messianic Sanctions for Terror," *Comparative Politics* 20 (1988) 195–213.

Reagan, Ronald. *An American Life*. New York: Simon and Schuster, 1990.

_____. *My Early Life or Where's the Rest of Me?* London: Sidgwick & Jackson, 1981.

Reed, Ralph. *Politically Incorrect: The Emerging Faith Factor in American Politics*. Dallas: Word, 1994.

_____. "We Can't Stop Now," *Christianity Today*, Sept. 6, 1999, 46–48.

Reed, Stanley. "Has Israel Played into Saddam's Hands?" *Business Week*, Oct. 22, 1990, 53.

Reese, Alexander. *The Approaching Advent of Christ*. Grand Rapids: Grand Rapids International Publications, 1975.

Reichley, A. James. *Religion in American Public Life*. Washington: The Brookings Institution, 1985.

Republicans Court Religious Right," *The Christian Century*, Aug. 26–Sept. 2, 1992, 770.

Rhodes, Richard. *The Making of the Atomic Bomb*. New York: Simon and Schuster, 1986.

Richards, Jeffrey J. *The Promise of Dawn: The Eschatology of Lewis Sperry Chafer*. Lanham, Maryland: University Press of America, 1991.

Robbins, Thomas, and Susan J. Palmer (editors). *Millennium, Messiahs, and Mayhem: Contemporary Apocalyptic Movements*. New York: Routledge, 1997.

"Robertson Bullish on Family Channel, UPI," *Christianity Today*, June 22, 1992, 51–52.

"Robertson Buys UPI," *The Christian Century*, May 20–27, 1992, 537, 539.

"Robertson Calls Lawyers 'Inept.'" *The Christian Century*, April 13, 1994, 378–379.

"Robertson Delivers Pep Talk to Coalition," *The Christian Century*, Oct. 8, 1997, 865–866.

Robertson, Pat. *The New World Order*. Boston: G.K. Hall, 1992.

"Robertson's Lawyers," *The Christian Century*, Oct. 21, 1992, 930.

"Roof, Wade Clark, and William McKinney. *American Mainline Religion: Its Changing Shape and Future*. New Brunswick: Rutgers University Press, 1987.

Rubinstein, Danny. *The People of Nowhere: The Palestinian Vision of Home*. New York: Random House, 1991.

Russell, C. Allyn. "W. A. Criswell: A Case Study in Fundamentalism," *Review and Expositor*, Winter 1984, 107–131.

Ryrie, Charles Caldwell. *Dispensationalism Today*. Chicago: Moody, 1965.

Sandeen, Ernest R. *The Origins of Fundamentalism*. Philadelphia: Fortress, 1968.

_____. *The Roots of Fundamentalism: British and American Millenarianism, 1800–1930*. Chicago: University of Chicago Press, 1970.

St. Clair, Michael J. *Millenarian Movements in Historical Context*. New York: Garland, 1992.

Sappir, Susan. "Tensions Mount," *The Jerusalem Report*, Jan. 3, 2000, 42–43.

Scheer, Robert. *With Enough Shovels: Reagan, Bush and Nuclear War*. New York: Random, 1982.

Schell, Jonathan. *The Fate of the Earth*. New York: Alfred A. Knopf, 1982.

_____. *History in Sherman Park: An American Family and the Reagan-Mondale Election*. New York: Alfred A. Knopf, 1987.

Schieffer, Bob, and Gary Paul Gates. *The Acting President*. New York: E. P. Dutton, 1989.

Schiller, David Th. "A Battlegroup Divided: The Palestinian Fedayeen," in *Inside Terrorist Organizations*, edited by David C. Rapoport. London: Frank Cass, 1988. pp. 90–108.

Schmithals, Walter. *The Apocalyptic Movement: Introduction & Interpretation*. Nashville: Abingdon, 1975.

Schoenfeld, Gabriel. "Thinking about the Unthinkable in the Middle East," *Commentary*, December 1998, 34–39.

Scofield, C. I. *Oxford NIV Scofield Study Bible*, edited by C. I. Scofield. New York: Oxford University Press, 1984.

"Scrapping the Moral Majority," *Time*, June 26, 1989, 29.

Sennott, Charles M. "Put Meaning into the Millennium," *The Jerusalem Report*, Jan. 3, 2000, 54.

Shachtman, Tom. *Decade of Shocks: Dallas to Watergate, 1963–1974*. New York: Poseidon, 1983.

Shahak, Israel. "The Third Temple and a Red Heifer," in *All in the Name of the Bible:*

Selected Essays on Israel and American Christian Fundamentalism, edited by Hassan Haddad and Donald Wagner. 2nd ed. Brattleboro, Vermont: Amana Books, 1986. pp. 66–67.

Shapiro, Walter. "Politics and the Pulpit," *Newsweek*, Sept. 17, 1984, 24–27.

_____. "The Teflon Twins of 1988," *Time*, Jan. 11, 1988, 26.

Shargai, Nadav. "The Baby Priests and the Red Cow," *World Press Review*, June 1998, 46.

Sharot, Stephen. "Sociological Analyses of Religion," in *Israeli Judaism: The Sociology of Religion in Israel*, edited by Shlomo Deshen, Charles S. Liebman and Moshe Shokeid. New Brunswick, New Jersey: Transaction, 1995. pp. 19–32.

Sheler, Jeffery L. "Charges of Antisemitism: Mending Fences Between the Christian Right and Jews," *U.S. News & World Report*, April 24, 1995, 32.

_____. "The Christmas Covenant," *U.S. News & World Report*, Dec. 19, 1994, 62–71.

_____. "Dark Prophecies," *U.S. News & World Report*, Dec. 15, 1997, 62–71.

_____. "Stains on Stained Glass: Tales of Treachery and Deceit Inside America's Biggest Megachurch," *U.S. News & World Report*, Oct. 10, 1994, 97.

Shikaki, Khalil. "Peace Now or Hamas Later," *Foreign Affairs*, July/August 1998, 29–43.

Shindler, Colin. *Ploughshares into Swords?: Israelis and Jews in the Shadow of the Intifada*. London: I. B. Tauris, 1991.

"Should the Temple Be Rebuilt?" *Time*, June 30, 1967, 48.

Silver, Eric. "The 'War of the Jews,'" *Maclean's*, Jan. 18, 1988, 18–19.

_____. "The West Bank's Law of the Gun," *Maclean's*, April 26, 1982, 40.

Simon, Merrill. *Jerry Falwell and the Jews*. Middle Village, New York: Jonathan David, 1984.

Simon, Roger. "Miracle Worker," *The New Republic*, Oct. 7, 1996, 11.

Slone, Chris. "Robertson Shakes Up Empire," *Christianity Today*, July 14, 1997, 60.

Slosser, Bob. *Reagan Inside Out*. Waco, Texas: Word, 1984.

Smith, Goodman. "They Must Go ... In the Name of the Bible: Rabbi Meir Kahane's 'Apartheid' Zionism," in *All in the Name of the Bible: Selected Essays on Israel and American Christian Fundamentalism*, edited by Hassan Haddad and Donald Wagner. 2nd ed. Brattleboro, Vermont: Amana Books, 1986. pp. 50–58.

Smith, William E. "Attack at the Dome of the Rock," *Time*, April 19, 1982, 49.

_____. "Tension on the Borders," *Time*, April 12, 1982, 24–25.

Snowball, David. *Continuity and Change in the Rhetoric of the Moral Majority*. New York: Praeger, 1991.

Sontag, Deborah. "Apocalyptic Cultists Arrested in Jerusalem," *Globe and Mail*, Jan. 4, 1999, A1, A11.

Spencer, William David. "Does Anyone Really Know What Time It Is?" *Christianity Today*, July 17, 1995, 29.

Spring, Beth. "Rating Reagan," *Christianity Today*, Oct. 7, 1983, 44–50.

Sprinzak, Ehud. *The Ascendance of Israel's Radical Right*. New York: Oxford University Press, 1991.

_____. *Brother Against Brother: Violence and Extremism in Israeli Politics from Altalena to the Rabin Assassination*. New York: The Free Press, 1999.

_____. "From Messianic Pioneering to Vigilante Terrorism: The Case of the Gush Emunim Underground," in *Inside Terrorist Organizations*, edited by David C. Rapoport. London: Frank Cass, 1988.

_____. "Netanyahu's Safety Belt," *Foreign Affairs*, July/August 1998, 18–28.

_____. "Three Models of Religious Violence: The Case of Jewish Fundamentalism in Israel," in *Fundamentalisms and the State*, vol. 3, edited by Martin E. Marty and R. Scott Appleby. Chicago: University of Chicago Press, 1993. pp. 462–90.

Stafford, Tim. "Robertson R Us," *Christianity Today*, Aug. 12, 1996, 26–33.

Stark, Rodney, and Charles Y. Glock. *American Piety: The Nature of Religious Commitment*. vol.1. Berkeley: University of California Press, 1970.

Stern, Jessica. *The Ultimate Terrorists*. Cambridge: Harvard University Press, 1999.

Stoff, Michael B., Jonathan F. Fanton, and R. Hal Williams (editors). *The Manhattan Project: A Documentary Introduction to the Atomic Age*. Philadelphia: Temple University Press, 1991.

Straub, Gerard Thomas. *Salvation for Sale: An Insider's View of Pat Robertson*. Enlarged ed. Buffalo: Prometheus, 1988.

Strozier, Charles B. *Apocalypse: On the Psychology of Fundamentalism in America*. Boston: Beacon Press, 1994.

Stuckey, Mary E. *Playing the Game: The Presidential Rhetoric of Ronald Reagan*. New York: Praeger, 1990.

Tal, Uriel. "The Foundations of Political Messianism in Israel," in *All in the Name of the Bible: Selected Essays on Israel and American Christian Fundamentalism*, edited by Hassan Haddad and Donald Wagner. 2nd ed. Brattleboro, Vermont: Amana Books, 1986. pp. 59–65.

Taylor, Ann C. M. (editor). *International Handbook of Universities*. 14th ed. New York: Stockton, 1996.

Taylor, John. "Pat Robertson's God, Inc.," *Esquire*, November 1994, 77–83.

Teegarden, Kenneth L. *We Call Ourselves Disciples*. 2nd ed. St. Louis: Bethany, 1983.

Teresi, Dick. "Zero," *The Atlantic Monthly*, July 1997, 88–94.

"Terrible Swift Sword," *Newsweek*, June 19, 1967, 24–31.

Tharp, Mike. "Fringe Groups and Y2K: A Scary Mix," *U.S. News & World Report*, Sept. 6, 1999, 58.

Thomas, Evan, and Jon Meacham. "The Book on Reagan," *Newsweek*, Oct. 4, 1999, 22–25.

Tibi, Bassam. *Conflict and War in the Middle East: From Interstate War to New Security*. 2nd ed. New York: St. Martin's, 1998.

Toscano, Louis. *Triple Cross*. New York: Carol, 1990.

Tough, Paul. "That's the News and I Am Outta Here," *Mother Jones*, September/October 1998, 79–80.

Toulouse, Mark G. "W. A. Criswell," in *Twentieth-Century Shapers of American Popular Religion*, edited by Charles H. Lippy. Westport: Greenwood Press, 1989. pp. 96–104.

Tuveson, Ernest Lee. *Redeemer Nation: The Idea of America's Millennial Role*. Chicago: University of Chicago Press, 1968.

[Untitled article on Pat Robertson] *Time*, Sept. 11, 1989, 89.

Van der Linden, Frank. *The Real Reagan*. New York: William Morrow, 1981.

Vaughn, Eric. "Where's the Rapture?" *Skeptical Inquirer*, vol. 17, no. 4 (summer 1993), 367.

"Visiting Team," *The New Republic*, Nov. 5, 1990, 9–10.

Wagner, Donald E. *Anxious for Armageddon: A Call to Partnership for Middle Eastern and Western Christians*. Scottdale: Herald, 1995.

_____. "Anxious for Armageddon: Probing Israel's Political Support among American Fundamentalists," in *All in the Name of the Bible: Selected Essays on Israel and American Christian Fundamentalism*, edited by Hassan Haddad and Donald Wagner. 2nd ed. Brattleboro, Vermont: Amana Books, 1986. pp. 16–28.

_____. "Evangelicals and Israel: Theological Roots of a Political Alliance," *The Christian Century*, Nov. 4, 1998, 1020–1026.

_____. "The Prophet Who Would Be King," in *All in the Name of the Bible: Selected Essays on Israel and American Christian Fundamentalism*, edited by Hassan Haddad and Donald Wagner. 2nd ed. Brattleboro, Vermont: Amana Books, 1986. pp. 37–43.

Wald, Kenneth D. *Religion and Politics in the United States*. 2nd ed. Washington: Congressional Quarterly, 1992.

Walker, Richard. "Falwell Claims Victory, Dissolves Moral Majority," *Christianity Today*, July 14, 1989, 58–59.

Wall, James M. "Missing Connections," *The Christian Century*, July 14–21, 1999, 699.

Wallis, Jim. "Recovering the Evangel," in *Border Regions of Faith: An Anthology of Religion and Social Change*, edited by Kenneth Aman. Maryknoll, New York: Orbis, 1987. pp. 285–89.

Walters, Ray. [Hal Lindsey's books] "Paperback Talk," *The New York Times Book Review*, March 12, 1978, 45–46.

Walters, Stanley D. "Hal Lindsey: Recalculating the Second Coming," *The Christian Century*, vol. 96 (1979), 839–40.

"War Sweeps the Bible Lands," *Christianity Today*, June 23, 1967, 956–957.

Watson, Russell. "A Bill Comes Due Early," *Newsweek*, Oct. 22, 1990, 34–40.

Weber, Timothy P. "How Evangelicals Became Israel's Best Friend," *Christianity Today*, Oct. 5, 1998, 38–49.

_____. *Living in the Shadow of the Second Coming: American Premillennialism, 1875–1982*. Grand Rapids: Zondervan, 1983.

Weigert, Andrew J. "Christian Eschatological Identities and Nuclear Context," *Journal for the Scientific Study of Religion* 27 (1988) 175–191.

Weissman, Steve, and Herbert Krosney. *The Islamic Bomb: The Nuclear Threat to Israel and the Middle East*. New York: Times Books, 1981.

Wharton, Gary C. "The Continuing Phenomenon of the Religious Best Seller," *Publishers Weekly*, Mar. 14, 1977, 82–83.

Wieseltier, Leon. "Gog, Magog, Agog," *The New Republic*, May 15, 1995, 46.

Wilhelm, David. "Getting Ready," *The Christian Century*, Feb. 17, 1999, 174–175.

Willoughby, William. *Does America Need the Moral Majority?* Plainfield, New Jersey: Haven Books, 1981.

Wills, Garry. *Reagan's America: Innocents at Home*. Garden City, New York: Doubleday, 1987.

_____. *Under God: Religion and American Politics*. New York: Simon and Schuster, 1990.

Wilson, Dwight. *Armageddon Now!: The Premillenarian Response to Russia and Israel Since 1917*. Grand Rapids: Baker, 1977.

"Winding Up War, Working Toward Peace," *Time*, Nov. 5, 1973, 28–50.

Wojcik, Daniel. *The End of the World As We Know It: Faith, Fatalism, and Apocalypse in America*. New York: New York University Press, 1997.

Woodward, Kenneth L. "Arguing Armageddon," *Newsweek*, Nov. 5, 1984, 91.

_____. "The Boom in Doom," *Newsweek*, Jan. 10, 1977, 49, 51.

_____. "Dead End for the Mainline?" *Newsweek*, Aug. 9, 1993, 46–48.

_____. "From 'Mainline' to Sideline" *Newsweek*, Dec. 22, 1986, 54–56.

_____. "Playing Politics at Church" *Newsweek*, July 9, 1984, 52.

_____. "This Way to Armageddon" *Newsweek*, July 5, 1982, 79.

_____. "Uh-oh, Maybe We Missed the Big Day," *Newsweek*, Aug. 11, 1997, 15.

_____. "The Way the World Ends," *Newsweek*, Nov. 1, 1999, 66–74.

Wright, Lawrence. "Forcing the End" *The New Yorker*, July 20, 1998, 42–53.

Wuthnow, Robert. *Christianity in the Twenty-first Century: Reflections on the Challenges Ahead*. New York: Oxford University Press, 1993.

_____. *The Struggle for America's Soul: Evangelicals, Liberals, and Secularism*. Grand Rapids: William B. Eerdmans, 1989.

_____. "The World of Fundamentalism," *The Christian Century*, April 22, 1992, 426–29.

Yankelovich, Daniel. *New Rules: Searching for Self-Fulfillment in a World Turned Upside Down*. New York: Random, 1981.

"Zaire Trip Criticized," *The Christian Century*, April 15, 1992, 394.

Zuckerman, Mortimer B. "Temple Mount: The Real Story," *U.S. News & World Report*, Nov. 12, 1990, 95–96.

Zweig, Ferdynand. *Israel: The Sword and the Harp: The Mystique of Violence and the Mystique of Redemption*. London: Heinemann, 1969.

Index

200
New

New, David S.

Holy war.

DATE			